The Guide to U.S. Legal Analysis and Writing

ASPEN COURSEBOOK SERIES

The Guide to U.S. Legal Analysis and Writing

Third Edition

Deborah B. McGregor

Clinical Professor of Law Emerita
Founding Director, Master of Jurisprudence Program
Indiana University Robert H. McKinney School of Law

Cynthia M. Adams

Vice Dean and Clinical Professor of Law
Indiana University Robert H. McKinney School of Law

Katrina J. Lee

Director of LL.M. Legal Writing and Clinical Professor of Law
The Ohio State University Moritz College of Law

ASPEN PUBLISHING

Cover image: iStock.com/ThomasVogel

To contact Customer Service, e-mail customer.service@aspenpublishing.com, call 1-800-950-5259, or mail correspondence to:

Aspen Publishing
Attn: Order Department
PO Box 990
Frederick, MD 21705

Printed in the United States of America.

1 2 3 4 5 6 7 8 9 0

ISBN 978-1-5438-0779-0

Library of Congress Cataloging-in-Publication Data application is in process.

About Aspen Publishing

Aspen Publishing is a leading provider of educational content and digital learning solutions to law schools in the U.S. and around the world. Aspen provides best-in-class solutions for legal education through authoritative textbooks, written by renowned authors, and breakthrough products such as Connected eBooks, Connected Quizzing, and PracticePerfect.

The Aspen Casebook Series (famously known among law faculty and students as the "red and black" casebooks) encompasses hundreds of highly regarded textbooks in more than eighty disciplines, from large enrollment courses, such as Torts and Contracts to emerging electives such as Sustainability and the Law of Policing. Study aids such as the *Examples & Explanations* and the *Emanuel Law Outlines* series, both highly popular collections, help law students master complex subject matter.

Major products, programs, and initiatives include:

- **Connected eBooks** are enhanced digital textbooks and study aids that come with a suite of online content and learning tools designed to maximize student success. Designed in collaboration with hundreds of faculty and students, the Connected eBook is a significant leap forward in the legal education learning tools available to students.
- **Connected Quizzing** is an easy-to-use formative assessment tool that tests law students' understanding and provides timely feedback to improve learning outcomes. Delivered through CasebookConnect.com, the learning platform already used by students to access their Aspen casebooks, Connected Quizzing is simple to implement and integrates seamlessly with law school course curricula.
- **PracticePerfect** is a visually engaging, interactive study aid to explain commonly encountered legal doctrines through easy-to-understand animated videos, illustrative examples, and numerous practice questions. Developed by a team of experts, PracticePerfect is the ideal study companion for today's law students.
- The **Aspen Learning Library** enables law schools to provide their students with access to the most popular study aids on the market across all of their courses. Available through an annual subscription, the online library consists of study aids in e-book, audio, and video formats with full text search, note-taking, and highlighting capabilities.
- Aspen's **Digital Bookshelf** is an institutional-level online education bookshelf, consolidating everything students and professors need to ensure success. This program ensures that every student has access to affordable course materials from day one.
- **Leading Edge** is a community centered on thinking differently about legal education and putting those thoughts into actionable strategies. At the core of the program is the Leading Edge Conference, an annual gathering of legal education thought leaders looking to pool ideas and identify promising directions of exploration.

To my parents, William A. Matson
and Mary Katharine Geimer Matson.

—CMA

To my sons, Geoff and Dan, for their love, patience,
and never-ending humor, and to my grandsons, Blake
and Evan, who light up my life every day.

—DBM

To my mom, and to Phoebe, Sabrina,
and Dennis, for everything.

—KJL

SUMMARY OF CONTENTS

CONTENTS

PREFACE

The world is indeed becoming smaller. With the world becoming more interconnected through business, technology, and the need to address global-scale problems like climate change, understanding one another's legal systems is critical. Our goal is to help you, the international lawyer from a different legal system, to understand how U.S. lawyers communicate and how the U.S. legal system works.

Many of you work in a civil or mixed legal system and are most interested in learning about the U.S. common law system. While many texts exist that include instruction on common law analysis, there has been no book to date that provides the level of detail that this one does.

We wanted to focus on the types of communications that you are most likely to read from U.S. lawyers or need to write to U.S. lawyers. Cultural differences and tradition may influence how a single document — a contract, for example — is written in any individual country. With an introduction to the techniques U.S. lawyers use when drafting communications, you will have a better understanding of why something is written the way it is, and how, in turn, to most effectively communicate with U.S. lawyers. For these reasons, we have introduced techniques for drafting an objective legal analysis; writing persuasively and drafting documents to the courts; and crafting expository writings, such as client letters, demand letters, and email communications. We chose not to explore research sources and techniques in the United States, knowing there are other exceptional books available that provide that guidance. We are delighted that this edition will eventually be accompanied by online supplementary student learning materials, available at no additional cost on the Aspen Publishing website (www.AspenPublishing.com).

We are thankful to our assistant, Janice White, for her help throughout this process. We would also like to thank ESL Specialist M. Catherine Beck for her advice and support. Thanks, too, to Aspen Publishing's anonymous reviewers, who offered valuable commentary. And a special thank you to our research assistants, including Hongbin Bao, Shishir Deshpande, Anna Dyuzheva, Kristen Davis Edmundson, Nathan Lundquist, Koichi Nishioka, James Porter, and Thomas Vandenabeele, who helped with our first edition, and Stephanie Rivas, who assisted with the second edition. We are grateful to The Ohio State University Moritz College of Law research assistants Marissa Diver, Arata Kaku, and Katie Potrzeboski, who assisted with the third edition. Everyone named here helped shape the final version of this text. Thanks also to students at both of our law schools who were assigned editions of this book over the years and, through their comments and reactions, helped us refine both the substance and the style for this edition. Professor Lee is grateful to the Moritz College of Law for the summer research grant support.

Professors McGregor and Adams welcome as a co-author on this third edition Katrina Lee, a former law firm equity partner and the Director of the pioneering LL.M. Legal Writing Program at The Ohio State University Moritz College of Law. An experienced legal writing professor and the Immediate Past President of the Association of Legal Writing Directors, Professor Lee taught with the first and second editions and has brought refreshing perspective and energy to the third edition.

We welcome feedback from faculty and students who use this book. You may contact Professor Lee at katrinalee@osu.edu, Dean Adams at cmadams@iupui.edu, and Professor McGregor at dmcgreg@iu.edu.

In the meantime, enjoy!

Deborah B. McGregor, Cynthia M. Adams, Katrina J. Lee
November 2021

CHAPTER 1

The System of Government and the Litigation Process in the United States

A. Introduction

This chapter will provide an overview of the system of government and the litigation process in the United States. The U.S. has a dual system of government, consisting of the federal and state systems. At both the state and federal levels, the government operates through three branches: judicial, legislative, and executive. The judicial branch is made up of the courts. When someone has a problem in need of resolution and brings it to the attention of the court by filing a legal document called a complaint, they start the litigation process. That process can result in a judicial opinion, also known as a case. In U.S. law schools, students read cases produced by the courts.

B. A Dual System

The United States has a dual system of government: the federal system and the state system. The federal system derives its law from four main sources: the

U.S. Constitution, federal statutes, administrative regulations promulgated by federal agencies, and federal court decisions. State law is derived from four main sources: state constitutions, state statutes, administrative regulations promulgated by state agencies, and state court decisions. (See Figure 1-1.) Although states make their own laws, they still cannot disregard federal law.

Primary Sources of the Law

Federal System	State System
• United States Constitution • Statutory laws enacted by the United States Congress • Common law found in federal court decisions • Administrative regulations created by federal agencies (e.g., the Environmental Protection Agency)	• State constitution • Statutory laws enacted by a state legislature • Common law found in state court decisions • Administrative regulations created by state agencies (e.g., the Bureau of Motor Vehicles)

Figure 1-1

C. The Constitutionally Created Three Branches of Government

The U.S. Constitution, which consists of 7 articles and 27 amendments, is the foundation of the U.S. legal system. The Constitution allocates responsibility for governance between the federal and state governments. The Constitution has been amended 27 times. The first 10 amendments, known as the Bill of Rights, mandate fundamental rights and protections for people. The Bill of Rights limits the federal government's power by guaranteeing certain rights to the people, including freedom of speech, freedom of religion, freedom of assembly, freedom of the press, the right to bear arms, the right to be secure from unreasonable searches and seizures, the right to a speedy trial, the right not to make incriminating statements against one's self, the right to a trial by jury, and the right to protection against cruel and unusual punishment. A state constitution can grant additional or greater rights and protections than the U.S. Constitution to individuals within that state's boundaries. At a minimum, though, a state constitution must provide the same degree of rights and protections as is afforded under the U.S. Constitution.

Both federal and state constitutions also provide a framework for governing. The constitutions divide the responsibility of governance into three branches: the executive branch, the legislative branch, and the judicial branch. (See Figure 1-2.) Each branch is assigned a particular role, but all branches may create law. Each branch serves as a check over the other two to maintain a balance of power among the three branches.

U.S. Dual System of Government

The Constitutionally-Created Three Branches of Government

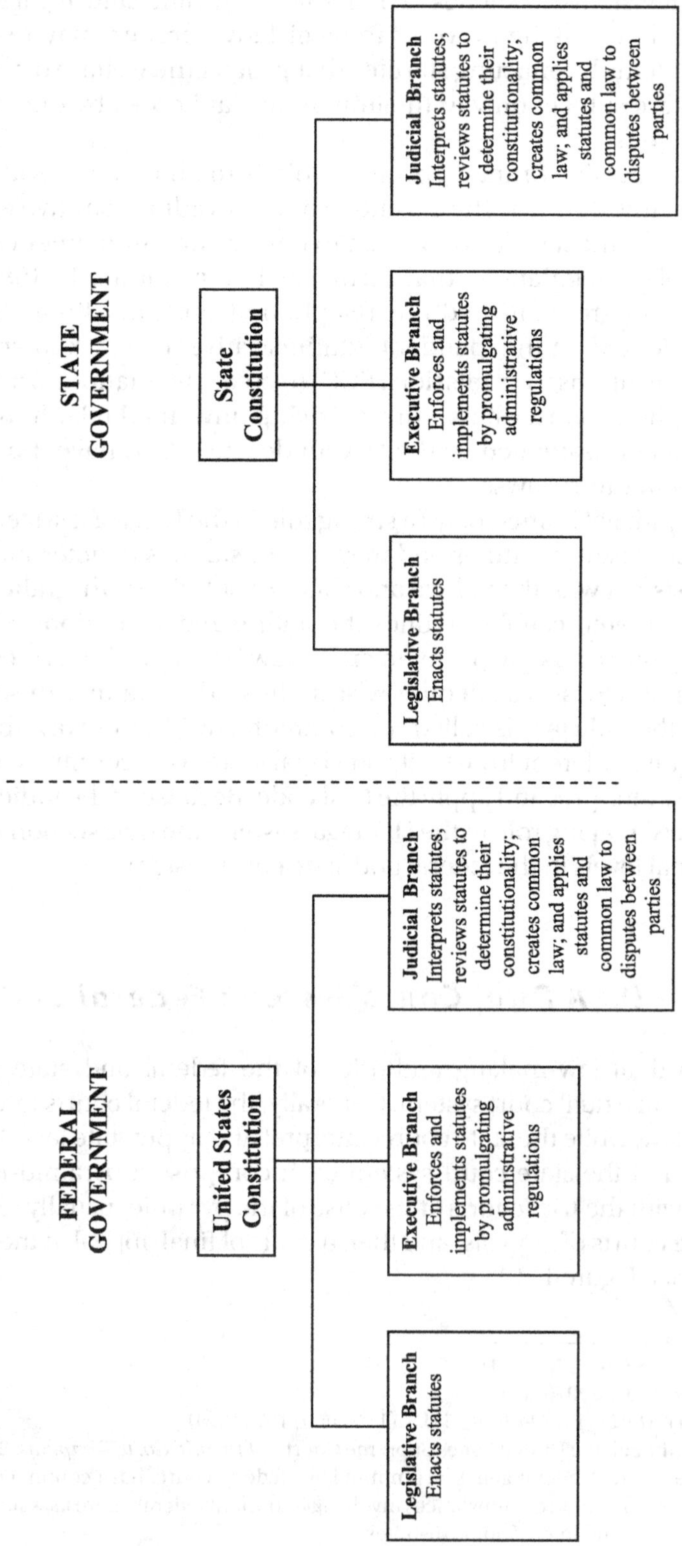

Figure 1-2

The legislative branches in both the federal and state legal systems possess supreme law-making powers. The legislative branch may respond to issues and problems by enacting statutes that protect the welfare of the public. These statutes are subject only to the limitations laid down by the federal and state constitutions.

The executive branch's primary role is to enforce the statutes created by the legislative branch. The executive branch's administrative agencies may be called on by the legislative branch to enforce and implement statutes by putting in place regulations that further define a statute. In 1991, for instance, the U.S. Congress enacted the Telephone Consumer Protection Act (TCPA) and mandated an independent administrative agency known as the Federal Communications Commission (FCC) to create regulations protecting residential telephone subscribers from receiving unwanted telephone solicitations.[1] The regulations created by the FCC under the TCPA have the same force and effect as statutory laws.[2]

The judicial branch plays a strong role in the U.S. legal system. The judiciary interprets existing statutes and may review statutes to determine whether they are consistent with the federal and state constitutions. The judiciary can declare a statute unenforceable if it finds the statute unconstitutional.[3] In addition, the judiciary possesses the power to create law by establishing rules and principles that respond to issues not otherwise addressed by statute. This body of law created by the judiciary is called the common law.[4] In this way, the U.S. legal system is quite different from civil code legal systems in countries where the courts may only interpret and apply the civil code. Because of the judiciary's unusually strong law-making role in the U.S. legal system, the next section will focus on the hierarchal levels in the federal and state court systems.

D. A Dual Court System: Federal and State

The dual law-making authority of the federal and state governments is reflected in a dual court system. Generally, the federal courts interpret and apply federal law, while the state courts interpret and apply state law. The federal court system and the state court system each comprise a pyramid-like hierarchy of courts, with the trial courts at the base of the pyramid, usually followed by intermediate courts of appeals, and then a court of final appeal at the apex of the pyramid. (See Figure 1-3.)

---

1. 47 U.S.C. § 227(c)(1-4).
2. 47 U.S.C. § 227(c)(5).
3. *See Marbury v. Madison*, 5 U.S. (1 Cranch) 137 (1803).
4. Although the United States Supreme Court in *Erie R.R. Co. v. Tompkins*, 304 U.S. 64, 78 (1938) stated there is no "federal general common law," federal courts have continued to develop federal common law in limited circumstances involving important federal interests, such as in admiralty and maritime cases and international disputes.

Court Hierarchy

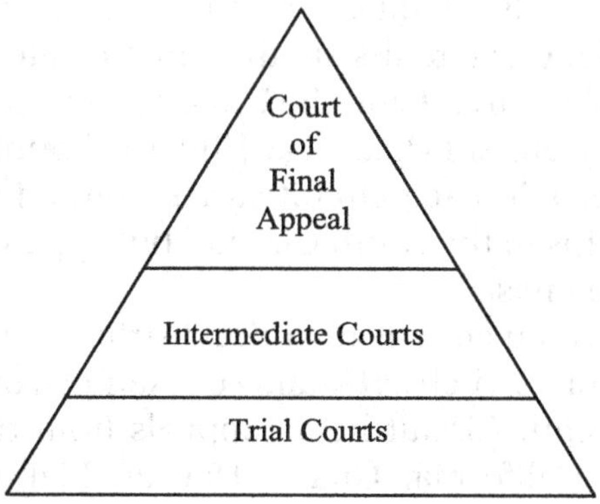

Figure 1-3

1. The federal court system

The federal courts hear disputes involving federal law, including disputes arising from the U.S. Constitution, federal statutes, and federal regulations. A federal court will also hear disputes where the United States is named as a party and can hear state law issues if the parties are citizens of different states and the dispute involves more than $75,000. For example, if two people, a citizen of Oregon and a citizen of California, are involved in a car accident resulting in injuries and damages exceeding $75,000, a lawsuit can be brought in federal court.

Issues involving federal law are usually heard in a federal trial court, called a district court.[5] Each state has at least one district court. The more sparsely populated states may have only a single district court and the more densely populated states may have several district courts. Oregon, for example, has only one district court, but California has four district courts. These courts may hear civil or criminal cases. The district court's jurisdiction is limited to the area within the territorial boundaries of its district. There are 94 judicial districts located in the United States, the District of Columbia (D.C.), the Commonwealth of Puerto Rico, and the 3 territories of the United States — Guam, the Virgin Islands, and the Northern Mariana Islands. (See Figures 1-4 and 1-5.)

A party has a right to appeal the final judgment of a district court or, if permitted by statute, certain orders of the court made during the course of the trial to the intermediate court of appeals having jurisdiction over the district court. In the federal court system, the intermediate courts of appeals are

5. In addition to district courts that hear disputes involving general federal law, the federal court system includes courts that have jurisdiction over special disputes, such as the military courts, the bankruptcy courts, and the United States Tax Court.

known as the United States Circuit Courts of Appeals. Congress has divided the United States into 13 circuits.[6] Eleven of these circuits are numbered 1–11. The two other federal circuits are the United States Court of Appeals for the District of Columbia Circuit and the United States Court of Appeals for the Federal Circuit. (See Figures 1-4 and 1-5.) The total number of judges serving on the court of appeals in each circuit varies from 6 judgeships in the First Circuit to 29 judgeships in the Ninth Circuit,[7] but appeals are generally heard only by three-judge panels.

Each of the numbered circuits includes district courts from various states and sometimes territories, such as Guam. For example, the United States Court of Appeals for the Ninth Circuit hears appeals from district courts located in Alaska, Arizona, California, Guam, Hawaii, Idaho, Montana, Nevada, Northern Mariana Islands, Oregon, and Washington. The United States Court of Appeals for the Second Circuit hears appeals from district courts located in New York, Connecticut, and Vermont. The numbered circuits and the D.C. Court of Appeals also hear appeals from decisions of some federal administrative agencies. (See Figures 1-4 and 1-5.)

Unlike the jurisdictions of the numbered circuits and the D.C. circuit that are based on territorial boundaries, the jurisdiction of the Court of Appeals for the Federal Circuit is nationwide and is based on special claims, such as those involving international trade disputes and patents. (See Figures 1-4 and 1-5.) In some instances, the Court of Appeals for the Federal Circuit also may hear cases against the U.S. government, including disputes arising out of U.S. government contracts, claims for money from the U.S. government, and claims related to veterans' benefits.

The U.S. Supreme Court has nine justices and is the court of last resort for appeals in the federal system and for appeals of state court decisions involving federal issues. (See Figure 1-5.) Most of the cases on the U.S. Supreme Court's docket[8] are discretionary. Thousands of petitions for appeal are filed each year with the Court. The Court is constrained by time, however, and grants permission to hear only a small number of these cases, usually those requiring an interpretation of federal constitutional or statutory provisions, or those requiring the resolution of pressing issues of federal law.[9]

---

6. 28 U.S.C. § 41.
7. 28 U.S.C. § 44.
8. A court docket refers to a record of the cases pending in the court.
9. In the 2012 Term, 7,509 cases were filed with the U.S. Supreme Court, and only 77 cases were argued before the Court. United States Supreme Court Chief Justice Roberts, *The 2013 Year-End Report on the Federal Judiciary* 12, http://www.supremecourt.gov/publicinfo/year-end/2013 year-endreport.pdf. In the 2019 term, the U.S. Supreme Court received 5,411 case filings, and 73 cases were argued before the Court. United States Supreme Court Chief Justice Roberts, *The 2020 Year-End Report on the Federal Judiciary* 5, https://www.supremecourt.gov/publicinfo/year-end/2020year-endreport.pdf

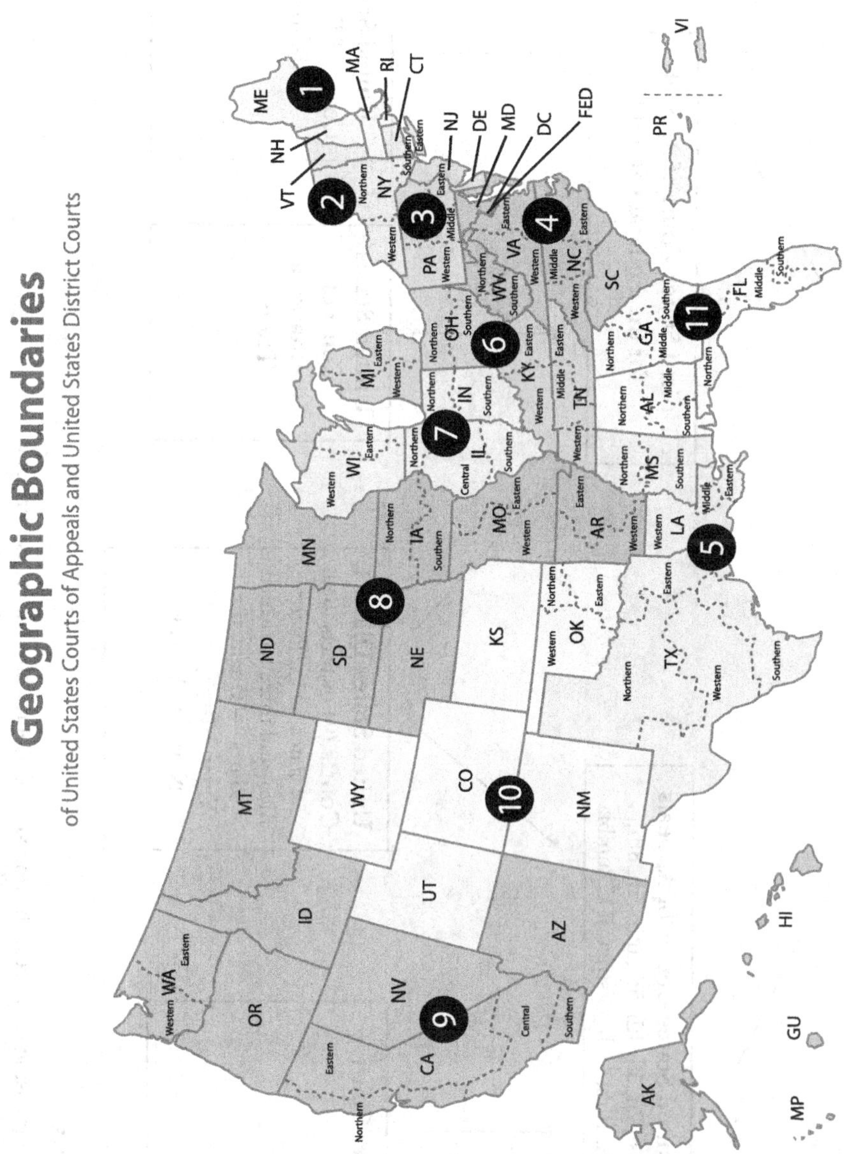

Figure 1-4
Source: Administrative Office of the United States Courts, https://www.uscourts.gov/sites/default/files/u.s._federal_courts_circuit_map_1.pdf (last visited, Aug. 13, 2021).

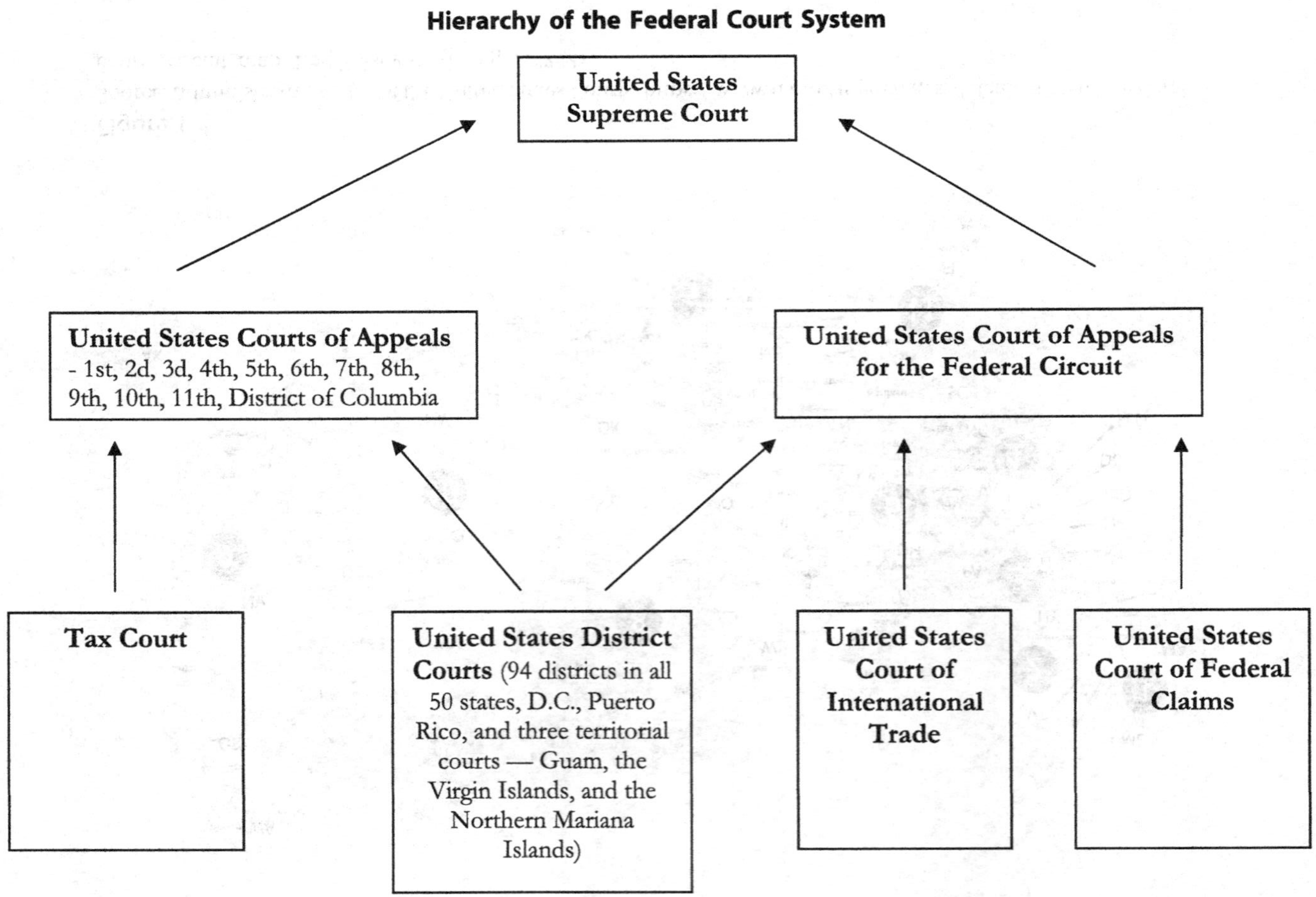

Figure 1-5

Source: Administrative Office of the United States Courts, http://www.uscourts.gov/

Note: Military, Bankruptcy, and Veterans Claims Courts are not shown.

2. *The state court system*

Each of the fifty states, as well as the District of Columbia and the Commonwealth of Puerto Rico, has its own court system. Similar to the federal system, many state court systems are composed of a three-tiered hierarchy consisting of a trial court, an intermediate court of appeals, and the highest court of appeals or the court of last resort. A minority of states with smaller populations, such as Maine, have two-tiered systems only, with trial courts and appellate courts. The names of the appellate courts vary from state to state. For example, California refers to its intermediate court of appeals as the court of appeal and its court of last resort as the supreme court. (See Figure 1-6.) Conversely, New York refers to one of its intermediate courts of appeals as the supreme court and its court of last resort as the court of appeals.[10]

A state trial court may be of general or limited jurisdiction. A court of limited jurisdiction can hear only certain types of cases. For example, a small claims court might hear only cases involving claims for small debts, and a state criminal court of limited jurisdiction might hear only criminal cases. Still other courts have specialized roles, such as domestic relations court, which might hear cases involving divorce, custody, and child support.

Similar to the federal court system, most states allow a right of appeal to the intermediate appellate court. A party that is dissatisfied with the outcome of a civil case decided by a state trial court may ask an appellate court in the state to review the trial court's judgment, order, or decision to determine whether the trial court committed a legal error that requires a reversal, a modification, or a new trial. If there is a third tier to the state court system, a party dissatisfied with the outcome in the intermediate appellate court may appeal the intermediate appellate court's decision to the state's highest court. In most instances, the highest court in a three-tiered court system is not required to hear an appeal. Like the United States Supreme Court, most dockets are discretionary in state courts of last resort. Unless the decision of a state court involves a federal constitutional question or federal law, the decision of the highest state court is final and cannot be appealed to any other court. For an example of one state's court system (California), see Figure 1-6.

---

10. A quick way to determine the names of the courts in the various state jurisdictions is to refer to Table 1 in THE BLUEBOOK: A UNIFORM SYSTEM OF CITATION (21st ed. 2020) or Appendix 1 in CAROLYN WILLIAMS, ALWD GUIDE TO LEGAL CITATION (7th ed. 2021). The states are listed alphabetically, and as a part of each state entry, the names of the courts in the state that publish decisions are identified along with the names of the reporters in which these decisions are published.

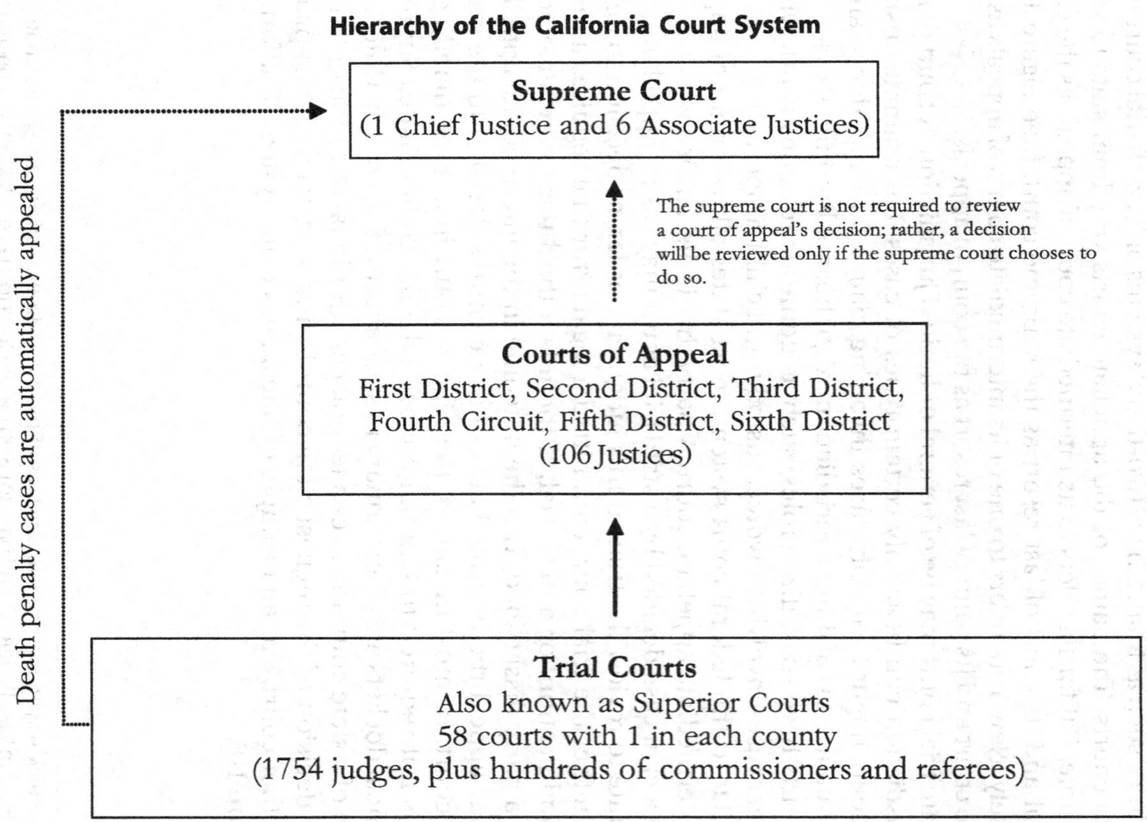

Figure 1-6

Judgeship numbers are current as of 2020. Source: The Judicial Council of California, http://ww.courts.ca.gov/2113.htm, and https://www.courts.ca.gov/documents/California_Judicial_Branch.pdf.

E. An Overview of the Litigation Process

Following is an overview of the basic civil litigation process. Not intended as an exhaustive discussion of civil procedure, this section is meant to help provide an understanding of the trajectory of a typical litigation matter.[11] Unless otherwise noted, this section focuses on the rules of procedure for a civil matter in federal court, though many states pattern their rules of procedure after the federal rules.[12]

1. The client interview

From a lawyer's perspective, the civil litigation process in the United States usually begins when a client meets with the lawyer for the first time to discuss a legal problem. The objectives of the client will vary. The client may want the lawyer to bring on their behalf a legal action against another person or entity. Alternatively, the client may have been named a party in a lawsuit and may want the lawyer to represent them in the matter. Or the client may want the lawyer to negotiate on their behalf a resolution to the legal problem without court involvement. In any event, the lawyer will want to collect the following information:

(1) The identification of the parties involved, including (if possible) addresses, telephone numbers, and email addresses.
(2) Where the key events of the problem arose.
(3) All facts related to or giving rise to the legal problem.
(4) When the events related to or giving rise to the legal problem occurred.
(5) Copies of all writings, papers, and documents related to the legal problem.

As part of assessing the client's case, a lawyer may summarize the major facts of the case gathered from the client before researching the problem. In this way, the lawyer brings some order to the interview notes, identifies follow-up questions that they need to ask, and becomes more familiar with the facts.[13]

---

11. This section does not focus on procedure in criminal law cases or special cases such as those presented in military court, bankruptcy court, and tax court.

12. *See, e.g.*, Charles Alan Wright, Law of Federal Courts 386 (8th ed. 2017). ("They [the Federal Rules of Civil Procedure] provide for the federal courts a uniform procedure in civil actions.... The impact of the rules has not been limited to the federal courts. The excellence of the rules is such that in more than half the states the rules have been adapted for state use virtually unchanged, and there is not a jurisdiction that has not revised its procedure in some way that reflects the influence of the federal rules.")

13. Those interested in learning more about client interviewing can consult books focused on lawyer counseling and advising, including Marjorie Corman Aaron, Client Science: Advice for Lawyers on Counseling Clients Through Bad News and Other Legal Realities (2012).

Lawyers meeting with clients should take great care to engage in active listening to elicit all relevant facts from a client. The client should be allowed time to tell the story of their problem without interruption, while the lawyer listens and takes notes. Often, the lawyer may wish to follow up with the client after reviewing materials from the client and their own notes. Only after communicating with the client and reviewing client materials can the lawyer have a preliminary grasp of the issues and sufficient information.

2. *Assessing the law and a course of action*

Once the lawyer has communicated with the client and reviewed client materials, the next step usually is to research the law to gain a stronger grasp of the legal issues and the strengths and weaknesses of the client's case.[14] Sometimes, a junior lawyer will be asked to do the research and write for a supervising lawyer's review a memorandum analyzing the client's legal question in light of the controlling law.[15] In a private meeting virtually or in person, or in a letter, the supervising or junior lawyer may discuss their analysis and conclusions with the client and make recommendations for possible courses of action. (Chapter 14 discusses drafting a client letter.)

A U.S. lawyer who finds that a client has a viable legal action may not always immediately file a complaint with the court. At this early stage, the lawyer's role is sometimes to be a negotiator on behalf of the client. As a negotiator, the lawyer may attempt to seek a resolution to the client's problem before initiating a legal action or proceeding to trial. For example, if the client wants another party to take a particular action, the lawyer may write a letter on the client's behalf to the other party insisting on this action. (Chapter 14 discusses drafting a demand letter.) Negotiating a resolution to the client's problem also can involve oral communication between the lawyer and the other parties or, if the other parties are represented by legal counsel, the other parties' attorneys. This informal negotiation process may continue even if the parties engage in the litigation process.

3. *Alternative dispute resolution*

Alternative dispute resolution (ADR) is commonly used to resolve civil disputes in the United States. For many reasons, parties may be reluctant to

---

14. While this book does not focus on legal research, many books do. *See, e.g.*, AMY E. SLOAN, BASIC LEGAL RESEARCH: TOOLS AND STRATEGIES (8th ed. 2021); KENT C. OLSON, AARON KIRSCHENFELD & INGRID MATTSON, PRINCIPLES OF LEGAL RESEARCH (Concise Hornbook Series) (3d ed. 2020).

15. *See* Chapters 6–12 for discussion of writing a predictive memo.

resolve a dispute through formal litigation. Litigation in court can be costly, time-consuming, and inconvenient. In addition, pleadings and accompanying documents are usually available to the public. This can give rise to concern if parties wish to keep certain information private. In some circumstances, ADR methods can lead to quicker private resolution of the dispute and result in less cost than court-centered litigation. Also, as legal technology, court processes, and laws evolve to allow people to access dispute resolution processes on their mobile phones or laptops, ADR may become more convenient and accessible.

ADR methods that can be used prior to or instead of commencement of formal litigation in court include mediation and the more structured process of arbitration. In mediation, the parties seek to resolve issues through cooperation and problem-solving with a neutral third party acting as a mediator. Arbitration follows a process similar to formal litigation in the courts, but the parties have more control over the arbitration procedure. In arbitration, the parties present their respective positions to a neutral party (one or more arbitrators) who then issues a decision in the matter.

Mediation and other ADR processes are also available in some jurisdictions after formal litigation has commenced. For example, courts may order parties to engage in mediation. The case would remain on the court's docket while mediation is pursued. The court may issue orders to ensure that the parties continue to participate in the ADR process. If no resolution can be reached, the ADR process may be abandoned, and the case would then move forward in court.

In the interest of conserving judicial resources in a busy court system, some jurisdictions also may allow parties to agree to additional ADR processes, such as mini-trial or summary jury trials.[16]

4. *Formal litigation in the U.S. civil court system*

Sometimes, the only way to obtain relief or bring public attention to an issue is to bring a matter to court. The following is a brief introduction to aspects of the civil litigation process. *See also* Figure 1-7, which charts the basic stages in the civil litigation process.

16. This section is not designed to provide an exhaustive review of ADR processes. Interested readers can consult books on ADR. *See, e.g.*, STEPHEN B. GOLDBERG, FRANK E. A. SANDER, NANCY H. ROGERS, & SARAH RUDOLPH COLE, DISPUTE RESOLUTION: NEGOTIATION, MEDIATION, ARBITRATION, AND OTHER PROCESSES (7th ed. 2020).

Basic Stages in Formal Civil Litigation

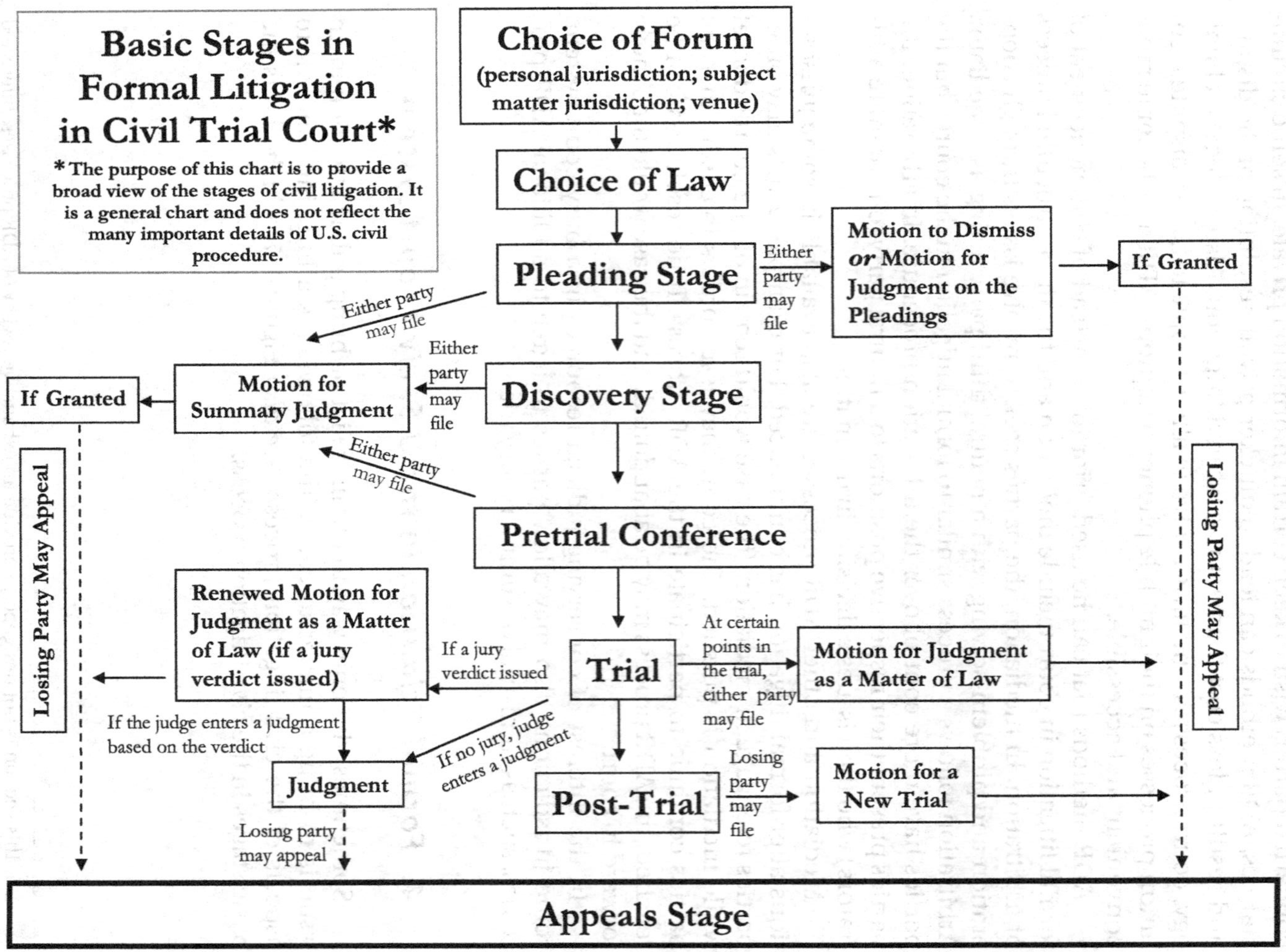

Figure 1-7

a. Choice of forum

In the preliminary stage of the formal litigation process, the parties must decide in which court to bring the lawsuit, known as the choice of forum. A court must have personal jurisdiction over the parties so the judgment reached by the court will be enforceable as to the parties.[17] A court must also possess the power to adjudicate the disputed claims, more commonly referred to as subject matter jurisdiction.[18]

In addition to the personal jurisdiction and subject matter jurisdiction requirements, the parties must give some thought to a variety of venue[19] considerations when deciding which court should hear the controversy. Considerations may include trying the case in a court presided over by a sympathetic judge, in a court that follows more favorable procedural court rules, or in a court situated in a location convenient to the parties, testifying witnesses, or physical evidence.[20]

The plaintiff, as the party bringing the action, will choose the court in which to file the complaint. The defendant in the action may object to the forum chosen by the plaintiff for a variety of reasons and may try to convince the court in the original forum that another court is more suitable to hear the dispute. For example, a defendant may request removal of a case originally filed in a state court to a federal court if the case involves a federal law question.

b. Choice of law

When deciding on a court in which to litigate a case, the lawyer must consider the procedural and substantive laws the court will apply to resolve the controversy. Substantive laws determine the parties' rights and obligations that are at issue in the pleadings. Procedural law governs the process that will determine these rights and obligations. A court applies the law of its own forum to procedural matters. But predicting which substantive law a court will apply is not always straightforward. It would be understandable to assume that a court will always apply the substantive law of its own forum. Indeed, this is the case where a state court is faced with a state law question, and the parties and the events giving rise to the dispute are within the state's jurisdictional boundaries.

In some instances, however, a court will use the substantive law of another jurisdiction. A federal court, for example, will apply state substantive law to a

---

17. *Ruhrgas AG v. Marathon Oil Co.*, 526 U.S. 574, 584 (1999).

18. *Id.* (citing FED. R. CIV. P. 12(h)(3)).

19. *See Japan Gas Lighter Ass'n v. Ronson Corp.*, 257 F. Supp. 219, 224 (D.N.J. 1966) ("Venue deals with the locality of the suit, that is, with the question of which [c]ourt, or [c]ourts, of those that possess adequate personal and subject matter jurisdiction may hear the specific suit in question.")

20. *See, e.g., Goggins v. Alliance Capital Mgmt.*, 279 F. Supp. 228 (S.D.N.Y. 2003).

state law question raised in a diversity jurisdiction action.[21] A state court will apply federal substantive law in actions where federal statutes permit a claimant to bring an action in state court for a violation of federal law.[22] And where transactions or occurrences surrounding the dispute have significant connections to more than one jurisdiction, the court will decide which jurisdiction's substantive law will determine the parties' rights and obligations.

c. The pleading stage

Once the plaintiff has determined the most appropriate forum for the dispute, the plaintiff will file a pleading with the court setting out the claims against the defendant, the basis for the court's jurisdiction, and a request for the court to grant specific relief.

In federal courts, a legal action commences with the filing of the complaint.[23] What constitutes the official commencement of an action in a state court varies from state to state. In some states, the legal action begins with the filing of the complaint. In other states, the action begins when all defendants to the action are served with a copy of the complaint along with a summons to appear in court and respond to the plaintiff's claims ("service of process"). The Federal Rules of Civil Procedure set out federal compliance requirements for service of process.[24] What constitutes adequate service of the complaint and summons on all state court defendants varies from state to state.

A defendant may respond to the complaint by either filing with the court an answer to the complaint, a motion for the court to dismiss the complaint, or both.[25] If the defendant fails to respond to the complaint in one of these ways within the period of time specified by the court rules, the clerk of the

---

21. The exercise at the end of this chapter provides an example. In the exercise, a client from Illinois seeks the return of a painting stolen from her home. The painting is in the possession of a doctor, a citizen of the fictitious state of East Carolina, who refuses to return the painting. The client will have to bring a legal action in a court that has jurisdiction over the doctor so that, if the client prevails, the court will have the power to order the doctor to return the painting. The client and the doctor are citizens of different states, and the painting is valued at more than $75,000. Therefore, although the return of personal property (such as the painting) is governed by state law, the client may consider bringing the action in a federal district court located in East Carolina, rather than a state trial court in East Carolina. Federal district courts located in the citizen's home state are sometimes viewed as being more impartial to a citizen than a state court from that citizen's home state. If the client brings the action in federal district court, the court will need to decide whether to apply the law of Illinois or East Carolina to determine the respective parties' rights to the painting.

22. *Schneider v. Susquehanna Radio Corp.*, 581 S.E.2d 603 (Ga. Ct. App. 2003), provides an example of a state court applying federal law. In this case, claimant filed a cause of action against a radio station for allegedly violating the federal Telephone Consumer Protection Act (TCPA). Under 47 U.S.C.S. § 227(b)(3) (LexisNexis, Lexis Advance through Public Law 117-47, approved October 8, 2021), a claimant can bring an action in state court for a violation of the TCPA.

23. FED. R. CIV. P. 3.

24. FED. R. CIV. P. 4.

25. FED. R. CIV. P. 12.

court will enter a default judgment in favor of the plaintiff.[26] Obviously, the defendant will want to avoid this outcome.

The defendant's answer will specifically respond to each allegation raised in the plaintiff's complaint. As to each allegation, the defendant may elect to admit, deny, or plead that they "lack knowledge or information sufficient to form a belief about the truth of an allegation. . . ."[27] The last response will be treated, in effect, as a denial.[28]

In addition, the defendant may raise available affirmative defenses.[29] An affirmative defense pleads a new matter not raised by the allegations in the complaint. An affirmative defense asserts that if this new matter is true, the defendant will prevail regardless of whether the plaintiff's allegations are true. For example, most claims have statutorily imposed time limits, or statutes of limitations, for filing a complaint. These statutes of limitations protect defendants from loss of evidence that might have helped defeat the claim and from "the emotional stress and financial uncertainty" of possibly being brought into court on an old claim.[30] The expiration of a statute of limitations is an affirmative defense that can be raised if the plaintiff fails to file the claim within the statute of limitations period. Rule 8(c) of the Federal Rules of Civil Procedure provides examples of affirmative defenses.

A defendant also may assert a claim against any codefendant, called a crossclaim, arising from an opposing party's claims.[31] A defendant may also bring claims against a plaintiff, called a counterclaim, which may or may not relate to the claims arising from the plaintiff's complaint.[32] In turn, the party against whom the counterclaim or crossclaim is asserted must file a reply to the claim.[33]

As an alternative or in addition to filing an answer, the defendant may file a motion to dismiss the plaintiff's complaint or a motion to dismiss some of the claims contained in the plaintiff's complaint.[34] A judge may dismiss a complaint because the complaint failed to state a valid claim on which relief can be granted; the court lacked personal jurisdiction over the defendant; or the court lacked subject matter jurisdiction over the dispute.[35]

In a motion to dismiss, the defendant asserts that even if the facts alleged in the plaintiff's complaint are true, the complaint must be dismissed as a

---

26. FED. R. CIV. P. 55(a).

27. FED. R. CIV. P. 8(b).

28. *Id.*

29. FED. R. CIV. P. 8(c).

30. GENE R. SHREVE & PETER RAVEN-HANSEN, UNDERSTANDING CIVIL PROCEDURE 342 (3d ed. 2002).

31. FED. R. CIV. P. 13(g).

32. FED. R. CIV. P. 13(a) & (b). A counterclaim is litigated between opposing parties in the original action, whereas a crossclaim is litigated by parties on the same side in the original action.

33. FED. R. CIV. P. 7(a).

34. FED. R. CIV. P. 12(b).

35. FED. R. CIV. P. 12(b).

matter of law because there is no legal basis for the claim.[36] If the court grants the defendant's motion to dismiss, a judgment is entered in favor of the defendant, dismissing the entire complaint or specific claims stated in the complaint. If the judge denies the motion to dismiss, the defendant must respond to the allegations in the complaint, if they have not already done so.

Additionally, any time between the close of pleadings[37] and prior to trial, a party may move for a judgment on the pleadings.[38] The party moving for a judgment on the pleadings asserts that, based on the pleadings filed by the parties, the court should enter judgment for the moving party as a matter of law. The basis for this motion and the standard the court uses for determining whether to grant the motion are the same as for a motion to dismiss. If the court grants the motion, a judgment is entered for the moving party. If the court denies the motion, the litigation proceeds with discovery or, if discovery has already begun, the discovery process continues.

d. The discovery stage

During the discovery stage, the parties have the opportunity to gather information related to any claims or defenses raised in the pleadings. The discovery stage not only assists the parties in preparing for trial but also helps the parties identify issues and determine the strengths or weaknesses of their respective positions.

There are several methods of discovery. Interrogatories are a series of written questions that must be answered in writing by the opposing party.[39] Depositions are a tool of discovery where a party or witness is questioned under oath about matters related to the controversy and the deposed person responds orally to the questions. A court reporter records the questions and answers, and then prepares a transcript of the deposition for the parties.

In addition to interrogatories and depositions, a party also may request documents relating to the dispute, such as a contract in the case of a contractual dispute.[40] A party also may request an inspection of a physical site, provided it is relevant to the controversy.[41]

As part of discovery, a party may also issue requests for admission to an opposing party. The requests for admission contain written fact statements, which the opposing party must admit or deny.[42] If any statement is admitted, then the admission is binding at trial, meaning that the court will treat the fact as established, making it unnecessary to prove it at trial.[43]

36. *See, e.g., Rippy v. Hattaway*, 270 F.3d 416, 419 (6th Cir. 2001).

37. Pleadings are deemed closed when the defendants have filed their answers to the complaint and the parties have filed replies to any crossclaims and counterclaims.

38. FED. R. CIV. P. 12(c).

39. FED. R. CIV. P. 33.

40. FED. R. CIV. P. 34.

41. *Id.*

42. FED. R. CIV. P. 36.

43. FED. R. CIV. P. 36(b).

e. Resolution of the dispute prior to trial

Most cases do not go to trial.[44] For example, a dispute can be resolved without going to trial if the plaintiff voluntarily withdraws the complaint as permitted under the trial rules or if all parties agree to dismiss the case because they have reached an out-of-court settlement.[45] A court also has the power to dismiss an action before it reaches trial in situations where the plaintiff fails to timely pursue the case or fails to comply with trial rules or court orders.[46]

An action can also be resolved prior to trial if the court grants a party's motion for summary judgment, and the judgment resolves all claims and requests for relief.[47] In a summary judgment motion, the moving party asks the court to enter a judgment in its favor on some or all of the claims. The moving party must assert that there are no genuine issues of material fact as to these claims and thus the moving party is "entitled to judgment as a matter of law."[48]

Either party may move for summary judgment. If the court grants summary judgment as to any or all claims, the court will enter judgment in favor of the moving party as to those claims. If the court denies the motion, the parties continue with discovery or, if discovery is complete, the trial may begin.

f. The pretrial conference

Prior to trial, the judge may order the attorneys representing opposing parties to attend a pretrial conference.[49] Pretrial conferences can help in the management and expedition of the trial. For instance, a conference gives the parties the opportunity to discuss such matters as limiting or restricting testimony at trial, stipulating matters of law, narrowing issues, identifying witnesses and documents, and reaching a settlement of the dispute.[50]

g. The trial

In situations where a party fails to make a timely demand for a jury trial or where a party waives the right to a jury trial,[51] the case will be tried before the judge in a "bench trial" unless the court, in its discretion, orders a jury trial.[52] In bench trials, the judge will make findings of fact[53] and issue rulings of

---

44. *See generally* Brooke D. Coleman, *The Efficiency Norm,* 56 B.C. L. REV. 1777, 1783 (2015) (percentage of civil cases that go to trial "hovers around 1.1%").

45. FED. R. CIV. P. 41(a).

46. FED. R. CIV. P. 41(b).

47. FED. R. CIV. P. 56(a).

48. *Id.*

49. FED. R. CIV. P. 16(a).

50. FED. R. CIV. P. 16(c)(2).

51. FED. R. CIV. P. 38.

52. FED. R. CIV. P. 39(b) & (c).

53. Findings of fact "generally respond to inquiries about who, when, what and where." Henry P. Monaghan, *Constitutional Fact Review,* 85 COLUM. L. REV. 229, 235 (1985).

law.[54] In jury trials, the jury makes findings of fact, and the judge issues rulings of law.[55]

The number of people serving on a civil jury varies. For example, the federal courts require at least 6 but not more than 12 jurors.[56] The members of a jury are determined by a proceeding known as voir dire. In voir dire, the attorneys or the judge asks questions of potential jurors and, based on the potential juror's response, the judge determines whether the potential juror will be fair and impartial when weighing the evidence.[57]

After the selection of a jury (if there is one), the trial begins with the attorney for the plaintiff making an opening statement, which is then followed by the opening statement by the attorney for the defendant. Next, the attorney for the plaintiff presents the plaintiff's case by asking questions of the plaintiff's witnesses on direct examination and introducing evidence to prove the claims alleged in the complaint. Throughout the trial, the judge supervises the conduct of those in the courtroom and determines what evidence is admissible. The attorney for the defendant may cross-examine any of the plaintiff's witnesses. Cross-examination of each witness occurs immediately after direct examination of each witness.

After the plaintiff's attorney has introduced all testimony or other evidence necessary to prove the allegations in the complaint, the attorney will "rest," or end their presentation of the plaintiff's case. At this point, the attorney for the defendant may move for a judgment as a matter of law (JMOL), asking the court to direct a verdict in the defendant's favor based on the argument that "there is no legally sufficient evidentiary basis for a reasonable jury to find for [the plaintiff]. . . ."[58] If the court grants the JMOL, then a judgment is entered in favor of the defendants. In essence, the matter for adjudication is taken away from the jury (if there is one), and the judge enters a judgment for the defendant as a matter of law. In the event the court denies the JMOL, however, the trial will proceed with the defendant's attorney presenting their case.

The attorney for the defendant will present the defendant's case through direct examination of the defendant's witnesses and by offering evidence into the record. This time, the attorney for the plaintiff has the opportunity to cross-examine any of the defendant's witnesses. Again, the judge presides over courtroom conduct and determines whether any evidence is admissible.

After the close of the defendant's case but before the case is given to the jury, either party can move for a JMOL, directing the court to rule in their

---

54. "Rulings of law" determine what law will apply to the facts.

55. To learn more about civil jury trial strategy and mechanics, readers can consult various publications on the topic. *See, e.g.*, TYLER G. DRAA, DORIS CHENG, MAUREEN HARRINGTON, & FRANKLIN E. BONDONNO, MASTERING THE MECHANICS OF CIVIL JURY TRIALS: A STRATEGIC GUIDE OUTLINING THE ANATOMY OF A TRIAL (2015).

56. FED. R. CIV. P. 48.

57. FED. R. CIV. P. 47(a).

58. FED. R. CIV. P. 50(a)(1).

client's favor.[59] If the judge grants the motion, then the judge will enter a judgment in favor of the moving party, and the trial ends. If the judge denies a JMOL after the close of the defendant's case, the plaintiff has the opportunity to present evidence that rebuts any evidence introduced by the defendant. The defendant, in turn, is given a chance to present evidence that rebuts the evidence introduced in the plaintiff's rebuttal. Finally, the attorneys for the plaintiff and defendant present their closing arguments to the jury or to the judge when serving the role of the fact-finder in a bench trial.

After the closing arguments in a bench trial, the judge considers the evidence presented in the case in light of the applicable law, reaches a decision, and enters a judgment. If it is a jury trial, the jury will deliberate over the facts of the case in light of instructions of law from the judge to reach a decision about the case.

When the jury returns its decision, called a verdict, the losing party may renew its motion for JMOL (often referred to at this stage as a renewed JMOL or RJMOL). The losing party moving for an RJMOL requests the judge to enter a judgment in that party's favor, despite the jury's verdict against that party.[60] If the judge finds insufficient evidence to support the verdict, then the judge grants the RJMOL.[61] If the judge finds the verdict reasonable, the judge enters a judgment reflecting the jury verdict.[62]

h. Post-trial stage

At the trial court level. The losing party may make a motion to the trial judge for a new trial.[63] This motion can be filed as an alternative motion at the same time as the filing of an RJMOL.[64] Although the trial judge has broad discretion to order a new trial, a judge will not liberally grant new trials in deference to the jury and in light of the time and cost of conducting a new trial.[65]

At the appellate court level. The losing party can also appeal any final judgment[66] of the trial court to a higher court in that court system. With some limited exceptions, judicial orders made by a judge during a trial, including most denials of summary judgment or partial summary judgments, may not

---

59. FED. R. CIV. P. 50(a).

60. FED. R. CIV. P. 50(b).

61. *Id.*

62. FED. R. CIV. P. 50(b)(1).

63. FED. R. CIV. P. 59(b).

64. FED. R. CIV. P. 50(b). In the case of alternative motions, the judge can decide whether to grant the RJMOL or the motion for a new trial, or to deny both motions.

65. *See also* FED. R. CIV. P. 61. ("Unless justice requires otherwise, no error in admitting or excluding evidence—or any other error by the court or a party—is ground for granting a new trial, for setting aside a verdict, or for vacating, modifying, or otherwise disturbing a judgment or order. At every stage of the proceeding, the court must disregard all errors and defects that do not affect any party's substantial rights.")

66. Fed. R. App. P. 4.

be appealed until the trial concludes and final judgment has been entered in the case.

i. The appeals stage

Usually the party seeking appellate review is the losing party. A prevailing party, however, may also seek appellate review if, for example, the prevailing party wants an increase in the amount of damages awarded by the trial court in its judgment. The party seeking the appeal must give notice of appeal in the manner and within a time period specified in the applicable appellate rules.[67]

On the federal level and in states where there are both an intermediate court of appeals and a final court of appeals, the case will be reviewed first by the intermediate appeals court. A copy of the trial court record, including witness testimony and documents marked as trial exhibits, will be sent to the appeals court for review. The court of appeals will not hear any additional testimony or admit new evidence into the case. The parties will also write briefs to the courts, arguing their respective positions. Sometimes the court will want to hear oral arguments to have an opportunity to ask the parties' attorneys questions about the issues raised on appeal.

The decision of the appeals court is issued in the form of a written opinion, explaining the court's reasons for affirming or reversing the trial court's decision and perhaps "remanding the case" (sending the case back to the trial court) for retrial. An appeals court reverses or modifies the trial court's decision only if it finds the trial court committed an error that affected the substantial rights of the parties, meaning that it must have affected the outcome of the case.[68]

The losing party on appeal may request the highest court in the court system to review the case. Except in strictly limited circumstances, the highest court, however, is not required to grant a review. In the event that the highest court in its discretion agrees to review a case, its judgment is final. On appeal, the parties again file briefs in support of their respective positions, and the court may hear oral arguments on the matter. The highest court then issues a written opinion, explaining the reason for its decision.

j. Res judicata

Once a claim has been fully litigated and a valid, final judgment on the merits has been issued, the parties cannot relitigate in a subsequent action an issue raised or an issue that could have been raised in this case.[69] The doctrine precluding relitigation of issues is referred to as res judicata.[70]

---

67. *See, e.g.*, FED. R. APP. P. 3, 4, & 5.

68. *Beck v. Haik*, 377 F.3d 624, 634 (6th Cir. 2004) (quoting *Kotteakos v. United States*, 328 U.S. 750, 765 (1946)); *Crabtree v. National Steel Corp.*, 261 F.3d 715, 719 (7th Cir. 2001).

69. *Allen v. McCurry*, 449 U.S. 90, 94 (1980).

70. Res judicata is based on "the generally recognized public policy that there must be some end to litigation and that when one appears in court to present his case, is fully heard, and the contested issue is decided against him, he may not later renew the litigation in another court." *Heiser v. Woodruff*, 327 U.S. 726, 733 (1946).

For example, a golfer (A) sues a homeowner (B) whose land abuts a golf course for injuries sustained when he went on the defendant B's land to retrieve his golf ball and was bitten by the homeowner's dog. This issue has never been decided by a court in defendant B's state. The trial court finds that defendant B owed no duty of care to A to protect him from B's dog. Plaintiff A appeals the case of *A v. B* all the way to the highest court in the state, and the highest court affirms the trial court's decision. The case is now res judicata, which means that plaintiff A can never sue defendant B again for these particular injuries.

Let us say that, after the decision in *A v. B*, another golfer (X) is injured when he is bitten by defendant Y's dog while retrieving a golf ball from Y's property. Plaintiff X pursues his claim to the state's highest court, which, after agreeing to hear the case, decides that its prior decision in *A v. B* does not reflect current public policy and so overturns the decision by finding that defendant Y owed a duty to plaintiff X to protect him from the dog. Plaintiff A (from the previous case of *A v. B*) cannot bring a new action against defendant B for his prior injuries, even though the law has changed in his state to allow for such an action. It would be possible, however, after the decision in *X v. Y* for plaintiff A to bring an action against defendant B if he is again injured by defendant B's dog while retrieving another golf ball from defendant B's land, since res judicata applies only to the injuries alleged in the original dispute.

• Exercise 1-A

You recently met with Edina Broward. Ms. Broward has asked your help in obtaining the return of a painting stolen from her home. You taped the interview. The following is a transcript of the interview. Prepare a summary statement of the situation. Include in your summary (1) the identity of the parties, (2) any important "when" facts, (3) any important "where" facts, and (4) all other facts you believe might be relevant.

Transcript of the Interview with Edina Broward

Lawyer: Good afternoon, Ms. Broward. We have talked briefly about your problem over the phone, but now I'd like to start at the beginning, if you don't mind.

Edina: Yes, that would be fine.

Lawyer: Good. Let's start by getting your full name and where you live.

Edina: I'm Edina Lawton Broward. I live at 303 Forest Drive, in Oak Park, Illinois.

Lawyer: And is this the same residence where you lived when the painting was stolen?

Edina: Yes. It happened in 1985 when I was moving out of my house. A temporary move, you see. The house was in need of repairs and major renovation. I thought it would be best to move everything out of the house so the workers could do their job, and I wouldn't have to worry about their ruining my antique furniture and rugs. I inherited the house from my father when he passed away in the 1970s. It's a lovely home; the famous architect Frank Lloyd Wright built it in 1903. Unfortunately, my father didn't keep up repairs during his final years.

Lawyer: Before we talk any further, tell me about the painting.

Edina: I inherited the painting from my father, just like the house. He was an attorney, just like yourself, though he practiced law in Chicago. Samuel Bryce Broward IV. He was the founding partner in the firm Broward & Fromm. He loved practicing law, but his real passion was art, especially the sketches and paintings of the Impressionists. The stolen painting was by the American Impressionist James Singer Sargent and had been his pride and joy. It was an oil on canvas of the Rialto Bridge, which Sargent had painted in 1913 during one of his many visits to Venice, Italy.

Lawyer: Do you remember when your father acquired it and how much he paid for it?

Edina: He kept documents on it. The records show he purchased the painting in 1925 for $800.

Lawyer: Did you ever have the painting appraised for insurance purposes?

Edina: No. I really don't know why. I thought the painting was covered by the insurance policy on the house. I didn't realize until the painting went missing that it wasn't covered under the policy. I do know that Dr. Warren, the man who has the painting now, paid $200,000 for it.

Lawyer: Let's go back to when the painting was stolen. You told me earlier that the painting was stolen when you moved your furnishings from the house.

Edina: Well, I didn't know immediately that the painting had been stolen. For several days, I thought the painting had just been lost in the move.

Lawyer: Do you remember the date you moved from the house?

Edina: October 5, 1985.

Lawyer: And can you tell me what you remember about that day?

Edina: I had taken the painting down from the wall. And I had wrapped it in brown paper and had tied it with a string. I wrote on the front of the paper, "Don't Move" in black marker and placed it in the corner of the room. I had planned for the movers to transport some of the furnishings down to my winter home in Florida, rather than risk putting them in storage. But I had planned to take the painting with me when I traveled to Florida. There were a lot of men from the moving company, packing and taking things out to the van. Also, some workers from the home restoration company were there that day, working on the second floor of the house. The workers sometimes passed through the front hall, next to the parlor, to get equipment and supplies from their truck. I was busy directing the movers on which furnishings to take to storage and which furnishings would be sent to Florida. When the movers were ready to leave, I noticed that the painting was missing. I asked the movers whether they remembered seeing the painting, and I even asked the workers from the restoration company whether they had seen the painting, but no one could recall. I assumed the painting must have been inadvertently put into one of the vans. The moving supervisor said that they would take careful inventory of my furnishings when they moved them off the truck into storage. If they found the painting, he would contact me. When the other van arrived at my Florida home several days later, they unloaded my furnishings, but the painting was not there.

Lawyer: Had the van stopped en route to Florida to pick up other transports?

Edina: No. The movers said that they had closed the van before it left my home, locked it, and had not reopened it until they arrived at my Florida home.

Lawyer: And what about the van going to the storage facility?

Edina: The moving supervisor told me that the painting had not been found in that van, either.

Lawyer: So what did you do?

Edina: I called a partner from my father's old firm, William McIntyre. He called the police. We filled out a theft report with the police. The police wanted a photograph of the painting, but I didn't have one. I just gave them a description of the painting. Mr. McIntyre also helped me hire a private investigator to track down the painting.

Lawyer: And what was the investigator's name?

Edina: James Morgan. He had done some work for Mr. McIntyre in the past. I doubt he is still in business. He was an older person. I suppose he's retired now.

Lawyer: Did Mr. Morgan find any leads?

Edina: No, he spent several weeks investigating the moving company, the restoration company, and their workers. He also questioned neighbors to determine whether they saw anything. He really didn't do any more than what the police did. Neither Mr. Morgan nor the police were able to turn up any information. It was about this same time that the insurance company told me that the painting was not insured.

Lawyer: When was that?

Edina: January of 1986. The police continued to investigate, though not as actively as before. I called them in October 1986, almost one year after the painting had disappeared, to see if they had turned up anything. But after talking with a detective, it became clear to me that finding the missing painting was not a top priority for them. I guess that the file remains open to this day. I was so sad. It wasn't so much the loss of the value of the painting. I'm not an art collector or art fan, and I don't subscribe to art magazines or regularly visit museums. For me, the painting had sentimental value. My father adored the painting. It was like losing a part of my father when I lost that painting.

Lawyer: Did you do anything else to try to find the painting?

Edina: Mr. McIntyre wrote the local museums, including the Art Institute of Chicago, the Terra Museum of American Art, and the Smart Museum of Art, and some local art dealers and auction houses. In the letters, he described the missing painting and requested that anyone who may have seen the painting or knew of its whereabouts contact the police, Mr. McIntyre, or me. I even offered an award of $25,000 for information that would lead to finding the painting. Mr. McIntyre followed up his letters with telephone calls to these places. No one had any helpful information.

Lawyer: Did you just give up looking for the painting at that point?

Edina: No, no. I never gave up looking for the painting. But Mr. McIntyre died in September of 1986. He was a close family friend, and, after he was gone, I never felt comfortable hiring another attorney. I never married, and I didn't have any family living nearby. I just didn't know who to ask to help me. Then I started suffering periodic dizzy spells that left me bedridden for days. I was only 55, but the doctor said that I had a disease of the inner ear. I had hoped that the police and Mr. McIntyre's letters would result in someone finding my painting.

Lawyer: But you, personally, haven't done anything else to find the painting?

Edina: Last year, I was reading the *Chicago Tribune* and came across an article reporting on the renewed popularity in artwork of American Impressionist painters. The article made me think that maybe, with the renewed popularity, whoever had my painting would try to sell it or exhibit it. I had kept copies of Mr. McIntyre's letters to the museums, auction houses, and art dealers. I wrote my own letters to these places, reminding them about my stolen painting and asking them to contact me if they saw or heard about my painting.

Lawyer: And did anything come of this?

Edina: No, but a curator at the Art Institute of Chicago recommended that I file a theft report with IFAR.

Lawyer: What is IFAR?

Edina: The International Foundation for Art Research. It's a global organization that reports stolen art to museums, galleries, auction houses, and other businesses and experts that deal in fine art.

Lawyer: Why didn't you do this earlier?

Edina: I didn't know about IFAR until then. It wasn't in existence when my painting was stolen.

Lawyer: When did you file the report?

Edina: July 25 of last year.

Lawyer: And is that how you learned about the painting's whereabouts?

Edina: No. My grand-niece, Susan Broward, has a friend, Mary Carter, who is an art student at the University of East Carolina. She attended an art exhibit last month at the university and saw my painting. She had talked with Susan some time ago about my stolen painting. A painting on exhibit at the university reminded Mary of my painting. Mary called Susan and told her about the painting. Susan gave my phone number to Mary, and Mary called me. Mary told me that the plaque by the painting noted that it was "owned" by Dr. Thomas Warren of Flora, East Carolina. I was able to track down Dr. Warren's phone number and called him. I explained to him what had happened to my painting and described my painting to him.

Lawyer: And what did he say?

Edina: He admitted that the painting I described was the painting in his possession. But, when I asked him to return the painting to me, he refused. He said that he had purchased the painting in June of 1988 from a reputable art gallery in Flora, the Nigel Townsend Gallery. The painting had been sold as part of the estate of Jeremy Thorne, a wealthy Flora art collector who had a special interest in American Impressionists. He died in 1987. There were no existing records as to where or how Mr. Thorne had acquired the painting. Dr. Warren purchased the painting for $200,000.

Lawyer: Did you ask Dr. Warren whether he looked into the prior history of the painting's ownership before he purchased it?

Edina: Dr. Warren said that Mr. Thorne was well respected. He didn't think Mr. Thorne would have a stolen painting in his collection, and the painting was in perfect condition. Dr. Warren said he had no reason to suspect the painting was stolen.

Lawyer: Was last month the first time Dr. Warren had publicly exhibited the painting?

Edina: He had exhibited the painting several times since he purchased it. He said that he had exhibited the painting in 1990, 1995, 2000, and 2005, mostly at local art galleries in Flora but once at the East Carolina Museum of Art. Each time the painting was on exhibit for about a month, except at the Museum of Art, where it was on exhibit for six months as part of a special show celebrating American Impressionist artists. Otherwise, the painting has been kept at Dr. Warren's private residence in Flora.

Lawyer: Is there anything else you can tell me about the painting and your search for it?

Edina: Not that I can think of. I want the painting back. It was my father's, and it was stolen from me. I don't care how much Dr. Warren paid for it or how long he has kept it, he bought a stolen painting. The painting belongs to me. If he refuses to give it back to me, I want to take him to court. Surely, a judge will order him to return it to me.

Lawyer: I will look into the matter and get back with you, Edina. Then, we can discuss what action you may want to take.

CHAPTER SUMMARY

- The United States has a dual system of government, composed of a federal system and a state system.
- Law in the United States, at the state and federal levels, comes from four main sources: (1) constitutions, (2) statutes, (3) case decisions, and (4) administrative regulations.

- The federal and state constitutions provide a framework for three branches at federal and state levels: the legislative branch, the executive branch, and the judicial branch.
- The legislative branch enacts statutes.
- The executive branch enforces and implements statutes.
- The judicial branch comprises courts that decide matters brought before them; the courts may interpret statutes and create law in situations not addressed by statute.
- The rules and principles created by courts are referred to as the common law.
- The federal system and the state system each have a set of courts including trial courts and appellate courts.
- Parties to a legal dispute may seek resolution of a dispute through informal negotiations, mediation, or arbitration, or a party may seek to resolve a dispute by filing a complaint in court and thereby initiating a lawsuit.
- At trial, each party to the dispute has an opportunity to present their case through witness testimony and the presentation of evidence.
- A losing party may appeal the trial court's final judgment.
- Once a dispute has been fully litigated and a final judgment is entered, the same parties are barred from re-litigating the same legal dispute.

CHAPTER 2

The Common Law in the United States

A. What Is the Common Law, and Why Does It Matter?

The judiciary in the United States plays a vital role in the law-making process. The judicial system in the United States differs from that of some other countries, since judges in the United States must look to previous decisions as part of their decision-making process. Even if there is an applicable statute, judges in the United States deciding a case cannot look only to the relevant language in a statute; they must also consider if judges in prior cases with similar legal issues or facts have applied the statute. The prior case decisions are referred to as precedent. Precedent makes up the common law. And so, the work of lawyers in either advising clients on a matter or preparing to argue before a court often does not consist of simply identifying a statute that might or should apply in their client's situation. The lawyer must also review judicial decisions.

B. The Judicial Doctrine of Stare Decisis

A judicial doctrine known as *stare decisis* underlies the decision making of courts in the United States. In Latin, *stare decisis* means "to stand by things decided."[1]

A court abiding by the doctrine of stare decisis is mindful of precedent and reconciles new decisions with its own prior decisions or with those of a higher court. Over the years, many reasons have been offered to support the use of the doctrine of stare decisis. Those reasons include:

1. *Certainty in the law:* When judges consistently apply the same rules to substantially similar fact situations, people can plan their actions with a measure of confidence because they are better able to predict the legal consequences of their actions.[2]
2. *Fairness:* The consistent application of rules will result in equal treatment of parties similarly situated.[3]
3. *Court efficiency:* Relying on precedent frees judges from the burden of recreating rules and principles with each new case.[4]
4. *Justice and judicial impartiality:* Judges who base their decisions on precedent promote the appearance of justice and judicial impartiality in the decision-making process. The public has greater confidence in the judiciary when there is less opportunity for judges' personal opinions to influence their decisions.[5]

Precedent that a court is bound to follow is called mandatory or binding precedent. Courts, however, can also seek guidance from non-binding precedent, which is frequently referred to as persuasive precedent.

1. Mandatory precedent

In the state court system, a trial court is bound by the previous decisions of the higher courts within its jurisdictional borders and federal statutory and constitutional decisions of the United States Supreme Court. If the state has a three-tiered court system, the intermediate appellate court is bound by (1) its previous decisions, (2) previous decisions of the court of last resort in the state, and (3) previous federal statutory and constitutional decisions of the United States Supreme Court. The state court of last resort—that is, the highest state

---

1. *Stare decisis,* Legal Information Institute, https://www.law.cornell.edu/wex/stare_decisis.
2. *See* Frederick Schauer, *Precedent,* 39 Stan. L. Rev. 571, 597-98 (1987).
3. *See id.* at 595-97.
4. Justice Benjamin N. Cardozo, a renown U.S. judge, noted that "the labor of judges would be increased almost to the breaking point if every past decision could be reopened in every case, and one could not lay one's own course of bricks on the secure foundation of the courses laid by others who had gone before him." Benjamin N. Cardozo, The Nature of the Judicial Process 149 (1921).
5. Earl Maltz, *The Nature of Precedent,* 66 N.C. L. Rev. 367, 371 (1988).

court—is bound only by (1) its own previous decisions, and (2) the previous federal statutory and constitutional decisions of the United States Supreme Court. (See Figure 2-1 for a chart of a state court system's general appeals hierarchy.)

For example, in the State of California, which has a three-tiered court system, a California trial court must abide by (1) previous decisions of the California Court of Appeal for its region, (2) the previous decisions of the California Supreme Court, and (3) the previous federal statutory and constitutional decisions of the United States Supreme Court. A California Court of Appeal, however, is bound only by (1) previous decisions within its own region,[6] (2) previous California Supreme Court decisions, and (3) previous federal statutory and constitutional decisions of the United States Supreme Court. The California Supreme Court is bound only by (1) its own previous decisions and (2) previous federal statutory and constitutional decisions of the United States Supreme Court. (See Figure 1-6 in Chapter 1 for a chart of the California court hierarchy. Please note that the California court system is used here as an example and that there can be variations among three-tiered state court systems.)

In the federal court system, a district or trial court is bound by (1) the previous decisions of the United States Supreme Court, (2) the previous decisions of the court of appeals of the circuit in which the district court is located, and (3) its own previous decisions. (See Figure 2-1 for the federal court system's general appeals hierarchy. A more descriptive federal court hierarchy chart is found in Figure 1-5 in Chapter 1.) Therefore, a federal district court in California must abide by (1) the previous decisions of the United States Supreme Court, (2) the previous decisions of the United States Court of Appeals for the Ninth Circuit (the circuit in which the California district courts reside), and (3) its own previous decisions.

Courts of appeals, such as the United States Court of Appeals for the Ninth Circuit, are not bound by previous decisions of district courts (federal trial courts) or previous decisions from other circuit courts of appeal. Nevertheless, these courts of appeals are required to abide by (1) their own previous decisions and (2) those of the United States Supreme Court. Of course, the United States Supreme Court is bound only by its own previous decisions.

A special situation, however, arises when a federal court is deciding a matter of state law. A federal court may have jurisdiction over certain disputes arising under state law when the claimed losses exceed $75,000 and the dispute is between:

"**(1)** Citizens of different [s]tates;
(2) citizens of a [s]tate and citizens or subjects of a foreign [country] . . . ;

6. *See, e.g., Cleveland v. Thomas*, 17 Cal. App. 4th 1700, 1709 (2d Dist. 1993) (the California Court of Appeal for the Second District stated that it was not bound to follow a prior decision of the California Court of Appeal for the Sixth District on a similar issue and rejected the Sixth District's decision). Also, another helpful source on mandatory and persuasive authorities is Barbara Bintliff, *Mandatory v. Persuasive Cases*, 9 No. 2 Persp.: Teaching Legal Res. & Writing 83 (Winter 2001).

Hierarchy of Appeals

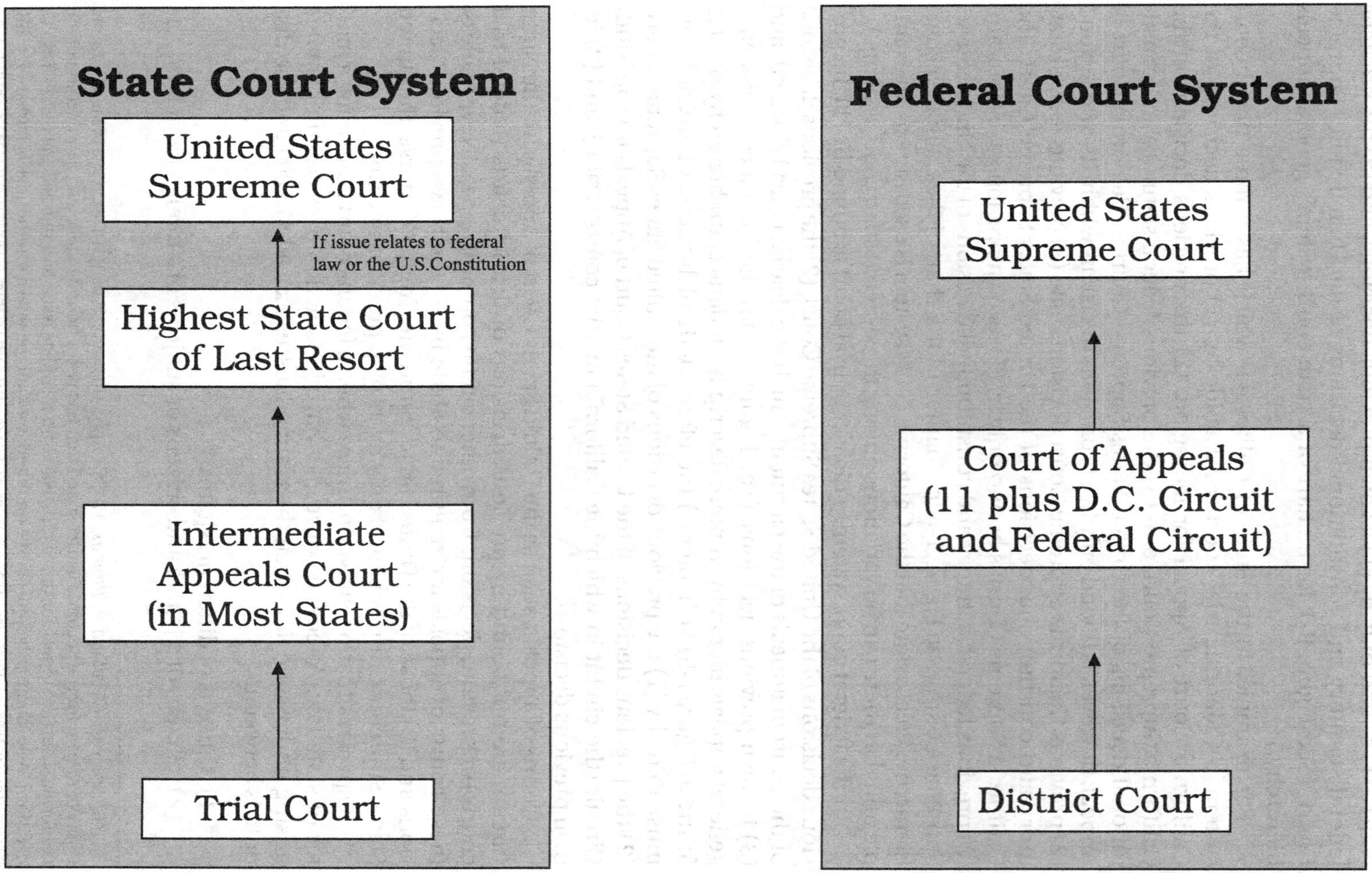

Figure 2-1

(3) citizens of different [s]tates and in which citizens or subjects of a foreign state are additional parties; [or]
(4) a foreign state . . . as plaintiff and citizens of a [s]tate or different [s]tates."[7]

A federal court's jurisdiction in these cases is based on the different citizenships of the parties and the amount in controversy. Here, the federal court applies the law that it determines the state's court of last resort would apply if the state court was faced with the same issue. While the federal court's decision is binding on the parties in that dispute, the state court is not bound by the federal court's decision. Remember, a state court is bound only by (1) previous decisions of its own court, (2) previous decisions of higher courts within its jurisdiction, and (3) previous federal statutory and constitutional decisions of the United States Supreme Court. The federal court is not within a state court's jurisdiction. As previously mentioned, the federal court system is a separate court system from the state court system. (See also Figure 2-1.) For example, assume a federal district court in California issued a decision in Case A based on the California state right of publicity and cases interpreting it. Assume that a year later a California state court was deciding a case concerning a similar right of publicity issue. That state court is not bound to follow the California federal district court decision from the previous year.

2. *Persuasive precedent*

If no mandatory precedent exists, a court may seek guidance from persuasive precedent, in addition to other sources.[8] Persuasive precedent is precedent that is not binding on the court. For instance, the California Supreme Court, especially when faced with a case presenting an issue the court has not addressed before, may be persuaded by a decision of the California Court of Appeal, even though it is not bound to follow that decision. A court may also look at persuasive case decisions outside its jurisdiction. The California Supreme Court, for example, may look to an Arizona decision on the same issue for guidance. In the federal court system, a comparable example would be the United States Court of Appeals for the Ninth Circuit being persuaded by a decision from the United States Court of Appeals for the Second Circuit.

---

7. 28 U.S.C. § 1332(a)(1)&(2).

8. For example, courts may seek guidance from statutes from other jurisdictions and from secondary authorities, including law review articles or treatises. Research texts provide extensive discussion of secondary authorities. *See* CHRISTINA KUNZ ET AL., THE PROCESS OF LEGAL RESEARCH (8th ed. 2012); AMY SLOAN, BASIC LEGAL RESEARCH: TOOLS AND STRATEGIES (8th ed. 2021).

C. The Evolving Common Law

1. Creating and developing the common law

The judge's role in creating and developing rules and principles that compose the common law can be challenging. The conscientious judge, when creating a new rule, will strive to do so in a way that brings a just result to the current dispute but also makes clear which future factual situations may be subject to the rule. During this decision-making process, the judge also may consider public policy—that is, the interest of the public and whether or not the rule will promote social, economic, moral, or other types of societal or legislative goals.

If a judge creates a rule using language that is drawn too narrowly, the rule will give insufficient notice to the public of its application. This could result in courts being overwhelmed with litigation involving similar situations. For the sake of certainty in the law and judicial efficiency, a court generally strives to create a rule that is not too narrow. For example, suppose Landowner A's property has an apple tree situated near the boundary line with Landowner B's property. Apples drop off the tree, and some fall in the yard of Landowner B. Landowner A walks onto Landowner B's property, picks up the apples, and takes them home. Landowner B sues Landowner A for trespass, claiming Landowner A entered onto Landowner B's property without permission. A court deciding this issue must first determine whether there is a statute governing this situation. If there is no applicable statute, a court will rely on prior similar court decisions to determine whether there is mandatory common law precedent on this issue. If no mandatory precedent exists, the court is faced with a new, unresolved issue in its jurisdiction, often referred to as an issue of first impression. During the decision-making process, the court may look to persuasive precedent and other law resources for guidance.[9] In addition, the court will consider how the decision will serve justice in the immediate situation and how the decision will support or further the goals of the public's interest in the future.

In Landowner A's situation, let's say the court decides that in the interest of fairness and in the interest of the public, Landowner A should have the right to go onto Landowner B's property to pick up the apples fallen from Landowner A's trees. In reaching its decision, the court should draft the language of the rule. A rule that states, "Owners of apple trees have the right to walk onto adjoining property to pick up apples that have fallen from their trees," certainly addresses the current case. But how does this rule affect future situations? Would this rule be too narrow? Should an owner of peach trees, for example, have the same right to pick up peaches that have fallen onto a neighboring

9. *See supra* text accompanying note 8.

property? Is there any critical difference between apples and peaches in this situation? If there is no critical difference between apples and peaches, then the rule likely was drafted too narrowly.

Conversely, a rule that is written too broadly can also create problems. A broadly constructed rule can unintentionally affect fact situations far outside the intended scope of the rule. As with a rule that is too narrowly stated, a rule that uses overly broad language can create uncertainty in the law. This can result in a flood of litigation attempting to weaken the rule by arguing for exceptions to the rule.

Referring again to the case of Landowner A's retrieval of apples from Landowner B's property, a rule that states, "A person has the right to enter the land of another in order to retrieve their property," is overly broad. This rule, as written, would seem to give anyone the right to walk onto someone else's land. This could be especially burdensome, for instance, to a homeowner whose land borders a recreational area where people play baseball, volleyball, and tennis. The broadly worded rule would give everyone playing in the recreational area the unlimited right to retrieve any of their baseballs, volleyballs, and tennis balls landing on the homeowner's land all the time. This scenario arguably gives rise to fairness and perhaps public interest concerns that are quite different than those in Landowner A's situation, which merely involves an adjoining landowner's right to retrieve his property.

A judge deciding the issue of whether a landowner can retrieve apples from neighboring property would probably not want to construct a rule that has such a far-reaching effect. Perhaps it would be better to leave the decision regarding the retrieval of baseballs, volleyballs, or tennis balls to a time when such an issue arises and the court is in a better position to contemplate the particular concerns implicated by that issue. Therefore, the court should carefully draft rules that are neither too narrow nor too broad. Ideally, it chooses words that include those groups intended to be affected by the rule and excludes all others. Limiting the landowner's right to enter another's property to retrieve only apples leaves open the question of whether the rule should also apply to retrieving other types of fruit. Conversely, permitting all persons the right to retrieve any of their property from another's land may give rights far beyond those implicated by the current situation before the court.

Ideally, a judge not only drafts a rule that provides a fair result for the parties in the current case but also provides guidance to potential parties in future cases. Lawyers in the United States must read cases closely and carefully until they have a full understanding of the scope of the rule created by the court.

2. The interaction between the common law and other forms of law

The federal constitution is the supreme law of the land. On the state level, a state constitution follows right behind the federal constitution in level of importance. All other laws—federal and state statutes, regulations created pursuant to statutes, and common law—cannot infringe on federal constitutional law. On the state level, a state's statutes, regulations created pursuant to state statutes, and common law cannot violate federal or state constitutional law.

Courts, as guardians of the federal and state constitutions, must ensure that constitutional rights and protections are not violated by statutes, regulations, or court decisions.[10] Sometimes legislatures enact a statute that may inadvertently infringe on rights and protections provided under the U.S. Constitution or a state's constitution. In these instances, the court must determine whether the statute violates the constitutional law. If the court finds a statute applied in any circumstance would be unconstitutional, then the statute will no longer be given effect. For example, the Washington Supreme Court in a 2003 decision found a Washington statute unconstitutional, and thus unenforceable, because it exempted in-state wine producers from a statute that required out-of-state wine producers to give notice and cause before terminating contracts with distributors in the state.[11] The court concluded that the statute violated the Commerce Clause of the U.S. Constitution[12] because the exemption impermissibly "protect[ed] in-state wine producers and discriminate[d] against out-of-state producers" by allowing in-state producers more flexibility to do business.[13]

If a statute is constitutional, a court must abide by the statute and should not create precedent that runs contrary to a statute enacted by the legislature. Sometimes, though, a statute can be ambiguous or vague as written or as applied to a certain factual situation. In these instances, the court's role is to interpret the statute to determine whether the statute applies to the case facts currently before the court.[14] If the legislature does not agree with the court's interpretation of the statute, the legislature may amend the statute to express more clearly the legislative intent behind the statute.

Even if a statute is not directly or explicitly applicable to the factual circumstances of a case before the court, the public policy that motivated the enactment of the statute may influence a court in determining whether to extend the law expressed in the statute to other factual situations.

In analyzing a client's case, law students and lawyers may find it helpful to consider these ways in which a court might use prior law in its analysis:

10. This principle stems from the early U.S. Supreme Court case, *Marbury v. Madison,* 5 U.S. 137 (1803).

11. *Mt. Hood Beverage Co. v. Constellation Brands,* 63 P.3d 779 (Wash. 2003) (finding section 19.126.040 of the Washington Code unconstitutional).

12. U.S. CONST. art. I, § 8, cl. 3.

13. *Mt. Hood Beverage,* 63 P.3d at 786–87.

14. A more detailed explanation of the court's role in statutory interpretation is given in Chapter 12.

a. A court may find that the same rule from a prior case applies to a present case before the court. When the court applies that rule to the facts of a present case, the result might be any of the following:

1. The outcome in the present case is the *same* outcome as the prior case because the important facts in both cases are sufficiently similar.
2. The outcome in the present case is a *different* outcome from the prior case because the important facts in the present case are sufficiently different from the important facts in the prior case.
3. The rule is expanded to include new, important facts of the present case.
4. An exception is created to the rule to exclude the new, important facts of the present case.

b. A court may find that the rule stated in prior case law has been replaced by a statute and thus is no longer applicable.

c. A reviewing court may find that the rule is no longer good law based on policy considerations and needs to be changed, so the prior case warrants overruling.

3. *The living law*

A court must adhere to the constraints of mandatory precedent, as well as constitutional and statutory law, but this does not mean that the common law is stagnant and unchanging. On the contrary, the common law is "living law." It is constantly evolving to keep current with scientific and technological advancements, as well as changing social customs and economic considerations. Traditionally, courts have used three rationales to depart from mandatory precedent:[15] (1) a development in the law has created a conflict between two precedents,[16] (2) the rule underlying the precedent is flawed[17] or

---

15. Amy L. Padden, *Overruling Decisions in the Supreme Court: The Role of a Decision's Vote, Age, and Subject Matter in the Application of Stare Decisis after Payne v. Tennessee*, 82 GEO. L.J. 1689, 1694 (1994).

16. *See generally* Maltz, *supra* note 5, at 383. Professor Maltz cites as an example the United States Supreme Court decision in *City of New Orleans v. Dukes*, 427 U.S. 297 (1976), which overruled the Court's prior decision in *Morey v. Doud*, 354 U.S. 457 (1957). *Id.* In *Morey*, the Court held that the special exemption of the American Express Company from the Illinois Currency Act was unconstitutional because the classification lacked a rational basis for doing so. *Morey*, 354 U.S. at 466-69, *cited in Maltz, supra* note 5, at 383 n.81. Since *Morey*, there had been an "unbroken line of cases that left states free to make classifications in cases involving purely economic regulations"; however, in an effort to avoid further confusion in the lower courts that sometimes relied on *Morey* to strike down local business regulations, the *Dukes* Court overruled *Morey*. Maltz, *supra* note 5, at 383 (citing *Dukes*, 427 U.S. at 306).

17. *See, e.g., Proctor v. State*, 967 S.W.2d 840, 845 & note 4 (Tex. Crim. App. 1998) (noting that prior decisions by the court were "poorly reasoned," the court overruled precedent requiring the state to prove beyond a reasonable doubt that prosecution was not barred by the statute of limitations, even when the defendant does not raise the issue).

has become unworkable,[18] or (3) the policy supporting the precedent does not reflect contemporary public policy interests and concerns.[19] When the highest court in the jurisdiction rejects the governing precedent by overruling the precedent and creates a new rule of law, that new rule will serve as precedent in future cases.

CHAPTER SUMMARY

- Under the doctrine of stare decisis, a court reconciles a new decision with that court's prior decisions and higher court decisions in the same jurisdiction involving similar legal issues and substantially similar facts.
- Mandatory precedents are prior court decisions that a court must follow when reaching a decision in a current case.
- Persuasive precedents are prior court decisions that a court may be persuaded to follow but is not obligated to follow when reaching a decision in a current case.
- A court need not follow its own or higher courts' prior decisions when the facts of the current case are substantially different from the facts of prior cases.
- A court may depart from precedent when (1) a development in the law results in a conflict between two precedents, (2) the rule relied upon in the precedent has become unworkable, or (3) the policy underlying the precedent does not reflect current public policy interests and concerns.

---

18. *See, e.g., Padilla v. State Farm Mut. Auto. Ins. Co.*, 68 P.3d 901 (N.M. 2003) (reasoning the prior rule unworkable, the court overruled precedent that upheld arbitration provisions in automobile insurance contracts providing for binding arbitration so long as the award did not exceed the limits under statute and would be subject to de novo appeal by either party).

19. *See, e.g., State v. Valentine*, 935 P.2d 1294 (Wash. 1997) (court relied on a perceived change in public policy to overrule prior common law that permitted citizens to resist unlawful arrests).

CHAPTER

3

The U.S. Legal Education System: Studying the Law and Briefing Cases

A. Why We Study Cases to Learn the Law

Studying U.S. law involves studying more than rules and codes. It requires critically reviewing U.S. constitutional provisions, statutes, and cases. The overriding goal is to learn (1) what legal principles and policies are relevant to a legal issue; (2) how to analyze and apply those legal principles and policies to a client's set of facts; and (3) how to create arguments on behalf of parties in a legal dispute.

In the U.S. legal system, the specific language of constitutional provisions, statutes, and legal principles developed through court decisions (the common law) is essential to a legal analysis.[1] And yet that language does not mean a great deal when studied in isolation. The language of a statute, for example, takes on real meaning when a court interprets that language and applies it to the facts in a case. And although the development of the common law results in rules or legal principles that look similar to statutes, these rules are more flexible; they change or are further defined each time a court applies them to a different set of facts. Benjamin Cardozo[2] once stated, "The rules and principles of case law have never been treated as final truths, but as working hypotheses [theories], continually retested in those great laboratories of the law, the courts of justice."[3]

Thus, while federal and state constitutions, statutes, and cases all provide the foundation for any legal analysis and argument, the outcome of each case depends on how the court interprets and applies the law to a new set of facts in a new case. In his book, *The Nature of the Judicial Process*, Justice Cardozo commented on the process from a judge's perspective. He longed for certain answers in the prior case law—clear mandates as to how to decide a new case before the court. He finally realized that

> [a]s the years have gone by, and as I have reflected more and more upon the nature of the judicial process, I have become reconciled to the uncertainty, because I have grown to see it as inevitable. I have grown to see that the process in its highest reaches is not discovery, but creation.... [The change is inevitable, where] principles that have served their day expire, and new principles are born.[4]

For example, consider the following statutory language:

> No person who intentionally causes the death of another shall in any way benefit by the death. All property of the decedent and all money shall pass as if the guilty person had predeceased the decedent.

1. *See* Chapter 1 on the U.S. legal system.

2. Benjamin Nathan Cardozo was an Associate Justice of the United States Supreme Court from 1932-1938. Before serving on the Supreme Court, he served as a justice with the New York Court of Appeals for 14 years (Chief Judge for his last 4 years). He has been described as the "great common law jurist of America... who spoke of the way the Constitution should be approached and the proper job of the judiciary in the American system." Sidney Asch, The Supreme Court and Its Great Justices 159 (1993).

3. Benjamin N. Cardozo, The Nature of the Judicial Process 23 (1949).

4. *Id.*

Since the statute does not include any definitions of the words used in the section, it's the judge's job to determine what the words mean. Determining how to interpret and apply the language of the statute raises a question of law (also referred to as a legal issue or law-based issue, discussed in Chapter 12). For example, what is not easily apparent from the statutory language above is what the word *intentionally* means. Thus, the court must determine what *intentionally* means as a matter of law.

The lawyer's job, then, is to argue to the judge what the correct interpretation of the law is and why, in applying that interpretation to the present case facts, the outcome favors the lawyer's client. To prove a client's case, a lawyer must show how the client's position conforms to the authority that is binding in the controlling jurisdiction.[5] In particular, a lawyer must show that the facts of the client's case are sufficiently similar to the facts of other binding cases addressing the same legal issue(s), so that the same outcome reached in the earlier cases should also be reached in the client's case. Further, the lawyer must show why the facts of a client's case are sufficiently different[6] from the facts in those cases decided in opposition to the client's position, so that a different outcome should be reached in the client's case.

Finally, once a judge interprets the language of a statute or a rule, it is the fact-finder's job to answer all questions of fact (also referred to as a fact-based issue or a fact-sensitive issue).[7] In the example referring to a "person who intentionally causes the death of another," the fact-finder would decide whether the defendant acted intentionally based on the judge's interpretation of what *intentionally* means. The judge reveals what *intentionally* means when the judge decides procedural issues or issues instructions to the jury.

Understanding court opinions is therefore essential to learning the law and the critical analytical thinking process. Law school professors will focus on the study of cases as a means to learn the law. Traditionally, each court opinion includes information essential to understanding what happened in the case, and how and why the court ruled as it did. Class preparation for the U.S. classroom may include writing case briefs prior to discussing those cases in class.

---

5. Note, however, that on occasion a legal issue is raised where there is no controlling authority in the jurisdiction. This is known as a case of first impression. Lawyers will look to authority (statutes and cases) from other jurisdictions to help argue the client's position, and judges will look to these outside authorities to decide a legal issue. (More on addressing cases of first impression is found in Chapter 12.)

6. When used in a legal context, the terms *factual similarities and differences* are used interchangeably with *factual analogies and distinctions*, and *comparing and contrasting facts*.

7. The U.S. jury usually decides questions of fact. Sometimes there is no jury, in which case the judge serves as the fact-finder and decides questions of fact as well as questions of law. *See* Chapter 1.

B. Preparing a Case Brief for Class

Students prepare case briefs for their own personal use for both class and exam preparation. The common sections of a case brief to prepare for class include the following:

1. Heading (with a note of the page where the case is located in your casebook)
2. Facts
3. Procedural History
4. Statement of the Issue
5. Holding
6. Judgment
7. Relevant Rules/Legal Principles Applied in the Case
8. Court's Reasoning
9. Concurrence and Dissent (if included in the opinion)
10. Personal Comments/Reactions

To introduce these sections of a court opinion, first read the following court opinion.

The heading below is as provided by the publisher. It includes the case name and the case citation. You will learn how to properly cite to a case using one of the legal citation manuals.

86 N.W. 2d 689
Supreme Court of Minnesota.
Morris LEFKOWITZ, Respondent,
v.
GREAT MINNEAPOLIS SURPLUS STORE, Inc., Appellant.

No 37220.

Dec. 20,1957

[Murphy is the Justice who wrote the opinion.]

MURPHY, Justice.

This is an appeal from an order of the Municipal Court of Minneapolis denying the motion of the defendant for amended findings of fact, or, in the alternative, for a new trial. The order for judgment awarded the plaintiff the sum of $138.50 as damages for breach of contract.

***690** This case grows out of the alleged refusal of the defendant to sell to the plaintiff a certain fur piece which it had offered for sale in a newspaper advertisement. It appears from the record that on April 6, 1956, the defendant published the following advertisement in a Minneapolis newspaper:

> 'Saturday 9 A.M. Sharp 3 Brand New Fur Coats Worth to $100.00
> First Come First Served $1 Each'

On April 13, the defendant again published an advertisement in the same newspaper as follows: 'Saturday 9 A.M. 2 Brand New Pastel Mink 3-Skin Scarfs Selling for $89.50

Out they go Saturday. Each . . . $1.00

1 Black Lapin Stole Beautiful, worth $139.50 . . . $1.00

First Come First Served'

The record supports the findings of the court that on each of the Saturdays following the publication of the above-described ads the plaintiff was the first to present himself at the appropriate counter in the defendant's store and on each occasion demanded the coat and the stole so advertised and indicated his readiness to pay the sale price of $1. On both occasions, the defendant refused to sell the merchandise to the plaintiff, stating on the first occasion that by a 'house rule' the offer was intended for women only and sales would not be made to men, and on the second visit that plaintiff knew defendant's house rules.

The trial court properly disallowed plaintiff's claim for the value of the fur coats since the value of these articles was speculative and uncertain. The only evidence of value was the advertisement itself to the effect that the coats were 'Worth to $100.00,' how much less being speculative especially in view of the price for which they were offered for sale. With reference to the offer of the defendant on April 13, 1956, to sell the '1 Black Lapin Stole * * * worth $139.50 * * *' the trial court held that the value of this article was established and granted judgment in favor of the plaintiff for that amount less the $1 quoted purchase price.

The defendant contends that a newspaper advertisement offering items of merchandise for sale at a named price is a 'unilateral offer' which may be withdrawn without notice. He relies upon authorities which hold that, where an advertiser publishes in a newspaper that he has a certain quantity or quality of goods which he wants to dispose of at certain prices and on certain terms, such advertisements are not offers which become contracts as soon as any person to whose notice they may come signifies his acceptance by notifying the other that he will take a certain quantity of them. Such advertisements have been construed as an invitation for an offer of sale on the terms stated, which offer, when received, may be accepted or rejected and which therefore does not become a contract of sale until accepted by the seller; and until a contract has

***691** below, known as star pagination, tells the reader that what follows is found on page **691** of the opinion, until you read ***692**.

been so made, the seller ***691** may modify or revoke such prices or terms. Montgomery Ward & Co. v. Johnson, 209 Mass. 89, 95 N.E. 290; Nickel v. Theresa Farmers Co-op. Ass'n, 247 Wis. 412, 20 N.W.2d 117; Lovett v. Frederick Loeser & Co. Inc., 124 Misc. 81, 207 N.Y.S. 753; Schenectady Stove Co. v. Holbrook, 101 N.Y. 45, 4 N.E. 4; Georgian Co. v. Bloom, 27 Ga. App. 468, 108 S.E. 813; Craft v. Elder & Johnson Co., 38 N.E.2d 416, 34 Ohio L.A. 603; Annotation, 157 A.L.R. 746.

The defendant relies principally on Craft v. Elder & Johnston Co. supra. In that case, the court discussed the legal effect of an advertisement offering for sale, as a one-day special, an electric sewing machine at a named price. The view was expressed that the advertisement was (38 N.E.2d 417, 34 Ohio L.A. 605) 'not an offer made to any specific person but was made to the public generally. Thereby it would be properly designated as a unilateral offer and not being supported by any consideration could be withdrawn at will and without notice.' It is true that such an offer may be withdrawn before acceptance. Since all offers are by their nature unilateral because they are necessarily made by one party or on one side in the negotiation of a contract, the distinction made in that decision between a unilateral offer and a unilateral contract is not clear. On the facts before us we are concerned with whether the advertisement constituted an offer, and, if so, whether the plaintiff's conduct constituted an acceptance.

There are numerous authorities which hold that a particular advertisement in a newspaper or circular letter relating to a sale of articles may be construed by the court as constituting an offer, acceptance of which would complete a contract. J. E. Pinkham Lumber Co. v. C. W. Griffin & Co., 212 Ala. 341, 102 So. 689; Seymour v. Armstrong & Kassebaum, 62 Kan. 720, 64 P. 612; Payne v. Lautz Bros. & Co., City Ct., 166 N.Y.S. 844, affirmed, 168 N.Y.S. 369, affirmed, 185 App.Div. 904, 171 N.Y.S. 1094; Arnold v. Phillips, 1 Ohio Dec. Reprint 195, 3 West.Law J. 448; Oliver v. Henley, Tex.Civ.App., 21 S.W.2d 576; Annotation, 157 A.L.R. 744, 746.

The test of whether a binding obligation may originate in advertisements addressed to the general public is 'whether the facts show that some performance was promised in positive terms in return for something requested.' 1 Williston, Contracts (Rev. ed.) § 27.

The authorities above cited emphasize that, where the offer is clear, definite, and explicit, and leaves nothing open for negotiation, it constitutes an offer, acceptance of which will complete the contract. The most recent case on the subject is Johnson v. Capital City Ford Co., La.App., 85 So.2d 75, in which the court pointed out that a newspaper advertisement relating to the purchase and sale of automobiles may constitute an offer, acceptance of which will consummate a contract and create an obligation in the offeror to perform according to the terms of the published offer.

Whether in any individual instance a newspaper advertisement is an offer rather than an invitation to make an offer depends on the legal intention of the parties and the surrounding circumstances. Annotation, 157 A.L.R. 744, 751; 77 C.J.S., Sales, § 25b; 17 C.J.S., Contracts, § 389. We are of the view on the facts before us that the offer by the defendant of the sale of the Lapin fur was clear, definite, and explicit, and left nothing open for negotiation. The plaintiff having successfully managed to be the first one to appear at the seller's place of business to be served, as requested by the advertisement, and having offered the stated purchase price of the article, he was entitled to performance on the part of the defendant. We think the trial court was correct in holding that there was in the conduct of the parties a sufficient mutuality of obligation to constitute a contract of sale.

***692** The defendant contends that the offer was modified by a 'house rule' to the effect that only women were qualified to receive the bargains advertised. The advertisement contained no such restriction. This objection may be disposed of briefly by stating that, while an advertiser has the right at any time before acceptance to modify his offer, he does not have the right, after acceptance, to impose new or arbitrary conditions not contained in the published offer. Payne v. Lautz Bros. & Co., City Ct., 166 N.Y.S. 844, 848; Mooney v. Daily News Co., 116 Minn. 212, 133 N.W. 573, 37 L.R.A.,N.S., 183.

Affirmed.

C. *The Basic Sections of a Case Brief with One Issue*

1. *Heading*

The heading of a court opinion includes the following information:

Case Name • Volume # • Reporter Abbr. • Page # • (Court Designation & Year Decided)

- **Case Name:** Case names are found at the beginning of each court opinion. The name provided in the actual case, however, may not be written using proper citation form. Specific instructions on what to include and how to write case names are found in citation manuals, such as Carolyn V. Williams, *ALWD Guide to Legal Citation* (2021), and *The Bluebook: A Uniform System of Citation* (2020).
- **Volume Number:** The volume number is found on the spine of each published Reporter and at the top of the page of the case online.
- **Reporter:** Court opinions are published in books in the library known as "Reporters." The abbreviations for these Reporters can be found in a citation manual or at the front of any Reporter in the library.
- **Page Number**: The page number in the citation refers to the page where the court's opinion begins.
- **Court Designation and Year (in parenthesis):** The court designation varies, depending on which court decided the case. The year is the year when the case was decided.

In the sample case, the heading would be:

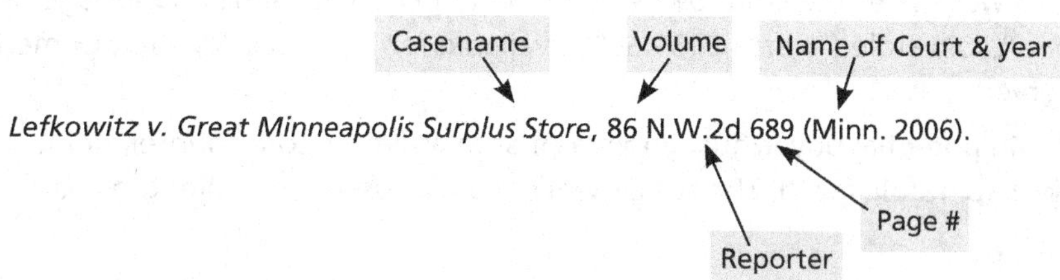

The reference to "Minn." is necessary to show that the case was decided by the Minnesota Supreme Court. The actual heading of the court opinion may include additional information that is not necessary when providing the case citation in a case brief or when referring to the case in a legal document.

Note: The heading of a case brief may also include the page number in the casebook where the case is located, so you can easily access the case if needed.

2. *Facts (F)*

This section provides the story of what happened before a plaintiff files a civil complaint in the trial court. The challenge is in determining which of the facts contained in the court opinion are legally significant to the issues addressed in the case. The ability to target the legally significant facts comes more easily with experience. To know which facts are legally significant requires first understanding the issues raised by the court, how the court resolved the issues, and why the court resolved the issues as it did. Reading carefully through the case prior to completing the Facts section is essential. The Facts section is usually one of the last sections of the brief to draft. Sample facts from *Lefkowitz* follow:

Facts:

- Seller store owner published Minn. newspaper ad announcing the sale of 3 fur coats ("worth *to* $100") for $1 each, available at 9 a.m. the following Saturday, and said, "First Come First Served."
- Potential buyer/husband arrived first on Saturday and presented money for the coat.
- The store owner refused to sell him the coat, citing a "house rule" limiting the ad only to women.
- One week later the store owner published an ad with similar language about one Lapin stole ("worth $139.50"), available for $1, and said, "First Come First Served."
- Again potential buyer/husband was first to arrive at store counter, demanding the Lapin stole for $1. The store owner again refused to sell him the coat.

When noting the key facts of the story, it's best to avoid writing the story word for word from the court's opinion. Using your own words will help you understand and remember the story during class and later when reviewing the cases while preparing for exams.

Since case briefs are for your personal use, the facts may be listed in bullet points, as set out above, rather than written in complete sentences. A list of the facts is fine, as long as the notes make sense to you later on.

3. *Procedural History (PH)*

This section states what happened once the case entered the judicial system, beginning when the plaintiff filed a complaint with the trial court. The complaint includes the cause of action that is the basis of the legal claim. For example, the cause of action may be to enforce a contract, to recover damages following an automobile accident, or to request a court injunction mandating that a neighbor stop trespassing onto someone's property. The procedural history may also include how the defendant responded to the plaintiff's claim, which could include filing procedural motions, discussed in Chapter 1. The defendant's response should also be included, along with any court rulings on the procedural motions. Separate the actions taken at the trial level from any other court actions, e.g., from the intermediate court, usually known as the court of appeals.

For example, when briefing a California Supreme Court decision, "Trial Court" can be shortened to "TC," and "Appellate Court" or "Intermediate Court" can be shortened to "AC" or "IC." State the judgment in each court below, the basis for the judgment, and the party appealing.

Note: The procedural history section does <u>not</u> include the holding in the case you are briefing.

The procedural history in *Lefkowitz* might look like:

Procedural History (PH):

Cause of Action (C/A): Plaintiff husband/buyer sued to recover damages for defendant/seller's refusal to sell potential buyer a fur coat and stole, arguing breach of contract based on the store's newspaper ad. Defendant store owner claimed the ad was not an offer but only an invitation to make an offer, so no contract existed until the store owner accepted the offer.

Trial Court (TC) found for Plaintiff, awarding $138.50 for the Lapin stole. The store owner filed a motion for amended findings of fact or a new trial, which the court denied. The store owner appealed.

4. *Statement of the Substantive and Procedural Issues*

This section of the case brief focuses on the specific legal issue(s) in dispute discussed in the case. The issue statement is usually written using neutral, generic terms rather than the personal names of the parties involved in the specific case. Identifying the parties in the cited case based on their relationship to one another rather than by name is more important. If the case involves a contract dispute, for example, instead of referring to the parties as "Smith" and "Jones," identify the parties by their relationship, e.g., "buyer" and "seller." If the case involves a medical malpractice claim, instead of referring to the parties as "Dr. Joe Brown" and "Cindy Carson," identify them as "doctor" and "patient." When first learning about the sections of a case, write out separately the Substantive Issue(s) (SI) raised in the case and the Procedural Issue(s) (PI) raised in the case.

Substantive Issue (SI):

The substantive issue states the issue based on the legal cause of action. Ideally, the substantive issue statement contains two parts:

a. The relevant legal question
b. The facts of the case relevant to the legal question
  i. If writing a fact-based question, state enough of the important facts to explain <u>why</u> the issue is in dispute. Doing so will likely require including facts supporting both parties.
  ii. If writing a law-based question,[8] state just enough of the facts to put the legal question in the proper factual context.

A sample Substantive Issue for *Lefkowitz* (addressing a fact-based issue) follows:

Substantive Issue (SI):

Did a store's newspaper ad reflect (1) a valid offer, revocable only prior to the buyer's acceptance, or (2) only an invitation for the buyer to make an offer, which becomes a contract only after the seller accepts the offer, when, on two occasions, the seller's ad said the clothing would be sold for $1 to the "First Come First Served," and the potential buyer arrived first on both occasions with the purchase price of $1, first for a fur coat worth "up to $100.00," and, second, for a Lapin stole worth "$139.50"; if a valid offer, was it revoked when the store owner on the first occasion told the potential male buyer verbally that under "house rules" the ad applied only to women buyers?

Procedural Issue (PI):

Separating the procedural issue from the substantive issue highlights whether the case went to the jury and was decided on the merits, or whether

---

8. A law-based question, for example, would be whether the court adopted the fault or no-fault rule when deciding who pays for damages in an automobile accident.

the case was dismissed by the judge before it went to the jury based on a motion by one of the parties, such as a motion to dismiss or a motion for summary judgment. The appeals court in *Lefkowitz* was focusing on a procedural issue raised by the potential buyer, so the procedural issue would read:

Procedural Issue (PI):
Did the trial court properly deny the store owner's motion for amended findings of fact or a new trial?

Combining the substantive and procedural issues into one statement is possible once the distinction between these two issues is fully understood. The single Statement of the Issue in *Lefkowitz* would then read:

Substantive Issue (SI):
Did the trial court correctly deny defendant store owner's motion for amended findings of fact or a new trial and rule in favor of the plaintiff buyer in finding that a store's ad reflected (1) a valid offer, revocable only prior to the buyer's acceptance, rather than (2) only an invitation for the buyer to make an offer, which would become a contract only after the seller accepted the offer, when, on two occasions, the seller's ad said the clothing would be sold for $1 to the "First Come First Served," and the potential buyer arrived first on both occasions with the purchase price of $1, first for a fur coat worth "up to $100.00," and, second, for a Lapin stole worth "$139.50"; if a valid offer, was it revoked when the store owner on the first occasion told the potential male buyer verbally that under "house rules" the ad applied only to women buyers?

5. *Holding (H)*

The holding of the case is the court's answer to the issue(s). The holding is the "legal principle to be drawn from the opinion (decision) of the court."[9] The holding in *Lefkowitz* on the substantive issue would read:

Holding (H):
The store's ad for the Lapin stole reflected a valid offer, since the terms were clear (value "$139.50"), but the fur coat ad was not a valid offer, since it was too speculative (value "*to* $100"); further, the verbal limitation to the potential male

9. Holding, BLACK'S LAW DICTIONARY (11th ed. 2019).

buyer that under "house rules" the offer in the newspaper ad applied only to women buyers was not part of the ad and could not be modified verbally.

The holding in *Lefkowitz* on the procedural issue could then read:

The trial court properly denied defendant buyer's motion for amended findings of fact or a new trial.

6. *Judgment (J)*

Imagine the judge pounding a gavel at the end of each case. The judgment is the final decision of the appellate court after reviewing the lower court's decision. The judgment is usually found at the end of the court's opinion and may state, for example, that the lower court's actions were affirmed, reversed, affirmed in part and reversed in part, reversed and remanded,[10] or modified.

The judgment in *Lefkowitz* is:

Judgment: Affirmed.

7. *Relevant Rules/Legal Principles Applied in the Case*

Separating into its own section the rules or legal principles the court applies in reaching its decision emphasizes the more general principles that a court is likely to apply when analyzing future cases. Separating the rules makes it easier to access this information later on when preparing an outline and studying for examinations.

Note: It may also be helpful to note the page in the casebook where each rule is located, in case you need to access the rule later.

10. To remand a case is to send it back to the lower court, with specific instructions on how to proceed.

The part of the case brief that reports rules or legal principles applied in *Lefkowitz* might read:

Relevant Rules of Law:

1. Where the offer to sell articles in a newspaper ad is "clear, definite, and explicit, and leaves nothing open for negotiation, it constitutes an offer, acceptance of which will complete the contract." *Johnson v. Capital City Ford Co.* (Louisiana) (court found newspaper ads re: the sale of automobiles constituted an offer, and acceptance of the offer established a contract) at pg. 691.
2. Williston, Contracts (Rev. ed. § 27): To determine whether an ad to the general public may be binding, ask "whether the facts show that some performance was promised in positive terms in return for something requested" at pg. 691.
3. Legal intention, based on the surrounding circumstances, distinguishes the offer from the invitation to make an offer [various secondary authority cited at pg. 691.
4. "While an advertiser has the right at any time before acceptance to modify an offer, once accepted the advertiser cannot then impose new or arbitrary conditions not contained in the published offer [citing persuasive cases at pg. 691.

8. Court's Reasoning

This is considered the heart of the court's opinion. When a court omits this section of the opinion, as it sometimes does, the case is not as useful as precedent as the opinion where the court thoroughly explains why the court decided the case as it did. In the reasoning section of the opinion, the court may address why it rejected the losing party's arguments or why certain rules, principles, and policies were not applied, or why other rules, principles, and policies were applied. The reasoning may also address why court opinions cited by the lawyers to support their clients' arguments were helpful to or distinguishable from the case before the court. A good explanation when addressing a fact-based issue will include references to both the key language of the rules or legal principles and references to those facts important to the court's reasoning.

In *Lefkowitz* the court's reasoning might be reported as:

Reasoning:

1. The court agreed that recovery of $100 for the fur coat was too speculative and uncertain, since the ad simply said, "Worth *to* $100." (*Emphasis added.*)
2. In contrast, the court said the sale of the Lapin stole worth a specific amount ($139.50) was clear, definite, and explicit, leaving nothing open for negotiation;

thus, when the buyer arrived first and offered the purchase price, he accepted and made a binding contract. "Sufficient mutuality of obligation" existed. The court rejected the ruling in *Craft v. Elder & Johnston Co.* (Ohio), where a seller published an ad offering a one-day special purchase of electric sewing machines at a set price. The court in *Craft* found that without consideration, the offer was unilateral and could be withdrawn at any time. The court in *Lefkowitz* disagreed and said the withdrawal had to occur before the acceptance.

3. Further, as to the seller's argument that the "house rule" that limited the sale to women modified the offer, the court found that since the restriction was not in the ad, while the seller could have, *prior* to acceptance, modified the conditions, he couldn't do so *after* the acceptance. [Case citations omitted.]

9. Concurrence and Dissent

In addition to the sections listed above, in some court opinions one or more judges other than the judge writing the majority opinion may choose to write a separate opinion. This opinion may be either (a) a concurring opinion or (b) a dissenting opinion. Always include a section that notes any concurring or dissenting opinion. Note, however, that if the concurrence or dissent is not included in the textbook, the author has concluded that it is not relevant for the point the case is illustrating; it is not, therefore, necessary to look up the case in order to note a concurrence or dissent that is otherwise not included in the textbook. Many concurrences and dissents, when provided, are the focus of classroom discussion and may later become majority opinions. Be careful, however, to separate any notes on the concurrence or the dissent from the other sections of the case brief. These opinions are not part of the majority opinion.

a. Concurring opinion

Judges write concurrences when they agree with the outcome of the case as decided by the majority of the court but do not agree with all or part of the majority's reasoning. The concurrence allows a judge to explain the concern with the majority court's reasoning and how the same result could be reached in a different way.

b. Dissenting opinion

A dissenting judge does not agree with the decision by the majority of the court. The judge may simply say, "I dissent," or the judge might explain why the majority opinion and its outcome is wrong. Dissenting opinions are especially important when the vote by the members of the court is close, such as in a 5-4 decision by the United States Supreme Court. The wise attorney knows that a single change in the membership of a court might affect the outcome in a future case when the same legal issue is addressed by the court.

The court in *Lefkowitz* did not include a concurrence or dissent.

10. Personal Comments/Reactions

This is the one section of the case brief that does not come directly from the court opinion. In this section you should state your own thoughts about the case. Consider, for example:

- Do you agree or disagree with the court's decision? Why or why not?
- Do you agree with the court's explanation of the relevant law or legal principles relied on in the case?
- How does this decision fit with other cases studied in class that address the same legal questions? What additional information did you learn from this case?
- Why did the author choose to include this case in the book? For example, you may find that the author included the case (1) because it helps explain the law you are studying, (2) because it is an example of poor or mistaken reasoning by the court, or (3) because it suggests an alternative approach to analyzing a particular legal issue.
- Does the court's interpretation and application of the rule advantage or disadvantage a particular group? If so, identify the group and explain how they are particularly affected.

Your personal comments and reactions can be especially helpful when preparing for class discussion and later when studying for exams.

D. Briefing a Case with Multiple Issues

When a court addresses more than one issue, it's essential to separate those issues once you have identified them, usually beginning in the Procedural History section. If there are two issues, for example, provide two separate sections for the Substantive Issue, the Holding, the Relevant Rules/Legal Principles Applied, and the Court's Reasoning. An outline of a two-issue case brief might look like the following:

(1) Case citation:
(2) Statement of the Facts
(3) Procedural History (identifying the two issues)
(4) Issue One:
  a. Substantive and Procedural Issue
  b. Holding on Substantive Issue and Procedural Issue
  c. Judgment
  d. Relevant Rules/Legal Principles Applied in the Case
  e. Court's Reasoning
  f. Concurrence/Dissent (if applicable)
  g. Personal Comments/Reactions
(5) Issue Two
  a. Substantive and Procedural Issue
  b. Holding on Substantive Issue and Procedural Issue

c. Judgment
d. Relevant Rules/Legal Principles Applied in the Case
e. Court's Reasoning
f. Concurrence/Dissent (if applicable)
g. Personal Comments/Reactions

Briefing a Case with Two Substantive Issues:

Any single case may include one or more issues in dispute, which should be reflected in the case brief. In fact, in *Lefkowitz* the court looked not only to whether the ad constituted a valid offer but also to whether the offer could be verbally modified. When more than one issue is identified, the best brief will set out those issues and then complete the remaining sections of the brief separately, since each issue will likely include its own holdings, judgments, relevant rules, and reasoning.

By example, consider this second case brief of *Lefkowitz,* beginning with the Substantive Issue section that separates the two issues:

Substantive Issues (SI):

I. Did the trial court correctly deny defendant store owner's motion for amended findings of fact or a new trial and rule in favor of the plaintiff buyer in finding that a store's ad reflected (1) a valid offer, revocable only prior to the buyer's acceptance, rather than (2) only an invitation for the buyer to make an offer, which would become a contract only after the seller accepted the offer, when, on two occasions, the seller's ad said the clothing would be sold for $1 to the "First Come First Served," and the potential buyer arrived first on both occasions with the purchase price of $1, first for a fur coat worth "up to $100.00," and, second, for a Lapin stole worth "$139.50"?

II. If a valid offer, was it revoked when the store owner on the first occasion told the potential male buyer verbally that under "house rules" the ad applied only to women buyers?

Procedural Issue (PI): Did the trial court properly deny the defendant seller's motion for amended findings of fact or a new trial?

Judgment: Affirmed.

Holding (H) on the Substantive Issues (SI):

I. The lower court ruled correctly, allowing the purchase of the Lapin stole and denying damages or recovery of the fur coat. The seller's offer to sell the fur coats "worth *to* $100" for $1 was too speculative to support a valid offer; however, the ad to sell the Lapin stole "worth $139.50" was sufficiently definite to support the accepted offer and award damages.

II. No, the offer was not revoked. The store's ad reflects (1) a valid offer, revocable only prior to the buyer's acceptance; the "house rules" that the sale applied only to women buyers verbally told to the potential male buyer were not part of the newspaper ad and did not preclude the male buyer from taking advantage of the sale.

Holding (H) on Procedural Issue (PI): Yes. The trial court properly denied the defendant seller's motion for amended findings of fact or a new trial.

Relevant Rules of Law:

I. A. Williston, Contracts (Rev. ed. § 27): To determine whether an ad to the general public may be binding, ask "whether the facts show that some performance was promised in positive terms in return for something requested."

B. **Legal intention** distinguishes the offer from the invitation to make an offer, based on the surrounding circumstances. [Various secondary authority cited.]

II. Where the offer to sell articles in a newspaper ad is clear, definite, and explicit, and leaves nothing open for negotiation, it constitutes an offer, acceptance of which will complete the contract. Citations omitted. (Cites *Johnson v. Capital City Ford Co.* (Louisiana): newspaper ads re: sale of automobiles constitutes an offer, and acceptance of the offer establishes a contract.)

Court's Reasoning:

I. A. The court agreed that recovery of $100 for the fur coat was too speculative and uncertain, since the ad simply said, "Worth *to* $100." (*Emphasis added.*)

B. In contrast, court said the sale of the Lapin stole worth a specific amount ("worth $139.50") was clear, definite, and explicit, leaving nothing open for negotiation; thus, when the buyer arrived first and offered the purchase price, he accepted and made a binding contract. "Sufficient mutuality of obligation" existed.

C. The court rejected the ruling in *Craft v. Elder & Johnston Co.* (Ohio), where a seller published an ad offering one-day special purchase of electric sewing machines at a set price. The court in *Craft* found that without consideration, the offer was unilateral and could be withdrawn at any time. The court in *Lefkowitz* disagreed and said the withdrawal had to occur before the acceptance.

II. The court quickly found that since the seller's "house rule" limiting the buyers to women only was not in the newspaper ad, while the seller could have, prior to acceptance, modified the conditions, he couldn't do so after the acceptance. [Case citations omitted.]

E. Additional Case Briefing Review

Preparing case briefs can be time-consuming, though they are well worthwhile. In many cases, the various sections of a case brief can be difficult to identify, taking more time than what was anticipated. To be prepared, plan sufficient time to complete all the briefs prior to class. Because understanding thoroughly how to brief a case is so important, another sample case, *In re Est. of Blodgett*, 147 P.2d 702 (Alaska 2006), is provided below, along with a sample brief of the case. Try to brief the case prior to looking at the sample brief; that way you will better understand which sections of the brief you have understood and what you might need to work on.

This is the heading as provided by the court. It includes the case name and the citation to the case. In citing this case name, however, you would shorten it as instructed in a legal citation manual such as the *ALWD Guide to Legal Citation or The Bluebook.*

Supreme Court of Alaska
In the Matter of the Estate of Richard Blodgett
147 P.3d 702 (Alaska 2006)

[This is the justice who wrote the majority opinion.]

CARPENETI, Justice.

*****

On September 14, 2003, Robert Blodgett caused the death of his father, Richard Blodgett. Blodgett was indicted for murder in ***704** the second degree, and in January 2004 he was convicted of criminally negligent homicide and given a three-and-one-half-year term of imprisonment.

Blodgett was named in the final Will and Testament (Will) of his father, which left "all properties, Bank accounts, stocks, and insurance policies" to his children. In April 2004 Blodgett petitioned the superior court for a hearing to determine his right to participate in the probate proceedings under the Alaska probate code and the slayer statute. The other beneficiaries of Richard Blodgett's Will consented to the hearing but argued that Robert intentionally killed his father, so the slayer statute precluded him from receiving any property under the Will.

The superior court denied Robert Blodgett's petition, preventing him from obtaining any benefits under the Will. The court explained that under the slayer statute he couldn't benefit unless he proved by a preponderance of the evidence that this would result in manifest injustice, which Blodgett failed to do. The court considered, and rejected, possible factors it thought might support finding manifest injustice, including past family relationships and Blodgett's monetary needs. The court found the "great deal of testimony about the nature of the past relationship" between Blodgett and his father "unhelpful" and irrelevant in determining "the justice of denying or allowing recovery." The court also concluded that "Blodgett retained sufficient income-earning capacity and property holdings that he would not be destitute if he did not receive these funds." Blodgett appeals.

Because the statutory subsection that governs this case provides that the superior court "may" set aside the application of the slayer statute if manifest injustice would result, we review the superior court's decision for abuse of discretion. We find an abuse of discretion "only if, based on a review of the whole record, we are left with a definite and firm conviction that a mistake has been made [by the trial judge]."

***705** The common law has long followed the policy that "no one should be allowed to profit from his own wrong." *Riggs v. Palmer*, 22 N.E. 188, 190 (N.Y. 1889). Over the years most legislatures enacted statutes covering these rules, known as "slayer statutes."

The original Alaska slayer statute, passed in 1972, prevented only those who feloniously and intentionally killed from benefiting. In 1988 the legislature passed an amendment removing the words "intentionally" from the statute, so the statute applied to crimes, including criminally negligent homicide. Ch. 164, §§ 3-8, SLA 1988.

Shortly after the legislature passed this amendment, the Alaska governor expressed concern that under unusual circumstances it might be unjust to prohibit a killer from taking the property of the victim, such as in the case of an unintentional felonious killing. Accordingly, another amendment was adopted in 1989, creating the manifest injustice exception for unintentional homicides now found in Alaska Stat. § 13.12.803(k):

> In the case of an unintentional felonious killing, a court may set aside the application of [the slayer statute] if the court makes special findings of fact and conclusions of law that the application of the subsection would result in a manifest injustice and that the subsection should not be applied.

*****

Thus, the legislature broadened the application of the slayer statute—by extending it to unintentional killings—and created an escape clause—by enacting the manifest injustice exception.

Under the current Alaska criminal code, all unjustified killings are considered felonies. This includes murders in the first and second degree, manslaughter, and criminally negligent homicide. Thus, Alaska's slayer statute encompasses intentional as well as unintentional homicides. Criminally negligent homicide occurs when "the person causes the death of another person." Alaska Stat. § 11.41.130.

***707** The legislature limited the broad reach of the slayer statute by giving trial court judges the discretion to allow killers to benefit from the victim's assets if manifest injustice would result otherwise. Should an inheritance be denied to the unskilled teenager who drives his car in a criminally negligent manner and accidentally causes the death of his sole remaining parent? The legislature clearly decided that in such a case there should be discretion in the court to consider the specific facts of the homicide and, if denial of the inheritance would be manifestly unjust, to permit it. Where the killer's act was not intentional, and especially where the act was not even reckless, and where other circumstances lessen the overall effect of the crime, the application of the slayer statute may lead to unnecessarily harsh results. Indeed, the unintended killing of a loved one, as in the example above, would likely cause the killer far greater personal ruin than monetary gain.

In this case, Blodgett was convicted of criminally negligent homicide, which is an unintentional homicide. Therefore, under subsection (k) Blodgett can avoid the effects of the slayer statute only if he proves by a preponderance of the evidence that applying the statute to him will result in manifest injustice.

***708** We have not had occasion to define the phrase "manifest injustice" as used in the slayer statute, or to set out the relevant factors that a trial judge should consider when ruling on this question. Similarly, because no other slayer statute contains a provision similar to subsection (k), out-of-jurisdiction case law provides no ready assistance. However, the Alaska Court of Appeals has interpreted this phrase in another, similar context, describing manifest injustice as something that is "plainly unfair" as applied "to a particular defendant." *Beltz v. State*, 980 P.2d 474, 480 (Alaska Ct. App. 1999). Before finding manifest injustice, the court held that the "judge must articulate specific circumstances making the defendant significantly different from a typical offender within that category or making the defendant's conduct significantly different from a typical offense." *Id.* We adopt *Beltz's* approach for the purpose of applying subsection (k) of Alaska's slayer statute.

Thus, the relevant comparison here is between Blodgett's conduct and that of a typical offender convicted of negligent homicide. In the criminal proceedings, Blodgett was sentenced to three and one-half years in prison, which is not the lowest possible sentence for negligent homicide. This suggests that the superior court did not believe Blodgett's acts fell at the lowest level of culpability and that the court below considered Blodgett's conduct in relation to other similarly situated defendants when it rejected his claim of manifest injustice.

To try and prove manifest injustice, Blodgett introduced evidence regarding (1) past family relationships, and (2) possible financial hardship if denied the benefits of inheritance. The court found that Blodgett failed to meet his burden of proving, by a preponderance of the evidence, extraordinary circumstances that would have made it manifestly unjust to exclude him from his father's Will. We agree.

The court described the evidence regarding his family relationships as "unhelpful." Witnesses testified that Blodgett and his father shared a "good relationship" marked with occasional fights typical of father-son relationships. Such testimony neither proves nor disproves the fairness of prohibiting Blodgett's inheritance. The court did not abuse its discretion in deciding that Blodgett failed to prove manifest injustice on this basis.

The court also examined Blodgett's argument that "it would be unjust to deny benefits under the Will to someone who is physically disabled, who faces unknowable future medical expenses, who has a compromised earning capacity, and who has ongoing psychological needs." The superior court noted that, although Blodgett suffered some medical disabilities, Blodgett's own witness testified that he "is capable at the operation of heavy equipment and has skills as a mechanic." The ***709** court found that these skills could lead to employment with yearly compensation ranging between $40,000 and $50,000 per year. It also found that Blodgett owns other property and that future medical expenses will likely be met through the Alaska Native Health Service. In light of this testimony, the court concluded that Blodgett would not endure financial hardship if he did not receive these funds. Consequently, the court found that Blodgett failed to prove manifest injustice based on monetary need.

While we believe the court did not abuse its discretion in making this determination, we are concerned that the court's analysis could lead to the conclusion that a showing of manifest injustice may turn on predictions concerning the future financial health of the defendant. Such an approach would allow slayers of their victims to inherit if they are poor, but not if they are financially stable. We doubt that this distinction—between different slayers based on their personal wealth—reflects the legislature's purpose in enacting the manifest injustice provision.

Despite these concerns, we conclude that the superior court did not abuse its discretion in finding that Blodgett failed to prove manifest injustice by a preponderance of the evidence.

*****

Affirmed.

What follows is a sample brief of *Blodgett*.

***In re Est. of Blodgett*, 147 P.2d 702 (Alaska 2006).**

Facts:

- Son Blodgett convicted of the criminally negligent homicide of his father.
- Father had executed a Will.

Procedural History:

Cause of Action (C/A): Son asked trial court to award him his share of father's estate as stated in his father's Will.

Trial (TC): Court applied Alaska's slayer statute and denied son's request because (1) he was convicted for his father's death, and (2) no "manifest injustice" would occur by denying his request.

Substantive Issue (SI): Under Alaska's slayer statute, which precludes certain killers from receiving the assets of their victims unless the preclusion would create a manifest injustice, can a son benefit from his father's Will when the son was convicted of the criminally negligent homicide of his father?

Procedural Issue (PI): Did the trial court abuse its discretion by denying a son's request for his father's assets under his father's Will?

Holding on Substantive Issue: Under Alaska's slayer statute, the son is precluded from benefiting from his father's Will after being convicted of the criminally negligent homicide of his father since no manifest injustice results.

Holding on Procedural Issue: The trial court did not abuse its discretion by denying the son's request to benefit from his father's Will after the son's conviction for the criminally negligent homicide of his father.

Judgment: Affirmed.

Relevant Rules:

Alaska's Slayer Statute (Alaska Stat. § 13.12.803)

(a) An individual who feloniously kills the decedent forfeits all benefits under this chapter with respect to the decedent's estate....

(k) In the case of an unintentional felonious killing, a court may set aside the application of section (a) if the court makes special findings of fact and conclusions of law that the application of the subsection would result in a manifest injustice and that the subsection should not be applied.

Court's Reasoning:

1. The court did not err in ruling that the son did not prove that a manifest injustice would occur if he was prevented from acquiring the assets of his father.
2. The Alaska Supreme Court had not previously defined "manifest injustice." In this case the court adopted the Alaska Court of Appeals' approach, considering manifest injustice as "plainly unfair" and more than a general finding. Now the court must find special circumstances to consider the defendant something other than a "regular" offender.

3. Here the TC imposed a three-year sentence, not the minimal sentence possible. This sentence suggests that the court considered the son more than minimally responsible. This finding alone supports the conclusion that the son's situation is no different from that of other regular offenders.
4. The lower court also found that it didn't make a difference that the son was physically disabled, requiring more finances and arguably more in need of his father's assets. The son could still operate heavy equipment and could work as a mechanic; he still had the potential of making $40,000-$50,000 per year.

Note: The Alaska Supreme Court was concerned, however, that future courts might think that a decision on manifest injustice could depend on the defendant's future financial health. The court made clear this consideration was not the intent of the legislature.

Personal Comments: [to be filled in by the individual student]

Note: In the sample brief of *Blodgett*, above, the relevant rule includes the main rule (any felonious killer forfeits any benefits of the decedent's estate), followed by an exception to that rule (unless denying those benefits would result in a "manifest injustice"). Thus, the rule has two parts. However, there is only one *disputable* issue in the case, which is whether the exception to the rule applies. Therefore, the Statement of the Issue is not separated into two issues; rather, the Substantive Issue subsumes the main rule and focuses on the single disputable issue. This follows the guideline to set out only substantive issues reflecting what's in dispute.

For an example of a case brief with multiple issues in dispute, *see Shrader v. Equitable Life Assurance Society*, 485 N.E.2d 1031 (Ohio 1985), found online in the Student Supplemental Materials for this book located on the publisher's website at http://www.aspenpublishing.com.

Note: Although initially you may follow this outline of the case brief sections, you may change how you prepare briefs for your individual classes. Different professors may expect different types of briefs. When first learning how to brief, it is better to include rather than exclude information. Once you understand the different sections of a brief, and also know what you need for each class, you may adjust your briefs accordingly.

F. Holding v. Dicta

A court must reach a decision about any disputable issue[s] raised by parties in each case before the court. Any comment addressing the specific issue before the court is part of the court's holding. Sometimes, however, a court will make statements beyond what is necessary to resolve the specific issue before the court. A court may comment, for example, on the likely outcome of a case with different facts than the case presently before the court. These comments are not part of the court's holding or binding on future cases, have persuasive value only, and are known as dicta or *obiter dicta* (plural for dictum). *Obiter dicta* is "a judicial comment made while delivering a judicial opinion, but one that is unnecessary to the decision in a case and therefore not precedential."[11] In *Blodgett*, for example, the court finished its opinion by suggesting that the legislature's purpose was not to focus on a slayer's personal wealth in deciding whether the manifest injustice exception applied. This statement was not necessary to the court's holding in *Blodgett* because the Alaska Supreme Court relied on the "more than minimal length" of the son's sentence in upholding the superior court's ruling finding no manifest injustice in denying the son his father's benefits. Thus, while the court's comment on the weight of a slayer's financial security in finding manifest injustice may be predictive of the court's rulings in future cases, it was not a part of the holding in *Blodgett*.

G. Class Participation: The Socratic Method

Preparing for class in a U.S. law school is essential. In many U.S. law classrooms, and especially in first-year courses, professors engage students in a dialogue known as the Socratic method.[12] The Socratic method is a way to promote a student's ability to think analytically and to create arguments in support of a party's position. Oftentimes, the professor will pose hypothetical situations based on the cases assigned for class, asking students to critically analyze what arguments could be presented for parties based on changing the facts of an assigned case. When using the Socratic method, a professor teaches by asking questions about what was assigned for that class rather than just lecturing. These questions will likely focus on the court opinions read and briefed for class. When a professor explores the issues raised in the cases and other material read for class with students through the Socratic method, the classroom becomes a cooperative environment where both professor and student work to help all students understand how to analyze and understand an issue more completely. Students likely can only participate in the Socratic exchange or follow along if they have read and briefed the cases.

The Socratic dialogue requires students to develop, state, and defend their positions. Lawyers are problem solvers, and the primary task in a U.S. law school is to learn the tools needed to solve problems. Laws will change, as will legal problems. Law professors don't have the answers to every legal situation, but they do try to help students develop critical reasoning skills that can be applied to any legal situation.

11. DICTUM , BRYAN A. GARNER, BLACK'S LAW DICTIONARY (11TH ED. 2019).
12. Socrates (469-399 B.C.) was a famous Greek philosopher.

Consider the following discussion between a professor and student about the court's decision in *Blodgett*:

Professor: Do you agree with the opinion in *Blodgett*?

Student: Yes, it doesn't seem fair that a son who kills his father could actually profit from that violent act.

Professor: But the statute does allow an exception—the manifest injustice exception. The legislature must have thought that a killer should be able to take assets under some circumstances. How could you argue that the facts in *Blodgett* support applying the exception?

Student: Well, a family relationship is special, different from the person on the street who kills someone. Also, the son was convicted of criminal negligence rather than murder, so there was no evil intent. Usually, parents want to provide for their children, and the father might have still wanted his son to receive some of his assets.

Professor: As you know, that's not what the court decided. Why did the court refuse to recognize the manifest injustice exception regarding the killer son?

Student: The court relied on the sentencing more than anything else. The lower court's sentence was more than the minimal sentence that could be imposed. This sentence suggested that the court viewed the son like anyone else—someone who did not deserve any kind of special consideration.

Professor: Did the trial court mention any other reasons for its decision?

Student: Yes, the court said evidence suggested that this father-son relationship was a typical relationship, which neither supported granting nor denying the exception. The court also addressed the son's need for the father's assets, mentioning that the son, although disabled, was able to take care of himself financially.

Professor: Were all these reasons part of the court's holding in the case?

Student: Not according to the appellate court. The appellate court in its opinion made a point to emphasize that it would be wrong to decide the manifest injustice exception based on an individual's income and didn't think that was what the legislature intended. The appellate court was able to affirm the lower court's opinion, however, because other valid reasons existed for not granting the exception.

Professor: So what if in the next case the defendant's sentence was the minimal criminal sentence allowed. Could the lower court then look at the manifest injustice question based on the financial need of the killer?

Student: Maybe. *Blodgett* says the issue shouldn't be decided based on financial need, but the court also said that wasn't at issue in that case since the ruling could be based on the length of the sentence, which was more than the minimal time permitted under the law. Therefore, the comments are only dicta, which is not part of the holding in the case and not binding in future cases.

H. Abbreviations in Note Taking

Remember that case briefs are used to help in preparing for class and later when studying for examinations. Strive to write a brief that is as complete as is necessary but is also as concise as possible. Creating a list of abbreviations for commonly used terms will shorten the time needed to brief cases and will also help when taking notes in class. Create your own list. Some suggestions are:

K	Contract
P	Plaintiff
D	Defendant
App'ant	Appellant
App'ee	Appellee
Pet.	Petitioner
Resp.	Respondent
BFP	Bona Fide Purchaser
SJ	Summary Judgment
C/A	Cause of Action
PH	Procedural History
SI	Substantive Issue
PI	Procedural Issue

I. Keeping Track of Legal Terminology

Students discover many new words and phrases when studying the U.S. law. Many of the new words and phrases will be legal terms that have special meaning. For this reason, quick access to a legal dictionary is imperative. There are paperback dictionaries small enough to keep handy during class or when studying. Alternatively, there are many legal dictionaries online.[13] Ideally, place your list of definitions in a file separate from your individual class notes. Many of the same legal terms will be raised in multiple classes; by keeping separate the list of terms, you can check the list for an unfamiliar word or phrase first. If the word or phrase is on the list, there's no need to look further. If not, you can then add the new definition to the master list. Taking the time to learn the terms while progressing through classes can result in eventually knowing their meaning without consulting the list of

13. *See, e.g.*, FindLaw Law Dictionary, at dictionary.findlaw.com, and LAW.COM at dictionary.law.com. Legal dictionaries are also available online through Westlaw and Lexis, two computer-assisted legal research databases.

words and phrases; at that point, those words and phrases can be eliminated from the master list. A glossary of terms is provided at the end of this book.

• Exercise 3-A

Read and brief *Everett v. Rogers*, found in the Student Supplemental Materials for this book located on the publisher's website at http://www.aspenpublishing.com.

CHAPTER SUMMARY

- The study of court opinions is essential to understanding the U.S. legal system.
- Most court opinions found in casebooks are appellate or reviewing court opinions.
- Preparing a case brief for class and using it later when studying for examinations is an essential part of the U.S. educational process.
- A court opinion includes mandatory information (pertinent to the "holding") and sometimes also includes comments that are not mandatory in answering the issue in the case ("dicta").
- Many law school professors use a question-and-answer method (Socratic method) in the classroom, in addition to lecturing to students.
- Tips for taking notes in class include the use of abbreviations and a system for keeping track of new language and definitions.

CHAPTER

4

The Legal Writing Process

A. Introduction
  1. The importance of legal writing
  2. Your responsibility as a legal writer

B. The Legal Writing Process from Task to Deadline
  Step 1: Collect the facts
  Step 2: Analyze the facts
  Step 3: Collect the law
  Step 4: Organize and analyze the law
  Step 5: Apply the law to the client's facts to complete the analysis

C. The General Writing Process from Task to Deadline
  1. Considerations when beginning to write
  2. The creative and critical stages in the writing process

A. Introduction

Law students' past writing experiences can be very helpful as they embark on learning legal writing. As with other forms of writing, careful attention to structure, content, and form are essential when writing a professional legal document. The same basic rules of English apply to writing a U.S. legal document; the same guidelines covering the structure of a paragraph apply; and the same general guidelines addressing the use of topic, thesis, and transitional sentences all apply.

However, in legal writing, one distinct characteristic stands out, which is the legal rule or principle used and applied in the document. Unlike most other types of professional writing, the relevant legal rules or principles dictate the basic structure of a legal analysis.

Anyone in the United States who practices law must write; therefore, any U.S. lawyer must develop the skills necessary to become a professional writer. Professional writers must strive to produce quality documents in both substance and form. Focusing on developing strong professional analytical and writing skills is crucial.

1. The importance of legal writing

The following job listings for law-related positions all over the country illustrate the importance of learning how to analyze the law and communicate an analysis both verbally and in writing.[1] Every listing includes a reference about the need for strong writing skills.

Title: Associate General Counsel for Health Sciences, Howard University Office of the General Counsel, Washington, D.C.

"Candidates for this position should possess a law degree from an ABA-accredited law school, a minimum of three to five years of health law experience, **well-developed analytical and writing skills, and excellent oral communication and interpersonal skills.**"

Title: Family Lawyer, Senior Associate or Partner, Birmingham, Alabama

"[S]ignificant Family Law experience, **strong writing and verbal skills,** and good academics are mandatory."

Title: Litigation Attorney, Tucson, Arizona

"Tucson, Arizona office of a prestigious Western U.S. law firm is seeking a mid-level commercial litigation associate. **Strong academics and well-developed research, writing, analytical, and advocacy skills are a must.**"

Title: Legislative Liaison, Washington State Bar Association

"Candidates must be able to show **excellent writing skills** around law and policy matters."

Title: Foreclosure Attorney, Fort Lauderdale, Florida

"Excellent oral and written communication skills are required."

---

1. These listings were taken from the website at Indiana University Robert H. McKinney School of Law.

> **Title: Compliance Consultant, Schaumburg, Illinois**
>
> "**Superb, proven, verbal and written communication skills** are necessary for this position."

> **Title: Litigation Attorney, Partridge, Snow & Hahn LLP, Providence, RI**
>
> "Qualified candidates should have outstanding credentials, two to four years experience in commercial litigation and **strong research, drafting, writing, and communication skills**."

Law students and lawyers are wise to pay attention to the details, both when preparing for and when writing about the law. They should pay careful attention not only to *what* they write but also to *how* they write. A lawyer's written document should withstand careful scrutiny. The lawyer's choices about overall paragraph structure, sentence structure, words, and punctuation can all matter.

A prime example of the need to pay attention to the details is found in the case, *Rogers Communications v. Bell Aliant.*[2] In this case, Rogers Communications representatives signed a contract to string cable lines across Aliant's telephone poles in the Canadian Maritime provinces. The language establishing the time frame for the contract was as follows:

> "This agreement shall be effective from the date it is made and shall continue in force for a period of five years from the date that it is made, and thereafter for successive five-year terms, unless and until terminated by one-year prior notice in writing by either party."

A few years after Rogers Communications began installing the lines, and prior to the end of the first five-year period, Aliant canceled the contract and increased the amount Rogers Communications would have to pay to use its telephone poles. The overall increase imposed by Aliant would cost Rogers Communications more than $2 million (Canadian dollars).

Rogers Communications filed suit, and the decision by the Canadian Radio-Television and Telecommunications Commission (Commission) was based on the language of the contract. Rogers argued that the contract could not be terminated within the first five years because the termination clause ("unless and until terminated by one-year prior notice in writing by either party") modified only the clause immediately preceding it—"and thereafter for successive five-year terms." Aliant argued that the termination clause

2. *Telecom Decision CRTC 2007-75*, http://www.crtc.gc.ca/archive/eng/2007/dt2007-75.htm (modified Aug. 20, 2007).

applied to *all* the language preceding the termination clause, so the contract could be terminated at any time, even in the first five years, provided Aliant gave one year's notice.

The decision turned on the placement of the comma, boldfaced below, and the rules covering punctuation.

> "This agreement shall be effective from the date it is made and shall continue in force for a period of five years from the date that it is made, and thereafter for successive five-year **terms, unless** and until terminated by one-year prior notice in writing by either party."

The Commission found the termination clause applied to all five-year terms, including the initial term. Careful drafting could have prevented this problem. The drafter could have either

- inserted a semicolon after the word "made," eliminated the conjunction "and," inserting instead "the contract shall continue." The provision would then read:

> This agreement shall be effective from the date it is made and shall continue in force for a period of five years from the date that it is made; the contract shall continue thereafter for successive five-year **terms, unless** and until terminated by one-year prior notice in writing by either party.

or

- turned the provision into two sentences. If two sentences, the provision would read:[3]

> This agreement shall be effective from the date it is made and shall continue in force for a period of five years from the date that it is made. Thereafter, the contract shall continue for successive five-year terms, unless and until terminated by one-year prior notice in writing by either party.

When a contract provision includes ambiguous language, its interpretation is left to a judge who may interpret the language in a way that was not

3. Rogers Communications appealed the Commission's decision, arguing that the French version of the contract had not been considered, and, under that version, the intent to disallow cancellation during the first five years of the contract was clear. In August 2007 the Commission overturned its decision and ruled for Rogers Communications. *Id.*

intended by the writer. The next section provides additional reasons for paying careful attention to choices about language when writing about the law.[4]

2. *Your responsibility as a legal writer*

Lawyers' words can have critical impact. Lawyers write documents that may matter, for example, for a client or in the development of a law or policy. And so, special considerations apply when writing about the law, including those below.

a. *Your readers may be impatient*

Legal professionals are oftentimes overworked and under severe time constraints. If an office memorandum, contract, last will and testament, or explanatory letter to a client is difficult to follow, the reader may be forced to follow up with questions, which can frustrate the supervisor. If a brief written to a trial judge is incomplete or unreadable, the judge may put down that brief and refer to opposing counsel's brief in hopes of understanding the case. Without question, these examples are not the desired results. Thus, the goal as legal writers is to make each point so clear that the reader can understand, upon the first reading, the story the legal writer is trying to convey and the legal issues and analysis the legal writer is explaining. The final document must be clear and clean.

b. *Legal writers often write about complex issues*

Legal writers oftentimes write about complex and difficult legal issues. The challenge is to write so that even the most complex legal issues can be understood by a reader who is not familiar with the information. This takes time. Writing a document at the last minute may result in realizing that, while the message is not as complete and logical as planned, there's insufficient time to revise the document before the deadline. To avoid this last-minute dilemma, draft early, and allow additional time to revise and edit.

c. *Others may read your documents in bad faith rather than in good faith*

In an adversarial legal system,[5] as in the United States, lawyers read opposing party documents in hopes of finding mistakes or weaknesses that can be challenged. These may be flaws in reasoning or gaps in arguments. Legal writers should strive to express their message so that it's unambiguous and not subject to any uncertainty.

---

4. These suggestions about language matters are based on a talk in the 1980s by Lauren Robel, when she was a professor of law at the Indiana University Maurer School of Law.

5. Adversary systems involve parties who oppose each other. Lawyers representing the parties argue their clients' cases using evidence such as witness testimony and documents before an independent decision maker. At trial, the lawyer for the opposing party may ask questions to challenge the strength of the other side's case.

d. *Lawyers' words can be powerful and have far-reaching effects*

As a lawyer, your words may mean more than they have ever meant before. Lawyers are in a position to exercise power, and much of that power is exercised through the written word. For example, as a result of a lawyer's words in a criminal case, individuals may lose their freedom; as a result of a lawyer's words in a civil custody dispute, parents may lose rights and access to their child; and as a result of a lawyer's words, the chief executive officer of a company may decide whether a product should be manufactured and introduced into the market, even though the new product carries a potential risk of harm. A lawyer's power comes with responsibility. That responsibility includes making careful choices about the substance of every message about the law and the way in which that message is presented to the reader.

B. The Legal Writing Process from Task to Deadline

Every writer likely has their own writing process. That writing process may have been developed carefully and consciously, or the process may have simply evolved without making conscious choices at all. Regardless of the prior writing process, now that students are writing about the law, beginning the process early and drafting, redrafting, revising, and editing will be essential.

Following is a suggested step-by-step approach to the legal writing process. The actual process, however, does not usually follow a step-by-step process in a linear manner as presented below. More likely, the list of issues and legally significant facts will change as research continues and more is learned about the law relevant to the client's case. Careful reading about the law may trigger more questions for the client. After acquiring the new facts and doing additional research, newly discovered legal issues may require additional, different research, which then requires even more questions for the client. So, while the legal writing process is set out below using a step-by-step, straightforward process, in reality the process involves repeating steps when necessary and is, therefore, quite recursive in nature.

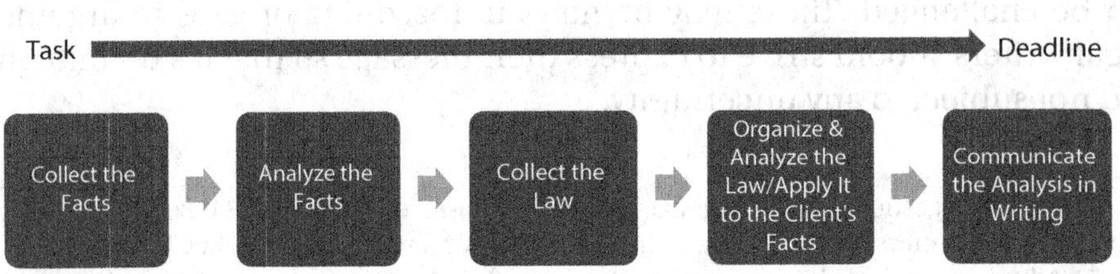

Figure 4-1

Step 1. Collect the facts

The first step is to talk with the potential client to learn what happened. The interview involves first collecting the facts by asking careful, probing questions. A good interviewer is an active listener who asks questions to learn the important facts and to make sure that, when the interview ends, the client's story is clear. For example, if the potential client, Travis Franklin, tells you he was hit in the face by John Smith, you would want to explore with him, among other things, the following:

- When and where did this encounter take place?
- What happened prior to your being hit; for example, were the two of you arguing?
- Did Smith threaten you first?
- Did you have any prior encounters?
- Did you do anything arguably to provoke Smith?
- Did you try to leave?
- Who is Smith—a friend? Stranger? Enemy? Employer?
- Did anyone else see the incident?
- Was the incident recorded?

Taking detailed notes during the interview is essential, as is reviewing the notes afterwards to determine whether any follow-up questions are needed due to gaps in the story.

Step 2. Analyze the facts

After collecting the client's facts, the next step is to analyze the facts by turning the simple language of the story into more generic terms that are helpful when researching. For example, the names Travis Franklin and John Smith will not be helpful when researching. Instead, before researching convert the personal names to their relationship status, using terms such as employer and employee; father and son; buyer and seller; coach and player; or landlord and tenant.

If familiar with legal actions that can be brought by one person against another, the lawyer may already know of potential legal claims such as a civil battery, which involves intentionally causing harmful or offensive contact with another. And if the story revealed that John may be able to argue that, even if he did hit Travis, he was acting in self-defense and, therefore, shouldn't be held liable, the term "self-defense" is a term the lawyer can use when researching. All these terms and perhaps more would be helpful when collecting the law.

Step 3. Collect the law

After analyzing the facts and considering the potential legal issues raised by the facts, it's time to research the legal issues. Using the list of words and phrases generated in Step 2, the next step is to create a plan before conducting the research. Determine in advance:

- What broad area of law is at issue (e.g., torts, which is a wrong committed by one against another that is not based on a contract);
- What specific question(s) must be researched (e.g., assault or battery);
- Do the potential issue(s) raise federal law questions or state law questions; and
- In which specific jurisdiction can the case be brought.

By planning the research in advance, the result should be a more thorough and efficient process, especially by taking careful notes while researching to avoid unnecessary duplication of the research steps.

Note: This book does not provide exhaustive guidance on how to conduct research. Numerous books cover the research sources available to those researching the law in the United States and provide further guidance on how to research.

Step 4. Organize and analyze the law

Researchers usually find relevant legal tests early in the research process. If the legal test is one that has its own subparts, the researcher can then expedite the research by breaking it down into those subparts and then inserting the relevant authority for each part of the legal test as the research continues. The result is research that takes less time and is analytical, allowing the researcher to know earlier when there's sufficient authority to stop researching. For example, if the case involves a torts issue, or a wrong committed by one person against another not based in contracts, and specifically both an assault and a battery, the research can immediately be separated into those two causes of action. Further, once the researcher learns that proving a battery requires showing the defendant (1) intentionally (2) caused a harmful or offensive touching (3) of another, without consent, the research regarding battery can be further separated into these requirements, knowing that each requirement must be proved separately to win the client's case. Thus, the structure of the legal test will further the research and analysis. A legal test may comprise, for example, (1) requirements (or elements) that must be met to prove liability, (2) a rule that imposes liability but includes one or more exceptions where no liability is imposed, or (3) the weighing of factors to consider in determining liability. The key to different legal tests and their basic structure when writing a legal analysis is discussed in detail in Chapter 8.

Once the preliminary research is completed, the relevant cases will need briefing. These briefs need only identify that portion of each case that is relevant to the legal issue(s) addressed in the client's case. A cited case may address multiple legal issues, for example, but may include only one issue relevant to the client's case. The research notes would then include any relevant statutes, rules, or definitions, along with the key facts, the court's holding, and the court's reasoning regarding the relevant issue, as well as any relevant statements of public policy.

Step 5. Apply the law to the client's facts to complete the analysis

At this point, the researcher has thoroughly collected and analyzed the facts, and has collected, analyzed, and organized the law. Now it is time to begin drafting the analysis by applying the relevant law to the specific facts of the client's case to assess the strengths and weaknesses regarding each legal issue, and to predict the likely outcome on those issues.

C. The General Writing Process from Task to Deadline

1. Considerations when beginning to write

As with any piece of writing, the writer must always consider (a) the purpose of the document, (b) the appropriate tone of the document, (c) the potential audience for the document, and (d) any constraints that may exist with respect to the document.

a. Purpose

Understanding the purpose of the document is vital. The document's goal might be to create a specific outcome (as in a contract or a last will and testament), to objectively analyze and predict the strength of the client's position (as in an office memorandum or e-memo for a supervising attorney), or to persuade (as in a document to the court or a demand letter). The document may also be in the form of correspondence, such as email communications or letters to clients or to opposing counsel, simply to inform, to make a recommendation, or to seek additional information. E-memos are discussed in Chapter 14.

b. Tone

The type of document dictates the appropriate tone when writing. Documents to a court are always written using formal language. Office memoranda may or may not be written as formally, depending on how well the writer knows the supervising attorney. However, if the document is an office memorandum, it may be filed away and eventually read by someone else. If any question exists regarding the appropriate tone, choose a more formal tone. And all legal documents, regardless of how formally written, should conform to the standard rules of grammar and style.

Communicating to clients and other lawyers through email and other forms of Internet media is also a frequent occurrence. Even though email communications are generally considered more informal, they must be written professionally and with an understanding that information contained in these forms of communication may be admissible as evidence. More on email communications can be found in Chapter 14.

c. Audience

Always consider who will read each document. The reader may be someone who has a law degree, for example, a lawyer or a judge, but who knows little about the specific law and nothing about the specific facts of the client's case. Or the reader might be a non-lawyer client who knows little about the law but everything about the facts of the case. Important choices are necessary regarding specific language and which legal and technical references might need to be further clarified. In particular, pay attention to the potential reader during the later stages of the writing process, when rewriting, revising, and editing.

d. Constraints

Lawyers are often constrained when writing a document. For example, supervising attorney assignments likely include specific deadlines for completing specific sections of a document as well as the complete document. Court rules will also set out page or word limitations as well as rules for properly formatting a document. Strive to set an individual schedule for completing assigned tasks and to ensure the court rules are followed.

2. The creative and critical stages in the writing process

The ultimate goal is a final written document; however, writing also influences the thinking process. Understanding that writing promotes thinking supports why it's important to draft early and allow time to redraft. Put another way, "Easy reading is damn hard writing."[6] If the writer is a procrastinator (someone who puts off completing a task), the shortened time will not allow the writer to use writing as a means to heighten analytical thinking. In the end, the analysis is likely not as in-depth and well reasoned as it could be.

The general writing process includes two stages:

Stage One of the writing process is the writer-based (creative) stage. In the list of the steps from task to deadline, many of the actions occur prior to writing the first draft. However, if begun early, there will be sufficient time to move through all of these writing stages and focus not only on the content of the message, but also on the presentation of the message to the reader.

Stage Two follows the creative stage. In this critical, reader-based stage, the writer works to ensure that the message is easy to read and understand.

---

6. Nathaniel Hawthorne (1804-1864), as quoted in https://www.brainyquote.com/lists/authors/top-10-nathaniel-hawthorne-quotes (last updated September 10, 2021).

Stage One: Writer-based (creative) focus

When beginning a task, focus on the substance of the message. Early drafting allows the writer to determine whether the message contains the correct substance and is structured appropriately. During this stage of the writing process, the writer need not worry about details such as using proper grammar or clear topic, thesis, and transitional sentences. If the focus is on the smaller details, the writer might overlook important substance. By drafting and redrafting early, the writer can focus on the relevant law and the critical analysis. Steps in the writer-based stage are shown in Figure 4-2.

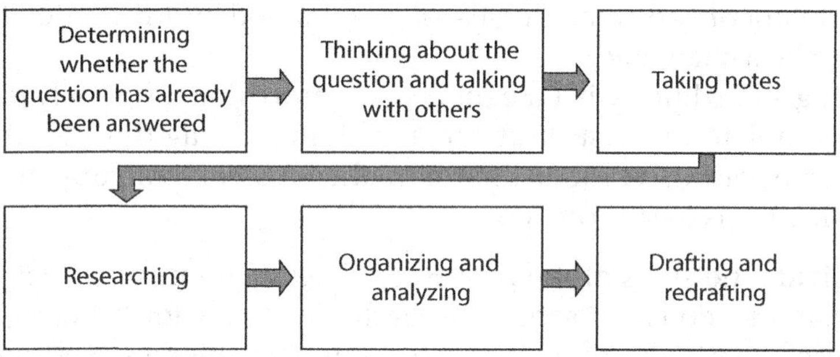

Figure 4-2

A well-written document typically reflects but a small part of what the writer knows and has considered throughout the writing process. Writing itself creates new thoughts that may be brought up from the far reaches of the writer's memory. And when one thought is rejected in a draft, that rejection oftentimes brings forth new thoughts.

Figure 4-3

Ernest Hemingway, an acclaimed U.S. fiction writer of the twentieth century, once compared the writing process to an iceberg: "The dignity of movement of an iceberg is due to only one-eighth of it being above water."[7] In other words, for every

7. Ernest Hemingway, DEATH IN THE AFTERNOON (1932).

one-eighth of an iceberg that is actually seen above the water, seven-eighths created the foundation below.

In the end, just as the tip of the iceberg above water rests on the solid foundation underneath the water, the final written legal document rests on the solid foundation of the writing and rewriting process to ensure the structure and message are accurate and complete.

Stage Two: Reader-based (critical) focus

After completing the writing process to ensure that the message is well organized and complete, Stage Two moves to the critical, reader-based stage of the writing process. At this stage the focus is on revising and editing so the analysis can not only be read but also is understood by any reader. Explaining the law can be a challenge.

Revising and editing will take time, likely more than originally anticipated. Strive to complete the first draft no later than halfway through the task-to-deadline time period. A procrastinator might consider applying one or both of the following steps to stay on task:

(1) Divide the steps of the process and set deadlines for each stage. For example, consider setting separate deadlines for (a) completing the research, (b) drafting, and (c) revising. Consider also setting your own deadlines for different sections of the document, depending on its length and complexity.

(2) Communicate the deadlines to someone else, for example, a supervising attorney, another attorney working on the same project, or an assistant.

Electronic editing tools can help in the polishing stage of legal writing. Both Word or Google Docs word processing platforms provide checks for spelling and grammar. Also, in addition to tools built into word processing platforms, software has been developed as add-ons to the word processing experience. BriefCatch (https://briefcatch.com/) is a legal editing tool designed for use with persuasive briefs. It provides suggestions to aid in areas including conciseness, clarity, and punctuation. For example, for conciseness, BriefCatch might suggest that the legal writer substitute the phrase "critically important" with "vital" or "crucial." WordRake is "automated in-line editing software" that can be used with documents on Word and emails on the Outlook platform. For example, WordRake software can review a document and strike out words that may not be needed and that may serve only to clutter the document. Before purchasing editing software tools like BriefCatch or WordRake, be sure to take advantage of any free trial offered so you can assess how helpful and user-friendly the tool is for you.

Note: Before using editing software for a law school class assignment, be sure to check with your instructor to confirm that the software tool you intend to use is permitted for work in that class.

CHAPTER SUMMARY

- Written legal documents must be professional and require drafting early to allow time to redraft until the structure and content of the message is thorough and clear.
- The legal writing process involves several stages necessary to achieve a complete, accurate, and professional document, including thoroughly understanding the client's story; obtaining the relevant law; organizing and analyzing the law by applying it to the client's facts; and then drafting, redrafting, editing, and revising to ensure readability.
- Lawyers and judges must use the laws set down by the state and federal legislatures and the courts when analyzing and writing about a legal issue.
- In any written document, and especially when writing legal documents, the writer must pay attention to the purpose of the document, the proper tone for the document, the audience, and any time or other constraints that must be followed.
- When first drafting, focus on the creative stage of writing to ensure the message is complete; then move to the critical stage of writing, revising, and editing to ensure that the message is clearly conveyed to the reader.

CHAPTER

5

The U.S. Concept of Plagiarism and Proper Attribution to Authority

---

A. Introduction: The U.S. View of Proper Attribution
   1. Plagiarism defined
   2. The importance of avoiding plagiarism
   3. Intentional or not, plagiarism jeopardizes careers
   4. "Common knowledge" exception
B. Ways to Avoid Plagiarism
   1. Accurate and thorough researching
   2. Special consideration for information found on the Internet
   3. Appropriate management of time
C. Components of Appropriate Attribution
D. Quoting, Summarizing, and Paraphrasing
   1. Quoting
   2. Summarizing
   3. Paraphrasing

A. Introduction: The U.S. View of Proper Attribution

1. Plagiarism defined

Plagiarism is the use of someone else's words or ideas, whether expressed in writing or orally, without proper attribution to the source.

Written words or ideas found in any public or private document, whether or not published, must be attributed to the source. Words or ideas taken from a website must be given proper attribution. Borrowed words or ideas originally expressed in a live, recorded, or broadcast speech, debate, or conversation must be attributed to the speaker. Charts, graphs, illustrations, photographs, and images, or information found in these sources, if borrowed by a writer, must also be properly attributed to the original source.

2. The importance of avoiding plagiarism

Plagiarism is considered a serious moral and ethical transgression in U.S. culture.[1] A student who plagiarizes can be subject to penalties under an educational institution's student code. Penalties range from failing a paper containing the plagiarized material or failing a course, to suspension or expulsion from school, to withholding a degree.[2] Plagiarists risk losing respect among their colleagues and peers, and, if employed, they may even lose their jobs.[3]

Software and online services aimed at detecting plagiarism are widely available.[4] Many instructors regularly use these aids to detect plagiarism in student papers. It is far easier today to spot plagiarized passages than in previous years.

Furthermore, giving attribution to respected authorities to support points or ideas in your writing significantly strengthens the likelihood that your reader will read and accept your legal analysis. Giving appropriate and frequent attribution results in more credible and persuasive writing.

3. Intentional or not, plagiarism jeopardizes careers

Plagiarism is a serious matter, whether or not a person is intentional about it. Intentional plagiarists knowingly use someone else's document, words, or ideas without attribution. Their intent is to deceive readers into thinking that they, the plagiarists, alone conceived and wrote the material. Some people do not intend to plagiarize and may assume that lack of intent will protect them from suffering the consequences of wrongdoing. That is not the case.

---

1. *See* JOSEPH GIBALDI, MLA STYLE MANUAL AND GUIDE TO SCHOLARLY PUBLISHING 166 (3d ed. 2008).

2. *DiPerna v. Chicago School of Professional Psychology*, 893 F.3d 1001 (7th Cir. 2018) (holding that student's dismissal for plagiarism where her paper was found to be 10% plagiarized on turnitin.com was not arbitrary or capricious); *Jaber v. Wayne State University Bd. of Governors*, 487 Fed. Appx. 995 (6th Cir. 2012) (denying plaintiff's due process claim where plaintiff's doctoral degree was revoked for plagiarism); *Napolitano v. Princeton Univ. Trs.*, 453 A.2d 263 (N.J. Super. App. Div. 1982) (upholding the university's sanction of withholding a student's degree for a period of one year because the student had quoted and paraphrased passages from a book in a class paper and failed to properly attribute these passages to the book's author).

3. *Wilson v. Cable News Network, Inc.*, 7 Cal. 5th 871, 444 P.3d 706 (2019) (while the issue in this case was not whether plaintiff plagiarized, the litigation arose because plaintiff was terminated from CNN for plagiarism); *Iowa Sup. Ct. Bd. of Prof'l Ethics & Conduct v. Williams*, 642 N.W.2d 296 (Iowa 2002) (the court suspended an attorney's license to practice law for filing a plagiarized brief in a federal district court); *Matikas v. Univ. of Dayton*, 788 N.E.2d 1108 (Ohio Ct. App. 2003) (the court granted a summary judgment in favor of the university, finding the university was within its rights to terminate a researcher's employment because he committed plagiarism in a manuscript submitted for publication).

4. Plagiarism checkers include iThenticate (iThenticate.com) and Turnitin (Turnitin.com).

When someone uses text and ideas from other sources without attribution to the original, whether intentionally or unintentionally, the writer commits plagiarism.

Also, in law school, unless the instructor says otherwise, students must submit their own work. While some students may find it tempting—especially if English is their second language—to turn to writing specialists, tutors, friends, or family members proficient in English to help them write or rewrite their papers, doing so would be plagiarism and therefore impermissible, unless specifically told otherwise by the instructor. Even if the student did the research and came up with the essential analysis for the paper, it is not permissible for another person to finish the paper by revising phrases, sentences, paragraphs, or sections to make it more readable. Anytime you borrow another person's words without making proper attribution—even when the idea behind the material is your own, you have plagiarized. A paper that you've written for an assignment in a course is expected to be the product of your individual effort, unless the professor states otherwise. Therefore, the temptation to have others write or rewrite papers, even merely for the purpose of correcting grammar or sentence structure problems throughout the paper, must be avoided. Otherwise, you risk incurring serious penalties that could jeopardize your educational pursuits and possibly your career.[5]

4. *"Common knowledge" exception*

In U.S. culture, matters of common knowledge to the writer's target audience do not require a citation to a source. Unfortunately, what constitutes common knowledge is confusing. This confusion is further compounded by cultural differences. Matters of common knowledge have been defined as "includ[ing] whatever an educated person would be expected to know or could locate in an ordinary encyclopedia."[6] At least one university website on plagiarism suggests that a fact or phrase may be of common knowledge if the information can be found undocumented in five different "credible" sources.[7] Still other university websites on plagiarism are not so specific in definition.[8]

---

5. *See, e.g.*, *supra* notes 2 & 3.

6. Robert A. Harris, Using Sources Effectively: Strengthening Your Writing and Avoiding Plagiarism 115 (2017).

7. *Should I Cite This?*, Purdue OWL, https://owl.purdue.edu/owl/research_and_citation/using_research/documents/20200617ShouldICiteChart.jpg (last visited June 23, 2021) (stating as one of its steps, "do at least 5 credible sources have the info without citation?").

8. *See, e.g.*, Academic Integrity at MIT, *What Is Common Knowledge?*, https://integrity.mit.edu/handbook/citing-your-sources/what-common-knowledge (last visited June 23, 2021) ("Information that most people know, such as that water freezes at 32 degrees Fahrenheit or that Barack Obama was the first American of mixed race to be elected president"); Ind. U. Writing Tutorial Servs., Plagiarism: *What It Is and How to Recognize It and Avoid It*, https://wts.indiana.edu/writing-guides/plagiarism.html#terms (last visited June 23, 2021) ("Common knowledge: facts that can be found in numerous places and are likely to be known by a lot of people").

Keep in mind that information someone in the United States considers common knowledge may not be considered common knowledge by someone from another country, and vice versa. Further complicating the situation is that what may be common knowledge to people educated in one particular discipline may not necessarily be common knowledge to people educated in another discipline. For example, it may be common knowledge among U.S. lawyers that there are 13 federal circuits in the United States, but this is likely not common knowledge to people in the medical field in the United States.

Therefore, when determining whether information is common knowledge, writers should consider their audience. If in doubt as to whether the information would be common knowledge to the writer's target audience, the writer should always cite to a source for the information.

B. Ways to Avoid Plagiarism

1. Accurate and thorough researching

Plagiarism often results from sloppy or hasty researching. You should give particular attention, therefore, to your note taking while researching. Do not trust that you will remember later which words in your notes are yours and which are an author's. As you research, mark the exact words you have copied, as well as those passages you have paraphrased or summarized. Also, do not trust yourself to remember the source or the page number where you found the information that you have marked in your notes. Write down the source where you found the information while you are creating your notes.[9] When recording the source, be sure to include the complete title of the source, the author's name, and the page number where you found the information. If you are researching in multiple places, such as in the law school library and online research databases like Westlaw or Lexis, note in which location you found the source so that you can easily return if you have questions later on. Creating a chart or log of your research, and filling it in as you research, can be especially helpful for recording information about a source. The chart or log will help you attribute and avoid plagiarism during the writing process.

2. Special consideration for information found on the Internet

If you found information on an Internet site, note the URL[10] address where you found it. Plagiarism has become especially troublesome with

9. Note taking also is discussed in Chapter 4.

10. Uniform Resource Locator, or the string of letters, words, and numbers that usually begins with *http*.

students' easy access to the Internet. The ease in copying online information and pasting it into your own document heightens the risk of plagiarism. Be especially mindful of noting the source of the language that has been pasted into your paper. When you are finalizing your paper, you may choose to take the highlighted words or passages and either summarize, paraphrase, or quote them; even so, you must always include a proper attribution to the website where you found the information.

Taking the time while you are researching to note whether you have quoted, paraphrased, or summarized information from a source will save time later, because you will not need to find the information again. More importantly, careful documentation while researching will prevent you from attributing text or ideas to the wrong source, or failing to give any attribution at all.

Technology has made keeping track of sources easier. Some legal research platforms, including Westlaw and Lexis, allow you to copy and paste an excerpt from a case or other source found on the platform with a citation automatically included. The citation will appear with your excerpt when it is pasted into your paper.

3. Appropriate management of time

Rushing to complete your research and then write your paper to meet a deadline can also give rise to incidents of plagiarism. Give yourself plenty of time to not only research but also to write your paper. (The writing process is discussed further in Chapter 4.) Most students in the United States who read and write English with ease still spend many, many hours researching, putting the information together, and drafting and revising their writing in an effort to create well-written papers containing strong legal analyses. If you are not fluent in English, this process may take longer. Be honest with yourself about your level of skill in researching and your proficiency in writing, and budget your time accordingly. The research and writing process almost always takes longer than originally anticipated, no matter your English language proficiency.

C. Components of Appropriate Attribution

Proper attribution has three basic requirements:

(1) The writer must accurately set out in their writing the words or ideas they are borrowing from another source;

(2) The writer must notify the reader about any quoted words or phrases by either placing quotation marks around the quoted text or, if the quotation is 50 or more words, by placing the quoted text in block format; and

(3) The writer must accurately and completely cite to the original source at all necessary points in their paper where they have used text or ideas from that original source.

The importance of accurate citations to the source cannot be overemphasized. Providing fictitious or incorrect citations to borrowed text or ideas is plagiarism because the writer has failed to give proper attribution to the original source.

D. Quoting, Summarizing, and Paraphrasing

A source can be used in a number of ways in legal writing. A lawyer might quote from the source. Quoting means using the exact language from the source. A lawyer might summarize part or all of a source. Or, a lawyer might paraphrase the source. Following is guidance on how to properly quote, summarize, and paraphrase.

1. Quoting

When using quoted text in your writing, keep the following criteria in mind.

a. The quoted material must accurately reflect the words in the original text.

If you modify anything within the quotation, such as changing the tense of a verb, replacing a proper noun with a pronoun, or omitting words or punctuation, you must note this using brackets or ellipses, as appropriate.[11]

Example:

The original text from *Blodgett* reads:

> The legislature clearly decided that in such a case there should be discretion in the court to consider the specific facts of the homicide and, if denial of the inheritance would be manifestly unjust, to permit it.

Someone quoting that text but adding clarifying language in brackets might write:

> In *In re Estate of Blodgett*, 147 P.3d 702, 707 (Alaska 2006), the court stated, "The legislature clearly decided that [where an heir commits a criminally

11. *See* Carolyn Williams, ALWD Guide to Legal Citation 403-13 (7th ed. 2021) (explanation and examples of the proper use of brackets and ellipses in a quoted passage).

> negligent act accidentally causing the deceased's death] there should be discretion in the court to consider the specific facts of the homicide and, if denial of the inheritance [from the deceased] would be manifestly unjust, to permit it."[12]

b. If the quotation contains fewer than 50 words, begin and end the quoted text with quotation marks.

Example:

"The legislature limited the broad reach of the slayer statute by giving trial court judges the discretion to allow killers to benefit from the victim's assets if manifest injustice would result otherwise." *Blodgett*, 147 P.3d at 707 (referring to Alaska Stat. § 13.12.803(k)).

c. If the quotation contains 50 or more words, place the quoted text in block format.

Indent both the left and right margins and use single spacing. Do not use quotation marks around the block quote. You may, however, use quotation marks if the block quote contains a quote within the block quote. The block format signals to the reader that the text is quoted material.

Example:

In *Blodgett*, the court reasoned:

> The legislature clearly decided that ... there should be discretion in the court to consider the specific facts of the homicide and, if denial of the inheritance would be manifestly unjust, to permit it.... Where the killer's act was not intentional, and especially where the act was not even reckless, and where other circumstances lessen the overall effect of the crime, the application of the slayer statute may lead to unnecessarily harsh results.

147 P.3d at 707.

12. The *Blodgett* passages given in this section were taken from the *Blodgett* case discussed in Chapter 3.

d. *Include a citation for the quoted language.*[13]

If you have quoted language from another source, place a citation to the source immediately after the sentence containing the quoted material, as in the example at 1.b. above.[14] When quoting material from another source, using quotation marks or a block format alone is not enough. The citation is necessary. The writer must provide quotation marks around the quoted text—or, in the case of a quote of 50 or more words, in block format—*and* a citation to the source in order to give proper attribution to the source. Without the citation, the writer has plagiarized the material.

e. *Avoid overuse of quoted language.*

Aim to use quoted material judiciously. Some students, especially those who don't give themselves enough time to complete a paper or are too uncomfortable to paraphrase or summarize information from a source, tend to string one quotation after another. Stringing one quote after another can result in a paper that essentially is not the writer's work product. Also, quotations can take up a lot of space in a paper, especially when extraneous words or information are included in the quoted text. Overquoting leaves little, if any, room for the writer's own ideas, thoughts, and analyses, which are a critical part of most written assignments in law school.

2. *Summarizing*

You may summarize the information contained in the original text. A summary is shorter in length than the passage in the original text, allowing more space for the writer to convey analyses or ideas. But you should also be aware that, by virtue of its brevity, a summary may not convey all the points made by the author in the original text. Therefore, you should use a summary when (1) it is important to be brief, and (2) it is unnecessary to convey all the points made by the author in the original text. A few quoted words or phrases may be included in a summary, in which case you must place quotation marks around the quoted text. When summarizing information from a source, keep the following guidance in mind.

---

13. For guidance on legal citation style, legal writers can consult CAROLYN WILLIAMS, ALWD GUIDE TO LEGAL CITATION (7th ed. 2021) or THE BLUEBOOK: A UNIFORM SYSTEM OF CITATION (21st ed. 2020).

14. However, if the writer quotes from another source in the same sentence, the writer should include the citation within the sentence. For example, if, in one sentence, the writer quotes from Case A and then in the same sentence quotes from Case B, the citation to Case A should be placed inside the sentence right after the quoted material from Case A. Here's a simplified example, with fictional quotes and cases: While one court has described a shallow pond in a park as "a scenic and harmless spot for children to play," *City Parks v. Gee*, 758 A.2d 28, 37 (Ohio 2005), another court described a similarly shallow pond in a park as "an unsafe attraction," *Merry Park v. Berkshire School*, 25 B.2d 98, 101 (Mass. 2007).

a. Make sure the summary accurately reflects information conveyed in the original text.
b. Quote any key words or phrases from the original text used in the summary.
c. Insert a citation to the source where you found the information you are summarizing.
d. Follow accurately an established legal citation style when writing citations to the information you are summarizing.[15]

Example:

The original text from *Blodgett* reads:

> The legislature limited the broad reach of the slayer statute by giving trial court judges the discretion to allow killers to benefit from the victim's assets if manifest injustice would result otherwise. Should an inheritance be denied to the unskilled teenager who drives his car in a criminally negligent manner and accidentally causes the death of his remaining parent? The legislature clearly decided that in such a case there should be discretion in the court to consider the specific facts of the homicide and, if denial of the inheritance would be manifestly unjust, to permit it.

A summary of a passage from *Blodgett* might read:

> The Alaska legislature expanded the coverage of the slayer statute to include unintentional killings but also limited its scope by creating an exception when its application would create a "manifest injustice," such as when a teen-aged child drives in a "criminally negligent manner" and accidentally kills the child's only surviving parent. *Blodgett*, 147 P.3d at 707.

Even if the summary had not contained quoted phrases, the summary must include a citation to the original text. Failing to cite to a source when summarizing a part or all of the source is plagiarism.

3. *Paraphrasing*

Rather than directly quoting or summarizing a passage, you may elect to paraphrase the information from the original text. A paraphrase restates the original text in your own words. If the original text is complex or awkwardly

15. *See supra* note 13.

worded, you may paraphrase the text rather than directly quoting it, to convey the information in wording that is easier for the reader to understand. You may prefer paraphrasing over summarizing the original text when you want to convey all the points made in the original text.[16] One way to draft a paraphrased passage is to read the original text over and over until you understand it, then put the text aside and draft the paraphrase, using your own words and sentence structure. Afterwards, check to make sure you have not used the original language in a way that needs to be changed or quoted. When paraphrasing information from another text, keep in mind the following guidance:

a. Make sure the paraphrased language accurately reflects information conveyed in the original text.

b. Using synonyms or just changing the tense of verbs, while keeping the same sentence structure of the original text without using quotation marks, would be plagiarism.

c. If a key word or phrase from the original text is used in the paraphrase, put that word or phrase in quotation marks.

d. Insert a citation to the source where you found the material you are paraphrasing.

e. Follow accurately an established legal citation style when writing citations to the information you are paraphrasing.[17]

Example:

An insufficient attempt at paraphrasing the passage from *Blodgett* might read as follows.

> The court in *Blodgett* noted that the Alaska legislature narrowed the reach of the slayer statute by giving the trial court judges the discretion to allow killers to benefit from the victim's assets if manifest injustice would result otherwise. In creating the exception, the legislature considered those instances such as when a child unintentionally kills his sole parent. Even though this act would fall within the slayer statute, prohibiting that child from receiving the parent's assets would be fundamentally unfair. The legislature decided that in instances such as this, the trial court may consider the specific facts of the homicide to determine whether denying the defendant the victim's assets would be manifestly unjust. *Blodgett*, 147 P.3d at 707.

16. It is suggested, however, that you quote all rules or relevant sections of a statute that are the focus of a legal analysis to avoid inadvertently changing the meaning of the rules or statutes.

17. *See supra* note 13.

This particular passage is plagiarized. The writer essentially has retained the sentence structure from the original text and merely replaced various words with synonyms.[18] Also, the phrase "reach of the slayer statute by giving the trial court judges the discretion to allow killers to benefit from the victim's assets if manifest injustice would result otherwise" has been quoted, and the writer failed to place quotation marks around this phrase. Finally, a citation to the case appears only at the end of the passage. This misleads the reader and may cause the reader to understand that only the last sentence of the passage represents the court's reasoning when the entire passage, in fact, represents the court's reasoning. A citation should have appeared at the end of each sentence. Any one of these errors—a failure to paraphrase the passage, a failure to place quotation marks around the quoted text, or a failure to insert a citation at the end of each sentence—would make a passage plagiarized.

Example:

A sufficient paraphrase of the passage from *Blodgett* might read:

> In *Blodgett*, the court stated that at the same time the Alaska legislature expanded the slayer statute to include unintentional killings, it also added an exception to the slayer statute. 147 P.3d at 707. The exception empowers the trial court to prohibit the application of the main provision of the slayer statute when to do so would be "manifestly unjust." *Id.* The court considered those instances such as when a child unintentionally kills their only parent. *Id.* Even though the child's actions would be a homicide and fall within the main provision of the slayer statute, prohibiting that child from receiving his parent's assets may be fundamentally unfair. *Id.* Thus, the legislature gave the trial court the ability to permit the defendant to take the victim's assets when a "denial of inheritance would be manifestly unjust. . . ." *Id.*

In the example immediately above, no language is taken directly from the original passage, but the message reflects the original message. A citation appears at the end of each sentence because each sentence communicates a part of the court's statement of a rule or its reasoning. Also, the writer has placed quotation marks around key phrases.

18. Another common way to plagiarize is by changing the tense of verbs in a passage from another source and failing to use brackets where the tense of verbs has been changed and failing to put quotation marks around the entire passage.

• Exercise 5-A

Using the following excerpt from the stolen art case, *Everett v. Rogers* (found in the Student Supplemental Materials for this book located on the publisher's website at http://www.aspenpublishing.com), write examples of (1) a summarized passage and (2) a paraphrased passage using the concepts learned in this chapter.

> The discovery rule is fact sensitive so as to adjust the level of scrutiny as is appropriate in light of the identity of the parties; what efforts are reasonable for an individual who is relatively unfamiliar with the art world, for example, may not be reasonable for a savvy collector, a gallery, or a museum. While Rogers could certainly have been more aggressive in his search—for example, making inquiries at galleries and museums rather than merely visiting them—Rogers' occasional visits to galleries and museums and his reliance on the services of the F.B.I. constitute a reasonable search effort under the discovery rule. Notably, the standard is not whether Rogers did everything that might have been done with the benefit of hindsight, but whether his efforts were reasonable given the facts of the case.

Everett v. Rogers, 836 F. Supp. 1030, 1033 (S.D.E.C. 1995).

CHAPTER SUMMARY

- Plagiarism is the use of someone else's words or ideas without properly attributing the source of them.
- Words or ideas taken from published or unpublished sources—including written text and websites; live, recorded, or broadcast speeches, debates, or conversations; or graphs, charts, illustrations, photographs, and images—must be given proper attribution to the original source.
- All quoted, summarized, and paraphrased information must be properly attributed.
- Steps to avoid plagiarism include taking accurate notes when researching; keeping track of passages copied and pasted from online sources; and allowing sufficient time for the writing process.
- Proper attribution includes (1) accurately reporting the borrowed words or ideas; (2) placing quotation marks around quoted text; and (3) accurately citing to the original source.

CHAPTER

6

Writing an Objective Discussion of an Office Memorandum Based on a Single Fact-Based Issue, Using Only One Case

A. Introduction to the Office Memorandum

A formal office memorandum, usually assigned by a supervising attorney, has two major goals:

- To explain the law that's relevant to any legal issues raised in a client's case.
- To predict a likely outcome regarding those legal issues, after applying the law to the facts of the client's case.

The objective analysis may be presented in the form of a formal office memorandum, the traditional form of communication, or in the form of an e-memo, which is more informal but still requires the same key information presented in a professional manner. E-memos are discussed in Chapter 14.

The supervising attorney may assign an office memorandum early on, for example, after the initial meeting with a potential client. The office memorandum would help the attorney decide how to proceed. The attorney may decide, for example, (1) not to represent the client; (2) to urge the client to negotiate a settlement; or (3) to proceed with the case by filing a complaint in a court. The supervising attorney may also assign an office memorandum to assess the likelihood of prevailing on a procedural motion that may be raised before or during trial.

The formal office memorandum usually includes the following sections:

- Questions Presented
- Brief Answers
- Statement of Facts
- **Discussion**
- Conclusion

This chapter focuses on writing the discussion section of the office memorandum. The other sections of an office memorandum are addressed in Chapter 13.

The heart of the office memorandum is the discussion, where the goal is to explain the issues and the relevant law, and then analyze and predict the likely conclusion regarding any issues raised in the client's case. Preparing a discussion section can be intimidating, especially when addressing a complex issue or multiple issues involving many facts and rules. To introduce the writing process for an objective legal analysis, this chapter focuses solely on analyzing a single fact-based issue using only one case. Later chapters introduce adding more issues and cases to the discussion section.

B. Learning the Client's Facts

As discussed in Chapter 4, the first step in resolving a client's legal problem begins with interviewing the client. The interviewer's goal is to collect the important facts and identify potential claims or defenses that will help answer the client's question. The interview requires the interviewer to ask careful questions and take copious notes. This chapter will explain this process focusing on a hypothetical potential client, Ana Hart, who has a legal problem. The following are the interviewer's notes from the interview with Ana.

Example of notes from client Ana Hart's interview:

- Ana and David Hart met while competing in a weightlifting competition, and both presently live in Flora, East Carolina. Flora is located in Marion County.
- Shortly after their marriage, they started a health and exercise club in Flora under the name of their business partnership, "Hart Fitness Center" (Center). Both Harts are active partners in the business.

- During the marriage the club thrived, and the Harts later purchased two other health and exercise clubs, one in Hamilton County and one in Johnson County, also known as Hart Fitness Centers.
- Recently, Ana and David decided to divorce.
- During the divorce proceeding, David petitioned the court to award him ownership of the couple's Centers.
- After the hearing on David's petition, the court ordered that, as part of the property settlement:
  - David will buy Ana's interest in the Centers by paying Ana an amount equal to one-half the fair market value in the Centers, and
  - In exchange for this sum, Ana will sell to David her interest in the Centers and sign a covenant not to compete (CNC).
  - In the CNC, Ana must promise "not to engage, either directly or indirectly, on her own or in the employ of another, in the health and exercise club business in any form for a period of five years in the counties of Hamilton, Hancock, Boone, Marion, Johnson, and Hendricks, plus the towns of Arcadia and Bloomtown, East Carolina." (*See* Figure 6-1 for a map of the fictitious state of East Carolina.)

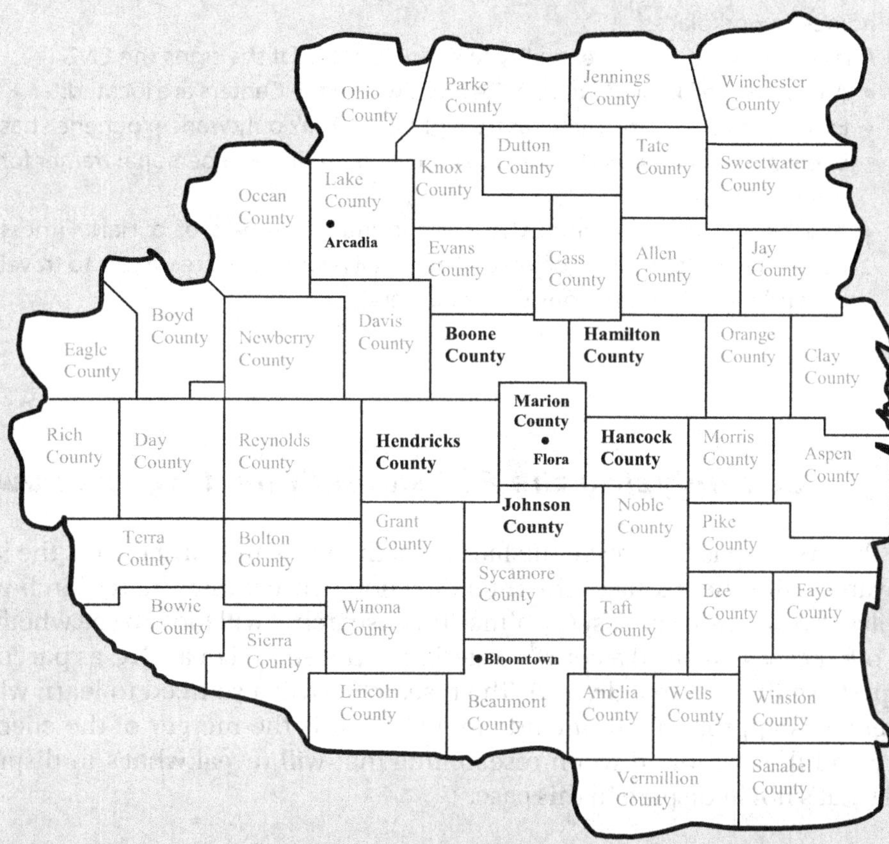

Figure 6-1
East Carolina (a fictitious state)

- Ana does not want to sign the CNC or abide by the terms of the CNC.
- The sellers of the clubs to David and Ana Hart in Hamilton and Johnson counties did not have any connection with members of the Hart Fitness Center prior to the sale.
- The purchase agreements for the clubs in Hamilton and Johnson counties included CNCs that restricted the sellers, for a period of five years, from engaging in the health and exercise club business in the counties where the clubs being sold were located.
- The Harts do not own any Centers in Boone, Hancock, or Hendricks counties, or any Centers in the towns of Arcadia or Bloomtown (all mentioned in the CNC as part of the divorce).
  - The Harts had planned to expand into these areas within the next three years.
  - The counties border Flora.
  - Bloomtown is located approximately 45 miles south of Flora, and Arcadia is located approximately 50 miles northwest of Flora.
- At the time of the divorce proceedings, the membership in the Hart Fitness Centers totaled 5,200 clients.
- A recent survey of Center members showed that, although members may use any of the Hart Fitness Centers, they usually attend a Center closest to their homes or workplaces.
- Ana is concerned about her ability to support herself if she signs the CNC.
  - Ana is not well known outside the areas where the Centers are located.
  - Except for her athletic career as a weightlifter, Ana's only work experience has been managing the Hart Fitness Centers and serving as a personal trainer for some of its members.
  - Ana has dedicated clients who are currently members of a Hart Fitness Center and who, because of job and personal restrictions, are unable to travel beyond the CNC restrictions to use her services

C. *Analyzing the Facts and Collecting the Law*

The first step is to analyze the facts, and then research and collect the law relevant to the client's case. The interview notes reveal that the research will involve divorce cases in East Carolina. The researcher will look to see whether any other cases involved a court's ordering a spouse to sign a CNC as part of a property settlement in a divorce. The researcher will also need to learn what generally is appropriate to include in a CNC. It is the merger of the client's story and the law found when researching that will reveal what's in dispute and what's not in dispute in this case.

D. Analyzing the Law

After researching, and based on the facts from the interview, the researcher learns that no court in East Carolina has previously ordered a spouse to sign a CNC as part of a property settlement. After researching East Carolina law on CNCs ancillary to or in connection with the sale of a business, the researcher found one court opinion addressing the reasonableness and enforceability of a CNC, *Mats Transport v. ABC Corporation*. Reading the relevant case law carefully and then briefing it is vital to the analysis. Immediately below is the full *Mats Transport* opinion.

Mats Transport (Plaintiff) v. ABC Corporation (Defendant)

824 S.E.2d 1467 (E.C. Ct. App. 1992)

Miller, Chief Justice.[1]

The plaintiff, Mats Transport, sued the defendant, ABC Corporation, alleging the defendant violated a covenant not to compete which was part of a purchase agreement it had signed when the defendant sold a part of its business to the plaintiff. Defendant moved for summary judgment, claiming the covenant not to compete was unreasonable because it was broader than necessary for the protection of the plaintiff's business and therefore unenforceable. Following a hearing, the trial court granted the defendant's motion. We affirm.

Both plaintiff and defendant are trucking firms. On May 1, 1989, the plaintiff and defendant entered into a purchase agreement which provided that the defendant would sell to the plaintiff all goodwill associated with or related to its business, its trade name, its customer list, and its operating permits. The purchase agreement included a covenant not to compete with the plaintiff under the terms of which the defendant agreed that for a period of five years it would not compete directly or indirectly with the plaintiff's trucking business in the United States.

In consideration for the defendant's sale of its business and the covenant not to compete, the plaintiff paid $50,000 to the defendant.

Shortly after the Agreement went into effect, the defendant leased seven trucks to Todd Stern, a former truck driver for the defendant. Stern began operating his own trucking firm. The plaintiff argues that Stern's operations compete with it, and that the defendant's leasing of trucks to Stern violated the covenant and has substantially diluted and impaired the value of the goodwill purchased by the plaintiff, resulting in lost revenues and lost profits for the plaintiff.

***1468** Under Rule 56(c) of the East Carolina Rules of Civil Procedure, summary judgment is proper "if the pleadings, depositions, answers to interrogatories, and admissions on file, together with the affidavits, if any, show

1. Created from *Ridgefield Park Transp. v. Uhl*, 803 F. Supp. 1467 (S.D. Ind. 1992).

that there is no genuine issue as to any material fact and that the moving party is entitled to a judgment as a matter of law." E.C. R. Civ. Proc. 56(c). In passing on a motion for summary judgment, the judge's role is not to evaluate the weight of the evidence or determine the truth of the matter, but it is instead to decide whether there is a genuine issue for trial. Summary judgment is especially appropriate where the issues in dispute are purely legal. In these circumstances, the need for trial is avoided because there are no genuine issues of material fact that must be resolved. The defendant argues that summary judgment should be entered in its favor because the CNC is unreasonable as a matter of law.

This court begins its analysis by noting that covenants not to compete are not favored by the law. The reason for this is not difficult to fathom; they impede trade and distort the market mechanism which allows our economy to function. Covenants not to compete consequently are strictly construed against the party seeking to enforce them. They are not per se unlawful, however, and will be enforced if they are reasonable, which is a determination made by the court.

Courts in this state apply a three-pronged test to determine whether a covenant not to compete ancillary to the sale of a business is unreasonable: (1) the covenant must not be broader than necessary for the protection of the covenantee's[2] legitimate business interest; (2) the covenant cannot have an adverse effect on the covenantor;[3] and (3) the covenant cannot adversely affect the public interest. *Hanson v. Albright*, 539 S.E.2d 500, 501 (E.C. Ct. App. 1989). If the covenant not to compete fails any prong of this test, then it is unreasonable as a matter of law.

This court finds that the covenant not to compete contained in the purchase agreement signed by the defendant fails the first prong of the test because it is broader than necessary to protect the plaintiff's interest. Whether a covenant is overly broad depends, in part, on the extent of the territory restricted. *See id.*

When a party sells a business to another, the seller often will agree not to compete with the buyer for a certain period of time within a certain area. This covenant not to compete protects value of the business's goodwill, which represents the value of the customers' relationship with the business at the time of the sale. *Matthews v. Acme Tax Consultants*, 470 S.E.2d 756, 763 (E.C. Ct. App. 1984).

While the trucking operation which the plaintiff purchased had permits to operate in 48 states, the record indicates that the defendant was primarily a regional shipper that operated out of a terminal in the southern part of East Carolina. Although the defendant at times hauled freight across the United States, this activity was sporadic; its business consisted primarily of serving a handful of major clients over established routes in East Carolina and the states on its border.

All parties were aware at the time of sale that the defendant was not a national concern and that it did not preside over an elaborate shipping network. This was implicit in the fact that the defendant had only one truck terminal and a small number of trucks. The covenant not to compete, however, constrains the defendant in a way that contemplates a far different organization—one that has its own developed markets coast to coast and a shipping

2. The party for whose benefit the covenant not to compete is made.

3. The party who agrees not to compete.

> infrastructure to support them. Nothing in the record supports such a finding.
>
> The covenant not to compete signed by the defendant prevents the defendant from competing, directly or indirectly, anywhere in the United States. The activity that it seeks to prohibit is far more encompassing than is necessary to protect the plaintiff's interests because it amounts to a total prohibition on the defendant's entry into any trucking market in the United States.
>
> Because the covenant not to compete fails the first prong of the *Hanson* test, this court need not examine the other two prongs. We uphold the trial court's finding that the covenant was unreasonable as a matter of law.

Careful reading of the case reveals that, in Ana's case, the CNC may provide more protection for David's business than is necessary and may, therefore, be unreasonable and unenforceable. This hypothetical will initially address only this issue. Thus, the next step is to brief *Mats Transport,* dealing specifically with the reasonableness of a CNC.

Following the guidelines found in Chapter 3, below is an example of a case brief for *Mats Transport v. ABC Corporation,* focusing on the reasonableness of the CNC:

***Mats Transport* [seller] *v. ABC Corp.* [buyer], 824 S.E.2d 1467 (E.C. Ct. App. 1992)**

Facts:

- Seller sold its trucking business and all goodwill associated with the business (including trade name, customer list, and operating permits), and signed a CNC restricting seller from competing in the trucking business, directly or indirectly, in the U.S. for 5 years.
- At the time of the purchase, the seller had permits to operate in 48 states but had only one terminal, located in East Carolina, and had hauled freight primarily for a few major clients on routes in East Carolina and adjoining states.
- The seller had hauled freight elsewhere across the United States on an infrequent basis.
- After the sale, the seller leased several trucks to a truck driver who had previously been the seller's employee. The driver began operating a trucking business using the leased trucks in the territory covered by the CNC.

Procedural History:

Trial Court:

- C/A: Buyer's complaint contended seller's leasing of the trucks to driver violated the CNC signed by the seller by impairing the value of the goodwill, resulting in lost revenues.
- Seller moved for summary judgment, which the trial court granted.
- Buyer appealed.

Issue:

Substantive Issue: Is a CNC signed as a part of a sale of a trucking business unreasonable when (1) the CNC requires that the buyer not compete, directly or indirectly, with the buyer in the business anywhere in the U.S., and (2) at the time the seller signed the CNC, the seller's business was limited to several customers in the state or adjoining states, and the seller had engaged in business only infrequently elsewhere in the U.S.?

Procedural Issue: Did the trial court correctly grant seller's summary judgment motion?

Holding:

Substantive Issue: Yes. A CNC signed as a part of a sale of a trucking business is unreasonable when (1) the CNC requires that the buyer will not compete, directly or indirectly, with the seller in the business anywhere in the U.S., and (2) at the time the seller signed the CNC, the seller's business was limited to several customers in the state or adjoining states, and the seller had engaged in business only sporadically elsewhere in the U.S.

Procedural Issue: Yes. The trial court properly granted seller's summary judgment motion.

Judgment: Affirmed.

Relevant Rules:

1. CNCs are strictly construed against the party seeking to enforce them because CNCs restrict trade and undermine the free market system on which the U.S. economy is founded. *Id.* at 1468.
2. A CNC will be enforced if it is reasonable. *Id.*
3. East Carolina courts use a three-pronged test[4] when determining whether a CNC signed in connection with the sale of a business is unreasonable:

    "(1) the covenant must not be broader than necessary for the protection of the covenantee's [buyer's] legitimate business interest;
    (2) the covenant cannot have an adverse effect on the covenantor [seller]; and
    (3) the covenant cannot adversely affect the public interest."

   (quoting *Mats Transport*, 824 S.E.2d at 1468).
4. A CNC is unreasonable as a matter of law if it fails any of the prongs of the test. *Id.*
5. When determining whether a CNC is broader than necessary to protect the buyer, the court will consider "the extent of the territory restricted." *Id.*
6. The CNC represents the seller's goodwill, which represents the value of the relationship between the seller and its customers. *Id.* (quoting *Matthews v. Acme Tax Consultants*, 470 S.E.2d 756, 763 (E.C. Ct. App. 1984)).

4. The terms *legal principle, rule,* and *test* are synonymous and used interchangeably in this text.

Court's Reasoning:

When the seller sold its trucking business to the buyer, the parties knew the seller's trucking business operated in a limited geographic area, yet the CNC restrained the seller as though it was a national enterprise with a market, offices, and a fleet of trucks operating in all states. Because the territorial scope of the CNC exceeded the protection of the buyer's legitimate interests, the CNC was unreasonable as a matter of law and was, therefore, unenforceable. The dismissal based on the motion for summary judgment was appropriate.

Note: The list of legal principles under the relevant rules section, above, includes cites to where the legal rules are located in the court opinion, for quicker access if needed in class.

In the Harts' case, the rules applied by the court in *Mats Transport* reveal the key to Ana's case is focusing on the first prong of the test for reasonableness—whether the CNC is broader than necessary to protect the buyer's interest. Also, the court in *Mats Transport* looked at the size of the business at the time of the sale to determine whether the scope of the restraint in the CNC exceeded the buyer's legitimate business interests. Perhaps other facts that relate to the size of the Hart Fitness Centers may be relevant. In addition, the fact that the buyer and seller presently are partners may be important in determining whether the CNC was broader than necessary for David's protection.

E. Organizing the Law for the Discussion Section

Once the researcher gathers the law that is relevant to the client's case, the basic structure of the discussion section can be organized. Because this chapter addresses a single issue with a single case, there is no need to further organize the law in Ana's case. How to organize the law is discussed in more detail in Chapters 7, 9, and 10, which address structuring a discussion of and analyzing multiple issues using multiple cases.

F. Analyzing and Applying the Law to the Client's Facts

By applying the law to the client's facts, the researcher learns what, if any, issues are in dispute. An issue is considered in dispute if the law and facts support a legitimate argument for each party. In Ana's case, a dispute exists regarding whether the CNC is broader than necessary for the protection of David's legitimate interest.

An objective analysis of an issue in dispute includes support for both parties. Use the objective analysis as an opportunity to assess the strengths and weaknesses of the client's case by thoroughly exploring how the law can be used to support the client's case and how the law can be used to support the case for the opposing party. Once the objective analysis is completed, predicted conclusions along with any recommendations can be made to the supervising attorney. If litigation is necessary, this objective analysis can later be used to present a complete and accurate argument on behalf of the client. A complete argument can only be achieved by fully understanding the support for both sides in the dispute.

Three sources are available to support the client's position:

(1) the relevant law;
(2) the client's relevant facts; and
(3) the underlying policy reasons for the law.

The relevant facts in court decisions are important in a fact-based analysis. When analyzing, strive to show how the legally significant facts of the court opinion may be similar to or different from the client's legally significant facts. If the holding in a court decision reflects the preferred result for the client, *compare* the relevant facts in the court decision favorably to the comparable relevant facts in the client's case. If the holding in a court decision reflects an outcome different from what is desired for the client, *contrast* the relevant facts in the court decision from the comparable relevant facts in the client's case.

> **Note:** *Compare or contrast, analogize or distinguish,* and *similar to or different from* are terms used interchangeably when discussing how the facts of a client's case are similar to or different from the facts in a court opinion.

For instance, the court in *Mats Transport* found the CNC overbroad in the protection of the buyer's interest. To support Ana's position, any legally significant facts in *Mats Transport* that are <u>similar</u> to the legally significant facts of Ana's case and any reasonable inferences drawn from these similarities can be used to support her position that the CNC she is being ordered to sign is also overbroad in its protection of David's legitimate interest. Conversely, David's lawyer would note any legally significant facts in *Mats Transport* that are <u>different</u> from the legally significant facts of Ana's case and any reasonable inferences drawn from these distinctions to support David's position that the CNC is not overbroad. Reasonable inferences connect the factual analogies and distinctions in the two cases to the conclusion being supported. Ultimately, the court will rule in part on whether the relevant similarities in the two cases outweigh the relevant differences, or whether the factual differences between the two cases outweigh the factual similarities.

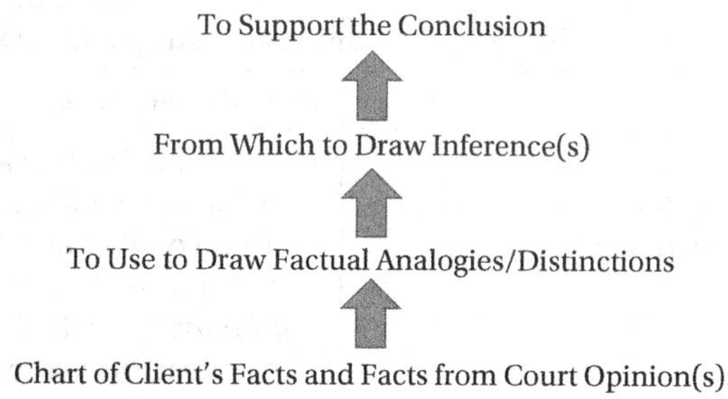

Figure 6-2

Beyond those facts that can be compared to or contrasted from the facts in the relevant case law, there may be other legally significant facts of the client's case that are not directly parallel to any of the facts from the court opinions but nevertheless may be used to draw reasonable inferences supporting the client's position. For example, Ana's facts reveal that sellers in prior sales of clubs to the Hart Fitness Center executed CNCs that restricted competition *only* in the area where the purchased clubs were already located. A reasonable inference can be drawn that the CNC should restrict the territory only where the clubs were located at the time the CNC was signed. Although there is no similar fact in *Mats Transport,* this fact should be used to support the argument that the CNC that Ana has been ordered to sign is overbroad.

Finally, public policy reasons, if noted by the court, may further support the key fact-based arguments. Public policy reasons are broad, underlying reasons that explain why a legal test exists and how to interpret and apply that test. In *Mats Transport,* for example, the court includes the point that CNCs are "strictly construed against the party seeking to enforce them," and that "covenants not to complete are not favored by the law" because they "impede trade and distort the market mechanism which allows our economy to function." *Mats Transport,* 824 S.E.2d 1467, 1468 (E.C. Ct. App. 1992). These public policy points may also be helpful in Ana's case. Public policy, however, should not be the key support for a fact-based analysis. Instead, public policy may be used to bolster the fact-based analyses. Public policy is used primarily to support a law-based analysis based on a question of law, discussed more in Chapter 12 on analyzing law-based issues.

Because lawyers are interested primarily in advocating for their client's position, they sometimes find it difficult to consider the opposing side's position. One way to avoid this problem is to adopt the role of the opposing lawyer, analyzing the opposing side's position first. In the role of the opposing lawyer in this CNC case, the focus would be on finding the law and facts that may be useful to David's position. Specifically, key would be any distinctions between the facts of *Mats Transport* and this case, along with additional facts in the CNC case from which to draw any reasonable inferences to support why the CNC Ana has been asked to sign is reasonable. For easier reference, consider charting this information. For example, the following charts the facts and inferences that support David's position:

Factual Distinctions and Additional Facts Supporting David's Position	
***Mats Transport* Facts**	**Facts of Client's Case**
• Seller never expressed to the buyer any intent to expand the business into additional areas covered by the CNC.	• David and Ana had agreed to expand the business within the next 3 years into 3 counties and 2 towns where the Harts presently did not operate a Center. ***Inference: The CNC protects David's legitimate future interests previously identified by both Harts.***
• The CNC restricted competition in every U.S. state, even though the business operated in only one state and had established trucking routes only in neighboring states.	• The CNC that Ana has been ordered to sign covers a limited geographic area in East Carolina where the business is located or where it will expand in the near future. ***Inference: The CNC protects David's legitimate interests.*** • Unlike the previous sellers of clubs who did not have any connection with Hart Fitness Center members prior to the sale of the clubs, Ana has developed a relationship with the Centers' members. ***Inference: Ana presents a greater threat to David's interest in the business, due to her history with the Centers and David's relying heavily on the continuing goodwill between the members and the Centers' employees.*** • Members usually use the club closest to their homes or workplaces. ***Inference: If Ana opens a club in the same county or town where a Center exists, Center members may join Ana's club if it is closer to their homes or workplaces.***

Notice that the distinctions between the facts from *Mats Transport* and the client's case are set side-by-side in the chart, making it easier to draft the discussion. Additional facts that support David's position are also listed. Finally, reasonable inferences are noted where appropriate.

Next, consider Ana's position using the same process. For example, consider the following support for Ana's position that the CNC is unreasonably overbroad for the protection of David's legitimate interest:

Factual Analogies and Additional Facts Supporting Ana's Position	
***Mats Transport* Facts**	**Facts of Client's Case**
• The CNC was overbroad for the protection of the buyer's interest when it restricted competition in territory beyond where the seller operated its business.	• The CNC Ana has been ordered to sign restricts Ana from competing in counties and towns where the Harts do not own any Centers. ***Inference: The CNC exceeds David's legitimate business interest.***

	• CNCs signed by previous sellers of clubs to the Harts restricted the sellers from competing in the counties only where the sold clubs were located. ***Inference: CNCs limiting the restricted territory to the counties where the Centers are located sufficiently protects the buyer's interest.*** • Members usually use the club closest to their homes or workplaces. ***Inference: Members will not travel a great distance to go to another club, so it is unnecessary to have a broad territorial restriction.*** • CNCs are "strictly construed against the party seeking to enforce them," and "are not favored by the law" because they "impede trade and distort the market mechanism which allows our economy to function." *Id.* at 1468.

Here, notice that the similarities between the facts from *Mats Transport* and the facts from Ana's case are set side-by-side in the chart, again to make it easier to recognize when beginning to draft the discussion. Additional facts that support Ana's position are also listed. Finally, reasonable inferences drawn from the factual analogies as well as the other facts are noted where appropriate.

Also note that the facts supporting Ana's position include some of the same facts that appeared when assessing David's position. Sometimes the same facts can be used to support the position for both sides of an issue. In these instances, different inferences can be drawn from the facts, as long as those inferences are reasonable.

> **Note:** While assessing each position, be careful not to engage in speculation or otherwise consider situations that are not supported by the facts. Sometimes in an effort to find additional support for the client's case, the writer might feel tempted to create circumstances that, if they existed, would help the client. However, do not "create" facts through speculation or imagination. The inferences and the analysis must be supported by the specific facts known by the writer.

• Exercise 6-A

Review your summary of the interview of Edina Broward from Chapter 1, the case, *Everett v. Rogers,* found in the Student Supplemental Materials for this book located on the publisher's website at http://www.aspenpublishing.com, and your brief of *Everett*. Complete the following.

(1) Chart the relevant facts in *Everett* and the facts in Ms. Broward's case supporting her position that she is not barred by the statute of limitations to bring her lawsuit, specifically because she did not wait too long to bring an action against Dr. Warren for the return of the painting.

(2) Chart the relevant facts in *Everett* and the facts in Ms. Broward's case supporting Dr. Warren's position that Ms. Broward is barred by the statute of limitations because she waited too long to bring an action against him for the return of the painting.

When preparing the charts of facts in (1) and (2), above, write the facts from *Everett* and Ms. Broward's case side-by-side so the set of facts can be directly analogized or distinguished. Include any additional facts of Ms. Broward's case that are not directly comparable to or distinguishable from those in *Everett* but nevertheless support the position being presented. Where appropriate, state any reasonable inferences that can be drawn to support the conclusion being analyzed.

G. Structuring an Objective Legal Analysis Based on a Single Issue and a Single Case

When drafting a legal analysis of a fact-based issue, remember its purpose. An objective legal analysis is used to inform the reader of the law on a particular issue and to predict the issue's probable outcome. A strong analysis carefully weighs the parties' respective positions and the support available for each party.[5] The reader, likely a supervising attorney, uses the information provided in an objective legal analysis to make a decision as to what future action to take in the case. The choice of words and the information provided to the reader will depend on the reader's knowledge of the facts and the law.

When writing a discussion section of a formal office memorandum, legal writers usually begin with the conclusion and then seek to prove that conclusion by presenting the relevant law and then applying the relevant law to the legally significant facts of the case in the analysis. For example, in Ana's case the predicted conclusion would reveal whether the CNC's territorial

5. A legal analysis is oftentimes written within the procedural context of the case. For example, the standard for granting a summary judgment is whether there is no genuine issue of material fact and the party moving for the summary judgment is entitled to that judgment as a matter of law. FED. R. CIV. P. 56(a). In Ana's case, a summary judgment motion would focus on whether there is no genuine issue of material fact that the CNC is unreasonable, entitling Ana to a judgment in her favor as a matter of law.

restriction is overly broad and thus unreasonable and unenforceable. Next, the conclusion would be supported by explaining the relevant law on the issue and then applying the law to the legally significant facts, as discussed in the remainder of this chapter.

The goal as a legal writer is to provide a complete, accurate, and concise analysis of the law that is understandable to the reader. This understanding likely can't happen if the analysis is disorganized, inaccurate, or confusing, or if it requires the reader to seek outside resources to clarify what is written or to fill in gaps or omissions in the analysis. To avoid these problems, legal writers often use a structural checklist to help organize their analyses. Using "CREAC" as a basic checklist will help ensure the analysis is structured in a logical manner and the substance is complete.

H. CREAC as a Structural Checklist

A good legal analysis always includes the following components.

C = The predicted conclusion on the issue, framed in the factual context in the case
R = Rule(s), including definitions, that may be relevant to the issue being addressed
E = Explanation(s) of the rules through an explanation of the relevant case law
A = Analysis/application of the law to the facts, including support for each position, where it exists
C = Conclusion, resolving the issue raised by the supervising attorney

> **Note:** Although it is not necessary to always organize the analysis in the exact order as CREAC presents, initially follow this order closely to gain confidence in structuring a legal analysis and in keeping track of the information included.
>
> CREAC is not the only acronym used as a recommended checklist in an objective analysis. Others, for example, include IRAC (Issue/Rule/Analysis/Conclusion), and CRAC (Conclusion/Rule/Analysis/Conclusion). The ultimate structure will be the same regardless of which acronym is followed.

1. C of CREAC: The predicted conclusion

The thesis sentence notifies the reader of the issue being analyzed and provides the predicted conclusion on the issue. For instance, read the following paragraph.

> Your shoulders should be in line with your seat bones. Your back must be straight but flexible. Your hips must remain supple. Your upper arms must rest next to your body, and your elbows must be slightly bent. Your legs must be relaxed with your knees and toes pointed forward, and your weight must rest in your heels.

What is the topic of this paragraph? It's not obvious, since the writer didn't first state what was being discussed. By clearly setting out the topic in the first sentence and also providing the predicted conclusion on that topic, the reader will know up front what is the point of the paragraph. Using the previous example, the paragraph would be better understood if a first sentence was added:

> The position of your body is a critical factor in becoming an effective horseback rider. Your shoulders should be in line with your seat bones. Your back must be straight but flexible. Your hips must remain supple. Your upper arms must rest next to your body, and your elbows must be slightly bent. Your legs must be relaxed with your knees and toes pointed forward, and your weight must rest in your heels.

In analyzing whether the CNC in Ana's case is broader than necessary to protect David's business interest, the discussion may begin with the following.

Thesis sentence (statement of topic at issue along with the predicted conclusion, provided in some factual context):

> The covenant not to compete (CNC) that Ana Hart has been ordered by the court to sign as part of her divorce settlement is likely overbroad in its protection of David's business interests and is therefore unreasonable. If unreasonable, the CNC will not be enforced.

• Exercise 6-B

Draft a thesis sentence for the issue that will be discussed in Ms. Broward's case about the stolen painting.

2. *R of CREAC: The rule*

Strive to inform the reader of any rule or definition as it becomes relevant in the analytical discussion. It is imperative to set out any legal tests apart from analyzing the facts of the client's case. Only the writer who researched this issue understands well the relevant legal tests or definitions. Therefore, the writer needs to provide the law to the reader in as clear a manner as possible.

If references to the relevant legal tests are cursory or mixed with references to the client's facts, the reader may not understand the significance of the legal terms in the explanation.

When providing relevant rules or definitions, quote the key words and phrases from the sources. For example:

Quoted three-pronged test directly from *Mats Transport*:

> In East Carolina, for a CNC related to the sale of a business to be reasonable, "(1) the covenant must not be broader than necessary for the protection of the covenantee's legitimate business interest; (2) the covenant cannot have an adverse effect on the covenantor; and (3) the covenant cannot adversely affect the public interest." *Mats Transp. v. ABC Corp.*, 824 S.E.2d 1467, 1468 (E.C. Ct. App. 1992). "A CNC is unreasonable as a matter of law if it fails any one of the prongs of the test." *Id.*

The above statement accurately reflects the three-pronged test by emphasizing that the court must make three separate and distinct determinations on each of the three prongs. This also means that if any of the terms of the CNC do not meet one of the three prongs, or requirements, the CNC is unreasonable and thus unenforceable.

By summarizing or paraphrasing a rule or definition, the writer may inadvertently change the meaning.[6] An inaccurately stated rule or definition creates a faulty foundation for the analysis and may lead to a flawed analysis. For example:

Inaccurately stated three-pronged test from *Mats Transport*:

> When determining whether a CNC signed in connection with the sale of a business is reasonable, East Carolina courts look to whether the covenant is broader than necessary to protect the legitimate business interests of the covenantee, and whether the covenant has an adverse effect on the covenantor and the public interest. *Mats Transp. v. ABC Corp.*, 824 S.E.2d 1467, 1468 (E.C. Ct. App. 1992).

The above at a minimum ambiguously reports the three-pronged test as stated in *Mats Transport*. First, the ambiguous rule as written does not state clearly that the court *must* make three separate and distinct determinations. Instead, the statement infers that these criteria are mere factors or considerations the court must weigh based on the language, "East Carolina looks to whether . . . ." Under the rule as ambiguously reported above, if a CNC is broader than necessary to protect the covenantee's legitimate business

6. *See* Chapter 5 for a discussion on summarizing and paraphrasing.

interest, the court is not necessarily required to find the CNC unreasonable. A review of the three-pronged rule as stated in *Mats Transport* reveals that this statement of the rule is flawed. Each of the three parts of the test are requirements or elements, and all three must be met in order to prove a CNC reasonable. If the court finds that any of the terms of the CNC does not meet any one of these prongs, then the CNC is unreasonable. An analysis based on the inaccurate statement of the rule would likely result in a faulty analysis.

3. E of CREAC: Explaining the key components of a court opinion

Providing an accurate rule explanation, where necessary, is also critical to a legal analysis. A rule explanation, as used in this book, is a concise description of a court's decision addressing the legal point at issue. The words of a rule may be subject to different interpretations by different courts. The purpose of the rule explanation is to help the reader better understand a rule. This happens by showing how, in prior binding decisions, the courts applied the rule in a case with different facts but with an issue identical to, or similar to, the issue being analyzed in the present client's case.

A rule explanation contains at least the following components:

- The ***Facts*** of the case relevant to the issue being analyzed;
- The *court's **Holding*** on the issue being analyzed; and
- The *court's **Reasoning*** for its holding on the issue being analyzed, explaining why the court ruled as it did.[7]

In addition to the legally significant facts, the court's holding and the court's reasoning (also known as the **F/H/R**), include the procedural facts, such as the cause of action or the legal basis for the claim. This information will show the reader that the same legal issues were being addressed in the cited court decision as in the client's case.

The components of a rule explanation (facts, court's holding, and court's reasoning) need not be presented in a particular order. The key is to present the information in a logical sequence and to include all the parts of the explanation. Include all facts relevant to the court's holding on the issue. Those legally significant facts that may not be comparable to any facts in the client's case should still be included because they might be used to support an argument

7. Sometimes a court does not explain the reasons for its holding. In this instance, the case may not be a good case to use in the analysis. However, if the facts of the case are sufficiently similar to the facts of the client's case and no other comparable case includes an adequate explanation of the court's reasoning, the former case may be used so long as the court made a specific ruling on the legal point being discussed. The case may always be used to set out the rule and from which to draw any policy support, as long as it remains good law.

that the case is significantly different from the client's case. An example of setting out the legal test followed by a rule explanation follows.

Example of a legal test and rule explanation from *Mats Transport*:

In East Carolina, for a CNC related to the sale of a business to be reasonable, "(1) the covenant must not be broader than necessary for the protection of the covenantee's legitimate business interest; (2) the covenant cannot have an adverse effect on the covenantor; and (3) the covenant cannot adversely affect the public interest." *Mats Transp. v. ABC Corp.*, 824 S.E.2d 1467, 1468 (E.C. Ct. App. 1992).

Rule for a valid CNC

A CNC is unreasonable as a matter of law if it fails any one of the prongs of the test. *Id.* This result occurred in *Mats Transport* where the court held that a CNC related to the sale of a business was unreasonable as a matter of law because it was broader than necessary for the buyer's legitimate business interest, thus failing the first prong of the three-pronged test. *Id.* The buyer in *Mats Transport* sued the seller for allegedly violating the terms of a CNC executed in connection with the sale of its trucking business to the buyer because the seller later leased several trucks to a prior employee. The prior employee used the trucks to operate a trucking business. The CNC prohibited the seller from competing in the trucking business with the buyer for a period of five years anywhere in the United States. The seller argued that the CNC was overbroad in its protection of the buyer's business interest and moved for summary judgment. The court of appeals affirmed the trial court's grant of the seller's summary judgment motion. *Id.*

Court's holding in the case.

Facts of the case (including key facts and background facts)

Procedural history

The court noted that when determining whether a CNC is broader than necessary to protect the buyer, the territory restricted is considered. *Id.* Also considered is "the seller's goodwill, which represents the value of the relationship between the seller and the customers." *Id.* (quoting *Matthews v. Acme Tax Consultants*, 470 S.E.2d 756, 763 (E.C. Ct. App. 1984)).

Further rule explanation

The court found that when the seller sold the trucking business to the buyer, the business hauled freight primarily for a few major clients on routes only in East Carolina, the adjoining states, and infrequently in other areas in the U.S. *Id.* The parties knew the seller's trucking business had only one terminal located in East Carolina, yet the CNC restrained the seller as though its business was a national business. Because the territorial scope of the CNC exceeded the protection of the buyer's legitimate interests, the CNC was unreasonable as a matter of law and was therefore unenforceable. *Id.* Subsequently, the case was properly dismissed. *Id.*

Court's reasoning in the case

a. Use descriptive generic names to identify parties in a reported decision

Note that the parties in the rule explanation of *Mats Transport* are referred to by generic names (buyer and seller) rather than by their personal names. In rule explanations and the analysis, do not confuse your reader by using the personal names of the parties from the court decisions. Instead, give the parties in the cited cases generic names that identify their respective relationships or status relevant to the dispute at issue. Use these generic names consistently throughout the rule explanation and analysis. Helpful generic names, inter alia, include the following:

Buyer and Seller
Parent and Child
Employer and Employee
Doctor and Patient

Avoid, however, using unhelpful generic terms such as *plaintiff, defendant, appellant, appellee, petitioner*, and *respondent*. These terms do not adequately identify the parties (unless you are referring to a criminal case, where *defendant is* the status of the party).

b. Use personal names when referring to parties in your case

Conversely, use only personal names when referring to the parties in the client's case. Referring to the parties in prior court decisions by generic names and the parties in the client's case by personal names emphasizes the distinction between the two and makes the case explanation and the analysis easier to follow. For instance, in the analysis of Ana's case, Ana and David are referred to using their first names, though, alternatively, they could have been referred to by their surnames, Mrs. Hart and Mr. Hart. Further, the Harts' business is referred to as the Hart Fitness Center or the Center. But ABC Corporation, the defendant in *Mats Transport*, is referred to as the *seller*, and the plaintiff in that case, Mats Transport, is referred to as the *buyer*. The business in *Mats Transport* is referred to as the trucking business.

c. Bring in information as it becomes relevant to the discussion

Also note in the above example that some rules were provided prior to the rule explanation of *Mats Transport*, while other rules were provided in the middle of the rule explanation. For example, note the third paragraph from the explanation of the rule in *Mats Transport*:

> The court noted that when determining whether a CNC is broader than necessary to protect the buyer, the territory restricted is considered. *Id.* Also considered is

"the seller's goodwill, which represents the value of the relationship between the seller and its customers." *Id.* (quoting *Matthews v. Acme Tax Consultants*, 470 S.E.2d 756, 763 (E.C. Ct. App. 1984)).

The rules provided in the rule explanation could have been provided with the other rules mentioned in the first paragraph, but it was more logical to bring them up later in the explanation of the case. These rules did not become important until that moment and were then more understandable to the reader within the context of the rule explanation. Let logic guide you in making this determination.

• Exercise 6-C

(1) Write down the rules from *Everett v. Rogers*, 836 F. Supp. 1030 (S.D.E.C. 1995), that are relevant for the discussion of the issue in Ms. Broward's case addressing her stolen painting. The facts of *Everett* are found at the end of Chapter 1, and the full court opinion is found online with the Student Supplemental Materials for this book located on the publisher's website at http://www.aspenpublishing.com.

If quoting the rules, place the quoted text in quotation marks and note the page in *Everett* where the quotation is located. When summarizing or paraphrasing a rule, (a) make sure that you are not actually quoting the text, (b) confirm that your words accurately reflect the rule, and (c) note the page in *Everett* where you found the rule. Chapter 5 speaks to quoting, summarizing, and paraphrasing rules.

(2) Draft a rule explanation of *Everett* that includes the F/H/R:

- The Key **F**acts
- The Court's **H**olding on the Issue
- The Court's **R**easoning on the Issue (explaining why, in applying the law to the client's facts, the court ruled as it did)

4. *The A of CREAC: Providing an objective analysis for a fact-based issue*

As previously noted, the objective analysis of any legal point in dispute must include a *complete* analysis of both parties' positions. If there are no legitimate ways to support both parties' positions, the legal point is not in dispute. Again, beginning legal writers tend to provide a thorough analysis of the client's position but do not give sufficient thought to support for the opposing party's position. The hallmark of a good lawyer is the ability to carefully analyze both sides.

A good legal analysis begins with the analysis of the predicted conclusion, or the position the court is likely to approve, which may not be the client's position. After providing the complete analysis of the predicted conclusion, the writer transitions to the support for the counteranalysis. The basic outline for the analysis of a single fact-based issue includes:

- The first sentence introducing the analysis for each party:
  - Begin the first sentence introducing the predicted conclusion the court will likely reach with a thesis sentence.
  - Begin the counteranalysis with a transitional sentence that signals a change in focus to the support for the other party's position.
- Any *analogies or distinctions* between the stated facts in the case law and related facts in the client's case, along with any *reasonable inferences* drawn from those analogies or distinctions; and
- Any *additional facts* of the client's case that support the position being analyzed, along with the *reasonable inferences* drawn from these facts.

When moving from the analysis of the position supporting the predicted conclusion to the counteranalysis, make the transition to the counteranalysis clear. An effective way to help the reader understand the change in focus is to provide a transitional word or phrase, such as one of the following.

- Alternatively
- But
- Conversely
- However
- In contrast
- Nevertheless
- Notwithstanding
- On the contrary
- Yet

When analyzing a fact-based issue, the reader needs to know how the facts of the client's case relate to the facts in each cited opinion. If a court in its opinion reached a result that is similar to the desired result of a lawyer's client, then compare favorably the relevant case law facts to the relevant facts in the client's case. Conversely, if a court addressed the same issue but reached a result that is contrary to the desired result of the lawyer's client, then contrast directly the relevant case law facts from the relevant facts in the client's case.

Ana's attorney, for example, would want the court to find the CNC she has been ordered to sign in the divorce settlement overbroad and thus unreasonable and unenforceable. To support this position, Ana's attorney would compare the relevant facts from Ana's case to the relevant facts in *Mats Transport* where the court found the CNC unreasonable, to show how they are analogous and support the same outcome. Conversely, David's attorney would strive to distinguish the relevant facts of *Mats Transport* from the facts in David's case to support why the CNC should be found reasonable.

Even though the relevant facts of the cited opinion were provided in the rule explanation, discussed above, when comparing or contrasting the facts from the cited case to the client's case, you must repeat those specific facts in the analysis. If the specific case facts are omitted in the analysis, then the reader may be unsure about which case facts the writer is using to compare to or contrast from the facts of the client's case. Even worse, the reader may find it necessary to return to the rule explanation of the case in an attempt to determine which cited case facts are relevant to the analogy or distinction drawn in the analysis. Consider the following examples.

Poor example of a factual comparison

> Similar to *Mats Transport*, the CNC that Ana has been ordered to sign restricts Ana from doing business in counties and towns where the Harts do not own any Centers.

After reading the above example, the reader will likely need to stop and recollect the facts of *Mats Transport* or return to the rule explanation of the case to ascertain the specific case facts that the writer is comparing to Ana's facts. This is especially true if there were multiple case explanations prior to beginning the analysis. *One of the goals of every legal writer is not to make the reader do the work that is the job of the writer.*

A better example of a factual comparison

> Similar to *Mats Transport*, where the buyer's business did not operate in all the places restricted by the CNC, the CNC that Ana has been ordered to sign also restricts Ana from doing business in counties and towns where the Harts neither own any Centers nor do any business.

This example states the specific facts from the cited case that the writer is comparing to the facts of Ana's case.

Oftentimes there are important facts present in the court opinion that are not present in the facts of the client's case. In this instance, consider whether the lack of these facts in the client's case will change the predicted outcome in the client's case. Explain to the reader why these facts probably will or will not change the outcome in the client's case.

Also be careful to not just compare a holding in a court decision to what is hoped to be a similar holding in the client's case. For instance, do not write this:

> Similar to *Mats Transport*, where the court found the CNC overbroad and unreasonable, the CNC the court has ordered Ana to sign is overbroad and unreasonable.

Making such a comparison is not a legal analysis of a fact issue. Rather, *show* the reader why the outcome in Ana's case will be similar to the outcome in *Mats*

Transport by explaining the similarities between the legally significant facts of Ana's case and the related facts in *Mats Transport* and then drawing reasonable inferences from those analogies or distinctions to support the conclusion.

Finally, check the internal organization of any analysis. Again, logic dictates that the analysis and support for the predicted conclusion be presented first before presenting the analysis and support for the counteranalysis. Thus, once the predicted conclusion is known, state that conclusion at the beginning of the analysis section. Then provide the *complete discussion* of the analysis of the predicted conclusion before transitioning to the counteranalysis. Avoid a "back and forth" pattern when writing, such as, "On the one hand . . ., but on the other hand, . . . but on the other hand . . . ." Although a writer might go through this mental activity while formulating support for each party's position, this wavering back and forth between the two positions in the written analysis confuses the reader and makes it extremely difficult to understand the strength of the arguments for each party.

Example of a "wavering" analysis, which must be avoided (the points supporting David's position are provided in boldface):

Similar to *Mats Transport*, where the CNC was overbroad for the protection of the buyer's interest when it restricted competition to territory beyond the location of the business at the time of the sale, the CNC Ana has been ordered to sign is probably overbroad because it restricts competition in three counties and two towns where the Harts do not own any Hart Fitness Centers. **But, unlike the seller in *Mats Transport*, who had no plans to expand beyond where the business was located, the Harts had plans to start additional Centers in the CNC-restricted areas where no Centers were presently located.** This is not persuasive, however, because the CNCs signed by sellers in prior sales of clubs to the Harts restricted competition only to the counties where the purchased clubs were located. **Even so, David may argue that a larger territorial restriction is needed in Ana's case because she has a relationship with the Centers' members**. But Ana can rebut this argument by pointing out that the goodwill represented in the CNC should be limited only to the present Centers' membership and not to future members.

The resulting structure of this analysis is:

- Point supporting Ana's position.
- **Point supporting David's position**.
- Point supporting Ana's position.
- **Point supporting David's position**.
- Point supporting Ana's position.

In contrast, the following example provides completely the support for Ana's position, the predicted conclusion, before the counteranalysis, providing completely the support for David's position. The presentation of the information in this order is clearer and easier for the reader to understand.

Example of an analysis supporting Ana's position, here the predicted conclusion:

The CNC that the court has ordered Ana to sign is likely unreasonable because it is overbroad in its protection of David's interest. The CNC restricts competition in three counties and two towns where the Harts presently do not own any Centers, so the business has not developed relationships with customers in these areas. Similarly, in *Mats Transport* the CNC was overbroad because it unreasonably restricted competition in every state, when the trucking business operated in only one state with established trucking routes in the surrounding states, extending beyond that territory only sporadically.

The CNC is also unreasonable because it extends beyond the one-county restriction of the CNCs signed by sellers in prior sales of clubs to the Harts. These previous CNCs restricted competition only to the county in which the purchased clubs were located. As the Center owners, both David and Ana Hart considered this a reasonable restriction in those prior transactions. Therefore, in Ana's sale of her interest to David, a CNC restricting competition in locations where the Centers are not currently located arguably exceeds what was considered reasonable in prior sales transactions.

Further support that the geographic restriction is too broad is that members usually use clubs that are closest to their homes or workplaces. Members probably will not travel great distances to go to another club; thus, it is not necessary to restrict competition over a geographic area that exceeds the present Centers' locations.

Analysis of David's position (shown here as the counteranalysis)

However, the CNC the court has ordered Ana to sign may be considered reasonable if more emphasis is placed on the planned expansion of the business, the nature of the business, and the importance of Ana's relationship with members of the Centers. Unlike the seller in *Mats Transport*, who never expressed to the buyer any planned expansion into other routes, Ana and David had planned together to expand the business in the next three years into the three counties and two towns covered by the CNC. The restriction also covers a limited geographic area in central East Carolina only, unlike the restricted area covered by the CNC in *Mats Transport* that extended to every state, even though the trucking business was located in only one state and operated a limited number of routes in the surrounding states.

Further, although the CNC to be signed by Ana is broader than the one-county restriction contained in the CNCs signed by sellers in prior club purchases, the broader restriction in Ana's case is arguably necessary to adequately protect David's goodwill interest in the business. Unlike the previous fitness club sellers, who had no relationship with members of the Center prior to the sales, Ana presents a greater threat to the business of Hart Fitness Center because she has developed a relationship with the Centers' members. Health and exercise clubs are service-oriented businesses that rely heavily on the good relationship between members and the employees of the clubs for the continuing success of the business. Arguably, David needs to protect his interest in the business, and the CNC would ensure that Ana did not compete with David's business and steal away members, which would lessen the value of the business. If Ana has a club near to or in the same county or town where Centers' members live or work, members may quit the Hart Fitness Center to attend Ana's club.

> **Note:** When analyzing an issue in dispute, be careful to not end the analysis of the predicted conclusion with an actual conclusion, such as "Therefore, the court is likely to find the CNC unreasonable and unenforceable." If the first analysis ends with this conclusion, there may be two sentences back-to-back that contradict each other, such as, "Therefore, the court is likely to find the CNC unreasonable and unenforceable. However, the court may find the CNC reasonable and enforceable." This creates a clear contradiction in back-to-back sentences, which will likely confuse the reader. Instead, wait to provide the predicted conclusion again in the overall conclusion, after the counteranalysis.

- **Exercise 6-D**

(1) Based on the fact chart you made in Exercise 6-A(1), write an analysis supporting Ms. Broward's position that her stolen painting should be returned.

(2) Using the facts of Ms. Broward's stolen painting from Exercise 6-A(2), write an analysis supporting Dr. Warren's position that he should retain the painting.

5. The final C of CREAC: Writing the conclusion

After providing a thorough analysis of the predicted conclusion followed by thorough support for the counteranalysis, provide a transition to the conclusion. Depending on the legal test applied, the conclusion may simply summarize the results of the legal test analyzed. For example, if in Ana's case the predicted conclusion is that the CNC was unreasonable, the conclusion could simply state that since the court is likely to rule that the third requirement was not met because the CNC was overbroad and unreasonable, the CNC is likely to be found unenforceable as part of Ana and David Hart's property settlement. In other situations, a more thorough explanation may be needed, focusing on the pivotal reason(s) why the predicted conclusion is stronger. Any policy that might help support the conclusion may also be introduced here, if not already used earlier in the analysis. Otherwise, refrain from adding new law or facts in the conclusion. If important to the outcome of the case, the law or facts should have been previously introduced and discussed in the analysis.

Be sure in the overall conclusion to answer the question originally asked by the supervisor. In some instances, the counteranalysis may seem equally as strong as the predicted conclusion — so strong that it may feel uncomfortable stating a conclusion. Rather than not concluding, especially if that's what the supervising attorney requested, state that strong support exists for both sides on the issue but, nevertheless, state the predicted conclusion. The conclusion can be qualified by using language such as *probably* or *likely*. For instance, if the writer concludes that a court would rule in Ana's favor, this conclusion may read, "The court will probably find that the CNC is overbroad for the protection of David's interest and thus is unreasonable. Therefore, the CNC is likely not to be enforced."

Example of a conclusion for Ana's issue when asked to predict a likely outcome:

> Nevertheless, the geographic restriction in the CNC extends into counties and towns where the Harts do not currently operate any Centers. This arguably exceeds the value of the goodwill Ana has in the current membership, which is what the CNC is meant to protect. The CNC is likely overbroad for the protection of David's business interest and is unreasonable. As a result, the CNC is likely not to be enforced, and Ana will not be required to sign the CNC as part of her divorce settlement agreement.

[Pivotal reason for predicted conclusion → "Nevertheless, the geographic restriction in the CNC extends into"]

[Overall conclusion → "interest and is unreasonable. As a result, the CNC is likely not to be"]

• Exercise 6-E

Decide whether the court is likely to support the position of Ms. Broward or Dr. Warren regarding the return of the painting. Note the reasons supporting the predicted conclusion, followed by the support for the counteranalysis.

6. *Putting it all together*

The complete analytical discussion of whether the CNC Ana has been ordered to sign is overbroad and unreasonable as to David's interest follows. As you read the sample, note the key elements of CREAC: the predicted conclusion reached to the question asked; the relevant rule and the explanation of the rule and relevant law, including the key facts, the court's holding, and the court's reasoning (F/H/R) of *Mats Transport*; the analysis of the predicted conclusion (why the CNC is not enforceable); the counteranalysis (support for why the CNC could be enforced); and the conclusion, answering the question posed by the supervising attorney. Note that the analysis begins with the predicted conclusion (thesis sentence), whereas the counteranalysis begins with a transitional sentence. Also, within the two analyses, note any factual analogies or distinctions as well as any additional facts that support Ana's or David's position, and any reasonable inferences drawn from those factual analogies or distinctions.

Sample Discussion

The covenant not to compete (CNC) that Ana Hart has been ordered by the court to sign as part of her divorce settlement is likely overbroad in its protection of David Hart's business interests and is therefore unreasonable. If unreasonable, the CNC will not be enforced. *Id.* In East Carolina, for a CNC related to the sale of a business to be reasonable, "(1) the covenant must not be broader than necessary for the protection of the covenantee's legitimate business interest; (2) the covenant cannot have an adverse effect on the covenantor; and (3) the covenant cannot adversely affect the public interest." *Mats Transp. v. ABC Corp.*, 824 S.E.2d 1467, 1468 (E.C. Ct. App. 1992).

C: The first sentence introduces & provides the conclusion to the legal issue within the story of the case.

R: The rule used to determine whether a CNC is reasonable follows.

A CNC is unreasonable as a matter of law if it fails any one of the prongs of the test. *Id.* This result occurred in *Mats Transport,* where the court held that a CNC related to the sale of a business was unreasonable as a matter of law because it was broader than necessary for the buyer's legitimate business interest, failing the first prong of the three-pronged test. *Id.* The buyer in *Mats Transport* sued the seller for allegedly violating the terms of a CNC executed in connection with the sale of its trucking business to the buyer because the seller later leased several trucks to a prior employee. The prior employee used the trucks to operate a trucking business. The CNC prohibited the seller from competing in the trucking business with the buyer for a period of five years anywhere in the United States. The seller argued that the CNC was overbroad in its protection of the buyer's business interest and moved for summary judgment. The court of appeals affirmed the trial court's grant of the seller's summary judgment motion. *Id.*

E: *Mats Transport* is explained, providing in the paragraph the holding and the key facts.

The court focused on the extent of the territory restricted in the CNC and emphasized that any CNC includes the seller's goodwill, which represents the value of the relationship between the seller and its customers. *Id.* The court found that when the seller sold the trucking business to the buyer, the business hauled freight primarily for a few major clients on routes only in East Carolina, the adjoining states, and infrequently in other areas in the U.S. *Id.* The parties knew the seller's trucking business had only one terminal located in East Carolina, yet the CNC restrained the seller as though

E: *Mats Transport* is further explained in this paragraph, providing the court's reasoning.

its business was a national business. Because the territorial scope of the CNC exceeded the protection of the buyer's legitimate interests, the CNC was unreasonable as a matter of law and was therefore unenforceable. *Id.*

The CNC that the court has ordered Ana to sign is likely unreasonable because it is overbroad in its protection of David's interest. The CNC restricts competition in three counties and two towns where the Harts presently do not own any Centers, so the business has not developed relationships with customers in these areas. Similarly, in *Mats Transport* the CNC was overbroad because it unreasonably restricted competition in every state, when the trucking business operated in only one state with established trucking routes in the surrounding states, extending beyond that territory only sporadically.

A: The analysis begins with a thesis sentence.

A: These 2 sentences draw a factual analogy between the facts in *Mats Transport* and Ana's case.

The CNC is also unreasonable because it extends beyond the one-county restriction of the CNCs signed by sellers in prior sales of clubs to the Harts. These previous CNCs restricted competition only to the county in which the purchased clubs were located. David and Ana Hart considered this a reasonable restriction in those prior transactions. Therefore, in Ana's sale of her interest in the business to David, a CNC restricting competition in locations where Centers are not currently located exceeds what was considered reasonable in prior sales transactions.

Further support that the geographic restriction is too broad is that members usually use clubs that are closest to their homes or workplaces. Members probably will not travel great distances to go to another club; thus, it is not necessary to restrict competition over a geographic area that exceeds the present Center locations.

A: Further facts found only in Ana's case are used in these two paragraphs to support why the CNC is unreasonable.

However, the CNC the court has ordered Ana to sign may be considered reasonable if more emphasis is placed on the planned expansion of the business, the nature of the business, and the importance of Ana's relationship with the members of the Centers. Unlike the seller in *Mats Transport*, who never expressed to the buyer any planned expansion into other routes, Ana and David had planned together to expand the business in the next three years into the three counties and two towns covered by the CNC. The restriction also covers a limited geographic area in central East Carolina only, unlike the restricted area covered by the CNC in *Mats Transport* that extended to every state, despite the business being located in only one state and operating a limited number of routes in the surrounding states and rarely beyond those states.

A: "However" alerts the reader that the focus is shifting to the counter-analysis.

A: These 2 sentences provide factual distinctions between the facts in *Mats Transport* and Ana's case, supporting why the CNC might be reasonable.

Further, although the CNC to be signed by Ana is broader than the one-county restriction contained in the CNCs signed by sellers

> in prior club purchases, the broader restriction in Ana's case is arguably necessary to adequately protect David's goodwill interest in the business. Unlike the previous fitness club sellers, who had no relationship with members of the Center prior to the sales, Ana presents a greater threat to the business of Hart Fitness Center because she has developed a relationship with the Centers' members. Health and exercise clubs are service-oriented businesses that rely heavily on the good relationship between members and the employees of the clubs for the continuing success of the business. Arguably, David needs to protect his interest in the business, and the CNC would ensure that Ana did not compete with David's business and steal away members, which would lessen the value of the business. If Ana has a club near to or in the same county or town where Centers' members live or work, members may quit the Hart Fitness Center to attend Ana's club.
>
> Nevertheless, the geographic restriction in the CNC extends into counties and towns where the Harts do not currently operate any Centers. This arguably exceeds the value of the goodwill Ana has in the current membership, which is what the CNC is meant to protect. The CNC is likely overbroad for the protection of David's business interest and is unreasonable. As a result, the CNC is likely not to be enforced, and Ana will not be required to sign the CNC as part of her divorce settlement agreement.

A: Further facts found only in Ana's case are used in this paragraph to support why the CNC might be reasonable.

C: "Nevertheless" signals the beginning of the conclusion, highlighting the key reasons for the predicted conclusion and answering the attorney's question.

When working on a particular document, it is helpful to have a generic checklist to review once your draft is written. This will help ensure that the structure and the substance of the final writing is complete and clear. A sample checklist for writing a discussion section of an objective analysis is included with the Student Supplemental Materials for this book located on the publisher's website at http://www.aspenpublishing.com.

• Exercise 6-F

Using your work from Exercises 6-A to 6-E, draft a complete discussion regarding whether Ms. Broward will be barred from bringing an action against Dr. Warren for the return of the painting. Include the following:

1. A thesis sentence introducing the issue and providing the predicted conclusion within enough factual context so that the reader understands why the issue is in dispute.
2. The relevant rule(s)/legal tests.
3. The explanation (F/H/R) of *Everett.*
4. The analysis of the predicted conclusion.

5. The support for the counteranalysis.
6. The overall conclusion, answering the question posed by the supervising attorney.

After you have completed your draft, check your work against the checklist.

• Exercise 6-G

This exercise provides you with another opportunity to apply the concepts presented in this chapter by drafting the discussion of a fact-based issue using a single case. Follow the drafting steps in Exercises 1, 2, and 3, below.

The senior attorney in your firm recently met with Derek and Iva Olson regarding the tragic drowning of their five-year-old son, Ricky, in a settlement tank maintained by Redwood Mobile Homes (Redwood), as part of its sewage treatment plant at Valley Vista Trailer Park, located in McCloud, California. The Olsons want to bring a negligence action against Redwood. The senior attorney is concerned about whether Redwood owed a duty to keep the tank and surrounding area safe for Ricky who was trespassing on Redwood's property at the time. The attorney has found the following rule from the Restatement (Second) of Torts Section 339, which has been adopted in California.

> A possessor of land is subject to liability for bodily harm to young children trespassing thereon caused by a structure or other artificial condition which he maintains upon the land, if (a) the place where the condition is maintained is one upon which the possessor knows or should know that such children are likely to trespass, (b) the condition is one of which the possessor knows or should know and which he realizes or should realize as involving an unreasonable risk of death or serious bodily harm to such children, (c) the children because of their youth do not discover the condition or realize the risk involved in intermeddling in it or in coming within the area made dangerous by it, and (d) the utility to the possessor of maintaining the condition is slight as compared to the risk to young children involved therein.

The attorney has asked you to research and draft an analytical discussion of whether 339(c) has been satisfied. For purposes of this discussion, you are to assume that the settlement tank is an artificial condition on the land and that Ricky was trespassing at the time of the incident. Do *not* address 339(a), (b), or (d) at this time; a discussion of these subsections will be drafted as an exercise in a later chapter.

1. Read the facts related to the accident that were gathered by the senior attorney. These facts are found in the client's file below. Identify which facts found in the file are likely relevant to the issue of whether 339(c) has been satisfied. Because you will not know all the relevant facts until after you have researched and read the law, you may find that you need

to reread the facts in the client file after you have researched and read the law to ensure that you have identified all the relevant facts.

2. After reviewing and making notes about the Olsons' case, you researched the issue and discovered the California Supreme Court case of *Garcia v. Soogian*, 338 P.2d 433 (Cal. 1959). For purposes of this exercise, you will need to read a copy of this case. You will find this case in the Student Supplemental Materials for this book located on the publisher's website at http://www.aspenpublishing.com.

   Read and brief *Garcia*.

3. Review the summary of your notes on the Olsons' case and your brief of *Garcia* and complete the following:

   (a) Chart the relevant facts in *Garcia* and the facts in the Olsons' case supporting the Olsons' position that 339(c) has been satisfied.

   (b) Chart the relevant facts in *Garcia* and facts in the Olsons' case supporting Redwood's position that 339(c) has not been satisfied.

When preparing the fact charts, set side by side the facts from *Garcia* and the Olsons' case that can be directly analogized or distinguished. Include any additional facts of the Olsons' case that are not directly comparable to those in *Garcia* but nevertheless support the position being analyzed. Where appropriate, state any reasonable inferences to support the position being analyzed. (Chart format examples are found earlier in this chapter.)

4. Draft a thesis sentence that reflects the predicted conclusion for the issue raised in the Olsons' case.
5. Write down the relevant rules that are important to the discussion of the issue in the Olsons' case. If quoting the rules, ensure that you place the quoted text in quotation marks and note the page in *Garcia* where you found the quotation. If you are summarizing or paraphrasing a rule, make sure that you are not quoting the text, confirm that your words accurately reflect the rule, and note the page in *Garcia* where you found the rule.
6. Draft a rule explanation (F/H/R) of *Garcia*.
7. Draft an analysis supporting the Olsons' position.
8. Draft an analysis supporting Redwood's position.
9. Determine the predicted conclusion and then draft a complete discussion regarding whether 339(c) has been satisfied.

After you have completed your draft, check your work against the Checklist in the Student Supplemental Materials for this book located on the publisher's website at http://www.aspenpublishing.com.

Olsons' Case File

The Olsons and their son, Ricky, were residents of a trailer park, which can accommodate up to 200 residential trailers. On the day of the tragic accident, May 5, 2022, only 140 lots were occupied. At the extreme northern part of the trailer park, Redwood maintained a sewage treatment plant, including on part of the property a settlement tank. The nearest resident's trailer was approximately 200 yards from this sewage treatment facility.

The settlement tank resembled a swimming pool; it was approximately 25 feet long and 11 feet wide, with vertical concrete reinforced walls 7 feet deep. The level of the water, which was dark and murky so as to be opaque, was maintained at a depth of 6 feet, which means the surface of the water was 1 foot below the top ledge of the tank. The top ledge of the tank was level with the ground. There was no ladder or other device at the side of the tank that would aid anyone who fell into the tank to climb out.

A 6-foot-tall, solid wooden flat fence had been erected around the tank. Between the inside of the fence and the rim of the tank lay a 3-foot-wide band of flat ground. There is a wooden gate preventing entry to the tank area. According to Redwood, the gate was always locked.

Last year, Redwood workers removed 60 trailers from the trailer park, leaving behind on the ground concrete blocks that had been used to support those trailers. Redwood's maintenance employees gathered up these blocks and piled them against the outside of the wooden fence enclosing the settlement tank. These blocks were stacked in such a way that they created a stair-like effect that led up to within 6 inches of the top of the fence.

A number of children lived in the trailer park with their parents, and they customarily played throughout the trailer park. Redwood's employees have admitted seeing children playing near the wood fence. However, no parent or Redwood employee ever saw a child on the concrete blocks or inside the sewage treatment facility.

There were no warning signs posted anywhere on the sewage treatment facility grounds to alert parents of any dangerous condition inside the wooden fence, nor were the tenants notified of the existence of the tank. The Olsons stated that they did not know what was inside the fence until after the fatal accident.

On the afternoon of the accident a number of children, ages five to eight, including Ricky, were playing in the trailer park in the vicinity of the wooden fence. At about 3:30 p.m. an older boy walking by was hailed by the children and was told someone was in the sewage tank. He climbed the blocks but could see nothing on the surface of the sewage tank. Other children went to notify Mr. Olson. Mr. Olson and the older boy probed the tank with a rake and succeeded in locating and removing Ricky's submerged body. Attempts at reviving Ricky were unsuccessful. Children who witnessed the drowning said that Ricky climbed the blocks, leaned over the rim of the tank, and fell into the water.

CHAPTER SUMMARY

- A supervising attorney may request a formal office memorandum. Completing the office memorandum will likely require researching and analyzing the legal issue(s) to inform the supervising attorney of the law relevant to the legal issue(s) and to predict any issue's likely outcome in the client's case.
- An objective discussion of a fact-based issue includes comparing and contrasting the facts in the relevant case law to the facts of the client's case to determine whether the outcome in the client's case will be similar to or different from the outcome reached in the relevant case law.
- Three sources used to support a legal analysis are (1) the relevant law, (2) the facts of the client's case, and (3) the underlying policy that supports the relevant law.
- CREAC (**C**onclusion, **R**ule, **E**xplanation of the Rule (where needed), **A**nalysis/Application of the Law to the Facts, and **C**onclusion) may be used as a structural checklist when writing a legal analysis.
- A rule explanation includes (1) the relevant facts of a reported case, (2) any additional facts that make the relevant facts understandable, (3) the court's holding on each issue, and (4) the court's reasoning for its holding, explaining why the court reached the conclusion it did.
- In a written legal analysis of a single issue, the support for the predicted conclusion is explained completely before explaining the support for the counteranalysis.
- The conclusion explains and answers the question(s) posed by the attorney.

CHAPTER

7

Analyzing the Law: Using Multiple Cases in Analyzing a Single Issue

---

A. Introduction

B. Analyzing the Law: Briefing the Cases

C. Organizing the Law Using More than One Case and Applying It to the Client's Case

1 Choosing which cases provide rules and definitions relevant to the client's case

2. Choosing which cases best explain how the relevant rules have been applied to facts in prior cases (rule explanations)

3. Choosing which cases are most helpful in supporting each party's position when applying the law to the facts of the case in the analysis

4. Based on the choice of cases in #1, #2, and #3, above, choose where to best explain the cases so they will be most helpful to the reader

---

A. Introduction

Chapter 6 introduced the case addressing whether Ana Hart could be forced to sign a covenant not to compete (CNC) as part of her divorce agreement with her husband, David. In that chapter, only one case, *Mats Transport v. ABC Corporation,* was used to analyze whether the CNC was overbroad and therefore unreasonable and unenforceable. However, usually more than one case is relevant to a legal issue. Using multiple cases creates new decisions. Determining how and where to use multiple cases is an important step in the analytical process. To explain the use of multiple cases in analyzing a single issue, *Hanson v. Albright,* 539 S.E.2d 500 (E.C. Ct. App. 1989), another case addressing the reasonableness of a CNC from the fictitious state of East Carolina, follows.[1]

1. Created from *Fogle v. Shah,* 539 N.E.2d 500 (Ind. Ct. App. 1989).

Hanson v. Albright

539 S.E.2d 500 (E.C. Ct. App. 1989)

Plaintiffs-appellants-sellers John and Karen Hanson (the Hansons) appeal the trial court's grant of a permanent injunction in favor of defendants-appellees-buyers Asad A. Albright, Employee Benefit Consultants of America, Incorporated (EBC), enforcing a covenant not to compete in connection with the sale of a business.

Hanson and Associates (H&A) was a pension consulting firm owned and operated by John and Karen Hanson. John held 80 percent of its stock. Albright wanted to take his 118 clients from a pension consulting firm he owned, buy H&A, and merge the two. Albright, after meeting John and Karen, began negotiations to purchase H&A. At that time, H&A had approximately 600 clients.

During these negotiations, Albright agreed to pay the Hansons a total of $1,000,000: $850,000 for John's stock and $150,000 for the covenant not to compete set forth below. Albright also agreed that John and Karen would become employees of EBC, Albright's new pension consulting firm. The CNC covered twelve states and lasted for three years, which coincided with the duration of Karen's employment contract (John's ran for fifteen months).

The covenant not to compete read:

> (a) For a period of three years from the date of closing, neither Sellers Karen Hanson nor John Hanson shall, directly or indirectly, engage in any activities within the States of East Carolina, Michigan, Ohio, Illinois, Kentucky, Missouri, Louisiana, Oklahoma, Wisconsin, Tennessee, Pennsylvania, or West Virginia, either as an owner, shareholder, director, officer, employee, or in any other capacity, on behalf of himself or herself or any third party, which are competitive with the services provided by the Seller prior to closing.

Approximately one year later Karen was terminated for insubordination, and John resigned. They formed another pension consulting business, naming it Actuaries and Benefit Consultants, Inc. (ABC). The Hansons began competing with Albright by contacting their former clients.

The Hansons filed a complaint, alleging that Albright materially breached the Stock Purchase and Pledge Agreements by firing Karen. Albright answered and filed a counterclaim for injunctive relief, requesting the court to enforce the CNC. After a trial on the merits, the trial court granted a permanent injunction against the Hansons, finding that the covenant not to compete was reasonable. The Hansons appeal. The only issue ***501** before this court is whether the covenant not to compete is reasonable.

Covenants not to compete created in connection with the sale of a business reflect the value of the customers' affiliation with the particular business, which is part of the bargain sought by the buyer. This "goodwill" is the protectable interest upon which the covenant not to compete focuses. The goodwill of a business is an intangible asset which may be transferred from seller to purchaser, and it becomes the buyer's right to expect that the firm's established customers will continue to do business with the newly purchased company. The seller reentering the market and competing with the buyer for customers prevents the buyer from receiving all that has been sold to him. Agreements in partial restraint of trade in connection with the sale of a business appear to be sanctioned because of the value of the goodwill purchased.

In East Carolina, the first step in analyzing a covenant not to compete in connection with the sale of a business is determining whether a protectable interest has been purchased. The parties here agree Albright has a protectable interest in the goodwill of H&A.

A three-pronged test is then applied in determining whether a covenant not to compete in connection with the sale of a business is reasonable. The factors of the test are:

(a) whether the covenant is broader than necessary for the protection of the covenantee (here, Albright) in some legitimate interest,
(b) the effect of the covenant upon the covenantor (the Hansons), and
(c) the effect of the covenant upon the public interest.

The Hansons present one issue for our review, that is, whether the three-year, twelve-state geographical restriction contained in paragraph 19(a) of the stock purchase agreement is broader than necessary to protect the goodwill purchased from the Hansons and the territories they serviced as employees of EBC.

H&A is a business that provides services. A covenant not to compete connected with the sale of a service-oriented business normally will be localized because services generally are performed within a small geographic area. However, there will be cases such as this case where the territory covered reasonably may extend over several states because of the nature of the business.

The undisputed evidence establishes that the pension consulting business depends on the employees' familiarity with clients. Customers have many consulting needs that occur time and again. Prompt service, integrity, and loyalty are of great importance to customers. Customers tend to rely on key personnel who have demonstrated these qualities in the past. The record here establishes that John and Karen had a successful relationship with their clients. Their clients kept returning and referred their friends to John and Karen. As a result, H&A grew as a business. If the Hansons were allowed to solicit their former pension consulting customers, the goodwill Albright purchased would be destroyed.

Albright notes that he paid valuable consideration, approximately $150,000, for the covenant and $850,000 for the goodwill and business, which included the Hansons' good working relationships with their former clients. Albright gave the price the Hansons wanted and sought to protect his purchase by having the Hansons' good name and expertise associated with his business. He did not want the Hansons competing for the clients he had purchased, those new clients he could attract, or those who did business with EBC. Clearly, a broad spatial restraint is justified here.

The Hansons contend it was unreasonable to preclude them from competition in twelve states in their geographic entirety. In states one through nine, H&A had a maximum of four clients; in states ten and eleven,

H&A had approximately 583 clients; and in the twelfth state H&A had no clients. The Hansons argue that territorial restraint ***502** is greater than necessary to protect the goodwill of H&A. We disagree.

The person who purchases a business with the purpose of extending its scope is entitled to bargain with the seller against competition within the territory into which he plans to extend his business. This type of contract does not violate public policy where the area it covers is not greater than that which the parties may fairly anticipate the extended business will cover.

It is readily evident that the parties thought EBC would geographically expand throughout the whole of the twelve states listed in the covenant. That Albright was attempting to expand EBC's client base is shown by negotiations with a major client in the twelfth state. John Hanson knew this fact and agreed to include that state in the purchase agreement. These facts establish that EBC was a growing business with plans to extend throughout the entire territory covered in the covenant. Further, by the plain words of their contract, the parties contemplated expansion into these areas.

Finally, Albright argues that with respect to the extent of the purchaser's original business, EBC's 128 clients in eleven states further support the argument that this covenant is territorially reasonable. John and Karen were employed by EBC immediately after H&A was sold to Albright. The record establishes that they would have contact with many of EBC's clients. Albright had a protectable interest in those clients, in addition to the goodwill purchased from H&A.

The second prong of the test to determine reasonableness addresses the effect of the promise upon the covenator (the Hansons). While the influence of this factor on the enforceability of employer-employee restraints is great, its importance in the sale or transfer of property is rather negligible.

In determining the sale price, the seller definitely puts a separate value on the goodwill of the business. Once specifically paid for his promise not to compete, the seller, whose bargaining power is usually similar to the purchaser's, has little appeal to the courts in a claim that the covenant is unduly harsh and covers too much territory. Courts are reluctant to help a "person who has voluntarily entered into an agreement not to compete, accepted the (frequently very considerable) consideration for his promise, and afterward wants to be absolved of his part of the bargain." Annotation, 46 A.L.R.2d 114, 261 (1951). Thus, policy supports every individual's right to work; however, policy also supports allowing any individual the option to sell anything he wants, including that right to work. We find the covenant is reasonable as to the Hansons.

The third factor, considering the reasonableness of the CNC as to the general public, is also met in this case because any restraint on trade will be minimal at best. Albright testified that pension consulting firms are everywhere and noted that there are twelve such firms in Flora, East Carolina, alone. Thus, the general public will not be harmed here by a restraint of trade. We find no error here.

Affirmed.

B. Analyzing the Law: Briefing the Cases

After collecting the relevant law, it's important to analyze the law by creating case briefs of the relevant cases. A full case brief of *Mats Transport* is set out in Chapter 6. Below is a brief of *Hanson.*

***Hanson v. Albright (H&A),* 539 S.E.2d 500 (E.C. Ct. App. 1989)**

Facts (F): Plaintiff's pension consulting firm H&A owned by sellers husband and wife (defendants).

- The buyer negotiated to take over seller's consulting firm to merge with buyer's consulting firm; the buyer paid sellers for the business and for signing a covenant not to compete (CNC).
- Under the purchase agreement, the sellers were to remain employees of the new company.
- The CNC covered 12 states and was to last 3 years, the length of the seller wife's employment contract with the buyer.
- Of the 12 states covered in the CNC, the sellers had approximately 583 clients in 2 states; no more than 4 customers total in 9 other states; and no customers in the last state; however, all parties knew the buyer planned to expand in all 12 states, and the seller husband knew the buyer had been negotiating with a major prospective client in the last state where there were no H&A clients.
- The CNC restricted the sellers from directly or indirectly soliciting or accepting any business competing with the new company.
- Approximately 1 year after the sale, the seller wife was fired, and her husband then resigned.
- The sellers opened a different pension consulting firm, competing with the buyer by contacting their former clients.

Procedural History (PH):

Cause of Action (C/A): The sellers filed suit alleging (1) breach of the agreement when the wife was fired, and (2) the 12-state restriction in the CNC was broader geographically than necessary to protect the buyer's interests and was, thus, unenforceable.

The buyer filed a counterclaim, requesting injunctive relief by ordering the sellers to abide by the CNC, since seller husband knew before the purchase that the buyer had been engaged in negotiations with a prospective client in the one state where, when buyer purchased sellers' business, there was no client.

Trial court (TC) granted a permanent injunction against the sellers, finding the CNC reasonable.

Substantive Issue (SI): Was the CNC, part of a sale of a consulting firm, overbroad and therefore unreasonable when (1) the CNC prohibited the sellers from conducting any direct or indirect business in competition with the new consulting firm for 3 years in 12 states, (2) there were few or no clients located in some of the restricted states, but (3) the sellers knew the buyer had plans to expand in all states, and (4) the husband seller knew the buyer was involved in negotiations with a prospective client in the one state where, when the buyer purchased the sellers' business, there were no clients?

Procedural Issue (PI): Did the trial court err in finding CNC reasonable and issuing a permanent injunction?

Holding (H):

Substantive Issue (SI). No. The CNC was not overly broad and was reasonable when (1) the CNC prohibited sellers from conducting any direct or indirect business in competition with the new consulting firm for 3 years in 12 states, (2) there were few or no clients located in some of the restricted states, but (3) the sellers knew the buyer had plans to expand in all states, and (4) the seller husband knew the buyer was involved in negotiations with a prospective client in the 1 state where, when the buyer purchased the sellers' business, there were no clients.

Procedural Issue (PI): No. The trial court did not err in finding the CNC reasonable and issuing a permanent injunction, since the decision was supported by the evidence.

Judgment: Affirmed.

Relevant Rules:

1. The test to determine whether a CNC is reasonable and, thus, enforceable, requires first, that a party shows that a protectable interest has been purchased. If so, three requirements, or prongs, are applied to determine if the CNC is reasonable:
   (a) Is the CNC broader than necessary for the protection of the covenantee in some legitimate interest?
   (b) Does the CNC have an adverse effect on the covenantor? and
   (c) Does the CNC have an adverse effect on the public interest?
   Hanson, 539 S.E.2d at 501.
2. "The goodwill of a business is an intangible asset which may be transferred from seller to buyer, and it becomes the buyer's right to expect that the firm's established customers will continue to patronize the purchased business." *Snider's Agency, Inc. v. Dixon*, 494 S.E.2d 77, 80-81 (E.C. 1985); *Hanson*, 539 S.E.2d at 501.
3. "Public policy supports every individual's right to work; however, policy also supports allowing any individual the option to sell anything he wants, including that right to work." *Day Cos. v. Patat*, 403 F.2d 792, 796 (5th Cir. 1969); *Hanson*, 539 S.E.2d at 501.

Court's Reasoning:

The CNC is not broader than necessary, and the first prong is met (along with the other two prongs), because:

1. While service businesses are usually localized and serve only a small geographic area, some businesses, such as this one, may extend over many states.
2. Here, the clients meet regularly with personnel, so their relationship is key to the business's success. Evidence supported that both sellers had good relationships with their clients; if allowed to solicit former clients, the goodwill the buyer purchased with the CNC would be destroyed.
3. Evidence supported that the sellers knew the buyer planned to expand the business to all states covered in the CNC and was actively negotiating with at least one major prospective client to expand in that area. The seller husband knew this and still agreed to include that state as part of the CNC's restriction. The public policy underlying this contract is not violated when the territory covered is restricted to areas all parties anticipate the business will cover.
4. The sellers were employed by the new company and had contact with many of the new company's clients, so the new owner had a protectable interest in both the older and newer clients in addition to the goodwill purchased in the sales agreement.

C. Organizing the Law Using More than One Case and Applying It to the Client's Case

After briefing the relevant cases, the next step is to organize and apply the law to the facts of the client's case. First, understand that there is no one way to use the relevant case law. Let logic guide all decisions every step of the way. Four decisions to make include:

1. Choosing which cases provide any rules and definitions relevant to the client's case

In deciding from which cases to draw the relevant legal principles or rules of law, consider the following:

a. Is the case binding or persuasive precedent?

Binding case law includes any case law that is relevant and was decided by the same court or by a higher court within the controlling jurisdiction.[2] In

2. In a few states, such as Indiana, there are no defined geographical regions for each intermediate appellate court, so all intermediate appellate court decisions are binding on all other intermediate appellate court decisions in the controlling jurisdiction. In contrast, in California a trial court is bound only by (1) the intermediate appellate court within its designated geographical boundaries and (2) the California Supreme Court.

contrast, persuasive precedent includes (1) any non-binding case from the controlling jurisdiction, such as a case decided by a lower court; and (2) any case that was decided in a court outside the controlling jurisdiction.

Address binding primary authority first, where it exists, within each section of the discussion. Thus, address any relevant rules from the controlling jurisdiction before mentioning any rules outside the controlling jurisdiction. Also explain and use in the analysis any case precedent from the controlling jurisdiction before discussing any case law from outside the controlling jurisdiction.

In the CNC case, both *Mats Transport* and *Hanson* were decided by a court in the controlling jurisdiction, the fictitious state of East Carolina, and are therefore binding on Ana's CNC case.

b. What is the level of the court deciding each case found in the controlling jurisdiction?

When analyzing a state law question, prefer a binding decision in the controlling jurisdiction from the state's highest court over an intermediate appellate court in the controlling jurisdiction. When analyzing a federal law question, prefer a United States Supreme Court case over a federal court of appeals case. Prefer both binding state and federal intermediate appellate court cases over a federal or state trial court case. Use a trial court case only if no other case is available or perhaps if a higher court in its opinion has referred to the trial court case. All federal court decisions are reported; however, most states do not publish trial court opinions. In the CNC case, both *Mats Transport* and *Hanson* were decided by the fictitious East Carolina state's intermediate courts of appeals. Therefore, these two binding cases are from the same level court.

c. What is the age of each case?

Consider the date of each court's decision. If two cases provide the same information and are from the same level court (for example, both are from intermediate appellate courts or both are from the highest appellate court), the more recent case is likely to be more helpful. Some cases, however, are considered landmark cases and are often cited for that reason. Landmark cases are those in which a court creates new law, such as when the United States Supreme Court decided that legislative decisions were supreme over all court decisions except those court decisions that decide the constitutionality of legislative enactments. *See Marbury v. Madison*, 1 Cranch 137, 5 U.S. 137 (1803).

Consider also whether the legal issue has been treated differently over time, because the common law test has evolved as it was applied to new cases with new facts. If so, the more recent cases will better reflect the rule to apply.

In the CNC case, *Mats Transport* was decided in 1992; *Hanson* was decided in 1989. Presuming *Mats Transport* represents the most recent case from the highest court in East Carolina addressing the CNC issue, it would be the preferred case to cite to the test used to determine the reasonableness of CNCs in East Carolina.

d. Does the case add important or relevant information about the applicable rule?

Rules may change as rules are applied, especially common law rules.[3] As courts apply the facts in the case precedent to a new set of facts, the court might further define what the former common law rule means based on the facts in the new case. The synthesis of the prior rule with the holding in the new case becomes a part of the new common law rule to be applied in future cases. More on synthesizing rules from multiple cases into a single rule is discussed in Chapter 8.

For example, the court in *Mats Transport* describes the goodwill of a business as that "which represents the value of the relationship between the seller and its customers." *Mats Transport v. ABC Corp.*, 824 S.E.2d 1467, 1468 (E.C. Ct. App. 1992). *Hanson* provides a bit more information by adding, "The goodwill of a business is an intangible asset which may be transferred from seller to buyer, and it becomes the buyer's right to expect that the firm's established customers will continue to patronize the purchased business." *Hanson*, 539 S.E.2d at 501. Both references are helpful to explain what constitutes the goodwill of a business.

2. Choosing which cases best explain how the relevant rules have been applied to facts in prior cases (rule explanations)

Deciding which cases to use for the rule explanations depends on the complexity of the law. If the legal test is a straightforward one, no case explanation or perhaps only one case explanation may be necessary to show how the court has interpreted and applied the relevant rule to a set of facts in a prior case. For example, in many common law burglary cases, the law requires that the crime take place during nighttime. The common law also may have provided a definition of nighttime, such as that time occurring one hour after the sun sets (dusk) and one hour before the sun rises (dawn). If in the case before the court, the alleged crime took place at 2:00 A.M. in New York City, and the common rule applies, only the definition is necessary to prove the nighttime requirement is satisfied.

---

3. Edward H. Levi, An Introduction to Legal Reasoning 143 (1948).

Case law explanations would be needed, in contrast, if the test requires analyzing a vague term. For example, in analyzing whether a CNC is broader than necessary based on its geographical restrictions and is, therefore, unreasonable, case law is needed to provide a thorough explanation of how in the past the court has interpreted and applied the legal concept of reasonableness. Some considerations when choosing which cases to explain include the following:

a. Whether two or more cases decide the same legal issue but reach different outcomes

Always provide the key legal rule or test addressing the issue in dispute before explaining the key facts, holding, and reasoning of any relevant case. If the relevant cases include at least one case where the court applied the rule of law at issue to a set of similar facts and concluded one way, and at least one other case where the court applied the rule of law at issue to a set of similar facts and concluded the opposite way, by explaining both cases, one after the other, the reader will better understand the parameters of the rule.

For example, in *Mats Transport* the court found the CNC too broad and thus unreasonable in protecting the covenantee buyer's legitimate business interest. In *Hanson*, however, the court addressed the same legal question but found the CNC was not too broad in protecting the covenantee buyer's legitimate business interest. When explaining the requirement that a CNC be reasonable and not overbroad, the best approach would be to explain both cases (facts, court's holding, court's reasoning) one after the other, so the reader will understand how the rule had been applied in different factual situations and the courts reached opposite results. The rule explanations regarding reasonableness may look like the following. Note that the three-pronged test for an enforceable CNC is provided, and the issue is narrowed to the first prong; the bracketed labels below show the different sections of the case explanation.

***Mats Transport* (CNC found unreasonable):**

[Court's Holding] A CNC related to the sale of a business was found unreasonable as a matter of law because the CNC was broader than necessary to protect the buyer's legitimate business interest. *Mats Transport v. ABC Corp.*, 824 S.E.2d 1467, 1468 (E.C. Ct. App. 1992). **[Key Facts]** The CNC restricted the seller from competing for five years with the buyer in the trucking business anywhere in the United States when, at the time of the sale, the business included only one trucking terminal in East Carolina and hauled freight to adjoining states and infrequently to areas across the United States. After the sale of the business, the seller leased trucks to a former driver, who began operating a trucking business. The buyer alleged a CNC violation, and the seller filed a motion for summary judgment, which the trial court granted. **[Court's Reasoning]** The appellate court affirmed, finding the CNC overbroad because the territorial scope of the CNC exceeded the protection of the buyer's legitimate interests. *Id.* Both parties knew there was only one terminal and yet the CNC restrained the seller as if it was a national business. Since the first prong was not met, the CNC was unreasonable as a matter of law. *Id.*

Hanson (CNC found reasonable):

[Transition and Court's Holding] In another case, however, the appellate court found the CNC was not overbroad. *Hanson v. Albright*, 539 S.E.2d 500, 502 (E.C. Ct. App. 1989). Since the other two prongs of the rule had also been met, the court found the CNC reasonable and enforceable, and the buyer's request for a permanent injunction was upheld. *Id.*

[Key Facts] The husband and wife sellers sold their pension consulting firm to a buyer, who then merged the sellers' firm with the buyer's other firms. The sellers signed a CNC covering twelve states and lasting three years. The sellers then became employees of the new company. One year later the wife was fired, and her husband quit. The sellers began a new consulting firm, soliciting their former clients. The sellers sued the buyer, alleging the twelve-state restriction in the CNC was broader than necessary to protect the buyer's interest since it extended to seven states where the buyer had only four customers and to one state where there were no customers. The buyer planned to expand to all twelve states, however, and was engaged in active negotiations with a prospective client in the state with no clients, which the sellers knew when they sold the business. The buyer filed a counterclaim, requesting an injunction that ordered the sellers to refrain from competing and to abide by the CNC.

[Court's Reasoning] In upholding the buyer's injunction, the court recognized that as a service business the consulting firm's good client relationships were essential. *Id.* at 501. Allowing the sellers to solicit former clients would destroy the goodwill the buyer purchased, especially since the former owners knew both the old and new clients. *Id.* Further, the sellers knew the buyer had been working to expand into all twelve states and had still agreed to the restricted states as part of the CNC, supporting its reasonableness. *Id.* at 502. The sellers received payment for this restriction and could not then later avoid it. *Id.*

b. Whether different cases provide additional relevant information based on the differing facts in the client's case

Sometimes multiple cases provide helpful information but in different ways. For example, two or more cases may describe and emphasize different types of facts in analyzing the same legal issue, and both types of facts are relevant to the story in the client's case. Thus, different cases may be chosen to help explain and support a different aspect of the client's case.

If, for example, a client's case in East Carolina addressed the reasonableness of a CNC, focusing on whether the territory restricted was too great, *Mats Transport* would be a useful case, since it also focused on the extent of the restricted territory in the CNC. If in the same client's case the seller, following the sale, worked for the buyer, *Hanson* would be particularly relevant, since in *Hanson* the buyer also employed the sellers in the new business.

c. Whether some cases provide useful public policy explanations

While one or more cases may be useful in drawing factual analogies and distinctions to support each party's position, other cases may be useful because they provide public policy support for the legal arguments raised by the parties.

It's apparent from *Mats Transport* how important it is that the buyer be able to rely on a seller's former business relationships and keep their former clients involved with the new ownership. The court in *Hanson* refers to the importance of former business relationships, relying on public policy not found in *Mats Transport*. Specifically, the court opinion in *Hanson* states, "Policy supports every individual's right to work; however, policy also supports allowing any individual the option to sell anything he wants, including that right to work." *Hanson*, 539 S.E.2d at 502. Even though *Hanson* is older, it's relevant, even if for no other reason than to provide the additional relevant public policy.

3. Choosing which cases are most helpful in supporting each party's position when applying the law to the facts of the case in the analysis

After assessing the value of each case, determine which cases are most helpful when drawing factual analogies and distinctions to the facts of the client's case to support each party's position in the analysis. In reaching a decision, (a) prefer a case with facts more similar to the client's facts over a case with facts that are dissimilar to the facts in the client's case; (b) prefer a court opinion that is well reasoned over one where the court's reasoning is superficial or nonexistent; and (c) prefer cases from the highest binding court in the controlling jurisdiction. Balance these guidelines with solid judgment and common sense.

a. Prefer cases with facts more similar to those facts in the client's case

When analyzing a fact-based issue, the closer the facts in a case are to the client's facts, the more germane is the analysis. If both sets of relevant facts are similar, reasonable factual analogies between the facts of the cited case and the facts of the client's case will be easier to explain and will be more convincing. Of course, this factor must be weighed against the other factors in this list.

For example, in *Mats Transport* the CNC restricted the seller from working in the same business anywhere in the United States. This fact is significantly different from the facts in Ana's case where the CNC prohibits Ana from working only in nearby counties and towns. If there was a third case—one where the CNC restricted territory closer in scope to the restriction in Ana's case and the outcome supported Ana's position—that case would be a stronger case from which to draw factual similarities.

This guideline also applies to providing support for the opposing party's position. It may be tempting to choose those cases where the facts are so different from the client's case facts that they are easily distinguishable. However, if only the easily distinguishable cases are used when other, more factually similar cases are available, those cases will be introduced by any competent attorney representing the other party. By ignoring these cases, there's a risk that the supervising attorney may not be fully prepared to later make a solid argument on behalf of the client, perhaps at the negotiations table or in court. A better approach is to choose those cases that are closest factually to the client's case but, for example, find the CNC in the case reasonable. That is the case that should be distinguished as part of the client's position; if that is possible, the client's case will be strengthened. So, when writing an objective analysis, carefully consider how to support each party's position using those cases that provide the strongest support for *each* party. The stronger analysis will include those cases that are hardest to distinguish from the client's.

b. Prefer a case where the court gave a well-reasoned basis for its decision over one where the court's reasoning is superficial or nonexistent

Also consider the extent of the court's reasoning in any potentially relevant case. Some courts in their opinions omit the reasoning entirely or provide only a superficial explanation for their holdings. The more thorough the court's reasoning, the more helpful the case will be when drawing factual analogies and distinctions to support the client's case. Be careful to avoid using a case *just* because the facts sound strikingly similar to the client's facts. If the court never explained *why* it concluded as it did, based on the facts—or even worse, never actually addressed the legal issue for which the similar facts are relevant—that case will not be helpful in the analysis. Pay careful attention to each court's reasoning, and use a case only when analyzing the same legal point the court analyzed in reaching its decision.

For example, in *Mats Transport*, found in Chapter 6, the court provided a three-prong test used to determine whether a covenant not to compete in a sale of a business was unreasonable and therefore unenforceable. The court then focused its reasoning only on the first prong of that test, because it concluded that, pursuant to the first prong, the covenant was "broader than necessary to protect the plaintiff's interest." *Mats Transport v. ABC Corp.*, 824 S.E.2d 1467, 1468 (E.C. Ct. App. 1992). Since all three requirements, or prongs, had to be met, and the CNC did not meet the first prong, the court did not need to address prongs two and three. Thus, even though the facts of *Mats Transport* may be relevant to prongs two and three, it would be unhelpful in analyzing either prong two or prong three, since the opinion included no holding or reasoning with respect to those two prongs. *Mats Transport* may be used only to draw factual analogies and distinctions regarding prong one or to provide other useful information, such as explanations of the rule or public policy considerations.

Hanson, in contrast, specifically addressed all three prongs of the CNC test in assessing the reasonableness of the CNC. The court's discussion on prongs two and three are not as thorough as the discussion on prong one, which was the requirement in dispute, but the court did quickly establish why prongs two and three were met. Therefore, *Hanson* could be used in analyzing all three requirements needed to show a CNC was unreasonable and thus unenforceable.

Note: Pay careful attention to what the court *says* it will address in its opinion and what the court *actually does* address in the opinion. Sometimes the court sets out an issue raised in the court below or on appeal but never actually addresses the issue in deciding the case. In *Hanson*, the husband and wife sued in part because the wife claimed she was wrongfully fired. While this is mentioned in the case, the court of appeals never addresses it, likely because it was not part of the appeal.

c. *When in the controlling jurisdiction there's no binding primary authority, referring to non-binding authority will be necessary*

As stated earlier in this chapter, when organizing the law and choosing cases to cite and explain rules, draw your factual analogies and distinctions from a case decided by the highest court in the controlling jurisdiction, where possible. If not, refer to an intermediate appellate court case in the controlling jurisdiction.

Sometimes outside authority is necessary, however, especially when there's no binding precedent in the controlling jurisdiction. When addressing a state law question, state court opinions from other jurisdictions are usually more helpful than federal court opinions where the federal court applied state law. This is because state courts outside the controlling jurisdiction address the same state issues more frequently than federal courts. For this reason, state courts have a greater ability than federal courts to reason through the state issues.

Any court decision that does not originate in the controlling state jurisdiction is only persuasive precedent. Further, any decision about a state law question issued from a federal court, where the court applied the controlling state's law, is persuasive primary authority only. Based on the same logic, when the client's issue involves a question of federal law, decisions by federal courts outside the controlling federal jurisdiction are more useful than decisions by state courts addressing the same federal question. Further, any state court decision resolving a federal law question is not binding on a federal court.

This choice of state versus federal court may arise, for example, when your client's case involves a constitutional question, such as whether your client's rights were violated under the Fourth Amendment to the U.S. Constitution, which protects citizens from unreasonable searches and seizures by the government. Where a court addresses the U.S. Constitution's Fourth Amendment (since all states are bound to the federal constitutional provisions), and also addresses a state's constitutional provision, the case could be brought in either a state or federal court.

d. Be careful about using unpublished opinions

Not all decisions are published officially, even though unpublished opinions are available online. Courts will decide whether to officially report a case; if so, that case will be considered precedent so long as it remains good law. Unpublished opinions, however, are treated differently in different jurisdictions. After finding a case that seems relevant to a client's case but is noted up front as an unpublished or unreported opinion, be sure to check the controlling jurisdiction's court rules to determine how that case is treated and how it can be used in that jurisdiction, if at all.

e. Refer to a majority opinion first; if referring to a concurring or dissenting opinion, be sure to identify that source

Finally, first and foremost cite to the majority opinion rather than to a concurring or dissenting opinion. If necessary, and only after citing to language in the majority opinion, language may be used from a concurring or dissenting opinion as long as the writer makes the source of the information explicit. After the statement from a dissent or concurrence, note that, for example, as "(Smith, J., dissenting)," or ("Evans, J., concurring)."

> **Note:** Be careful when pulling information from a case on the computer; always check to see whether the noted language is part of the majority, concurring, or dissenting opinion. It may not be obvious when looking at a computer screen.

Also note whether the language from the case is part of the actual holding or is merely dicta (extraneous to the holding). The persuasive value of the discussion is greater if it is part of the court's actual holding. If dicta, the information may still be useful in future cases, since it's predictive of the court's future reasoning, but it should be identified as dicta in any written document.

4. *Based on the choice of cases in #1, #2, and #3, above, choosing where to best explain the cases so they will be most helpful to the reader*

Determining where to place information from the case law depends on how each case will be used. The following are sample outlines of different ways a discussion of one legal issue may be structured.

a. Using two cases to support both parties' positions

Consider using the following CREAC structure when you have two cases, and both can be used to support each party's position:

- ***Conclusion*** (identifying the legal issue and providing the predicted conclusion in factual context)
- ***Rule*** (and, where available, general explanations of the rule, such as definitions of words and phrases in the rule)
- ***Rule explanations, where needed*** (key case facts, court's holding, and court's reasoning) provided one case at a time (e.g., Case A and Case B)
- ***Analysis/application*** of the law to the client's case.

  —assertion and support for the predicted conclusion, by comparing favorably the facts of the case with the same outcome (e.g., Case A) with the facts supporting the party's position in the predicted conclusion (e.g., Party 1), and contrasting the facts of the case with the undesired outcome (e.g., Case B) from the facts supporting Party 1's position

  —transition to support for the counteranalysis, comparing the facts of Case B to the facts of the present case to support Party 2's position and contrasting the facts of Case A to the facts of the present case to support Party 2's position
- ***Conclusion*** addressing the predicted conclusion and the overall question(s) posed by the supervising attorney

In Ana Hart's CNC case, both *Mats Transport* and *Hanson* would be used to support both parties' position. The best pattern to follow in the discussion of Ana Hart's case, therefore, is the above pattern, where both cases are explained one after the other and then used to support each party's position. When providing support for why the CNC is unreasonable, favoring Ana's position, the facts in Ana's case would be compared favorably to the facts in *Mats Transport* and contrasted from the facts in *Hanson*. When providing support for why the CNC is reasonable, favoring David's position, the facts in the case would be compared favorably to the facts in *Hanson* and contrasted from the facts in *Mats Transport*.

For easier reference, consider charting this information but now adding *Hanson* to the chart introduced in Chapter 6. Because the client in the CNC case is Ana Hart, first chart the facts and inferences that support David's position that the CNC was not overbroad and was, therefore, reasonable:

Facts and Inferences to Support Why the CNC Is Reasonable (David's Position):		
Facts of *Mats Transport* (unreasonable CNC)	**Facts of Ana's Case**	**Facts of *Hanson* (reasonable CNC)**
• CNC restricted competition throughout U.S. for 5 yrs.	• CNC covered 6 E.C. counties and two towns in other counties for 3 yrs. ***Inference:*** *David's CNC limited geographically and is not overbroad, supporting reasonableness.*	• CNC covered 12 states for 3 yrs.
• When sold, the company had only 1 E.C. terminal with routes in E.C. and adjoining states and hauled across U.S. infrequently.	• When sold, Harts owned 3 Centers in 3 counties named in CNC but no Centers in the remaining 3 counties or 2 towns listed. ***Inference:*** *Centers existed in sufficient areas named in CNC to consider the CNC not overbroad but reasonable.*	• When business sold, company had up to 4 clients in states 1-9; 583 clients in states 10-11; and no clients in state 12.
• Seller never expressed to buyer any intent to expand the business into any areas covered by the CNC.	• David & Ana agreed to expand the business within the next 3 yrs. into the 3 counties & 2 towns where Centers were not located, though no steps taken thus far. ***Inference:*** *Plans to expand to areas named in CNC, known by parties in CNC, supporting reasonableness.*	• Sellers husband & wife knew of buyer's plans to expand in all areas covered by CNC, and seller husband knew buyer was negotiating with major client in state with no clients.
	• Unlike previous sellers of clubs to David & Ana, who did not have any connection with the Centers' members prior to the sales, Ana had a relationship with the Centers' members. ***Inference:*** *Ana presents threat to David's business interest, which relies heavily on continuing goodwill between the owners and club members.*	• Husband & wife had successful relationship with clients, shown by clients returning & referring friends to the couple. Company provided a service where the goodwill between owners and clients was important to the business.

Facts and Inferences to Support Why the CNC Is Reasonable (David's Position):		
Facts of *Mats Transport* (unreasonable CNC)	**Facts of Ana's Case**	**Facts of *Hanson* (reasonable CNC)**
	• Members usually use the club closest to work or home. ***Inference:*** *If Ana opens a club in a nearby county or town, it may physically be closer to a member's work or home, resulting in direct competition, which CNC is designed to prevent.*	

Notice that distinctions between the facts from *Mats Transport, Hanson,* and the client's case are set side by side in the chart; this makes it easier to see the factual analogies and distinctions. Additional facts that support David's position are also listed. Finally, reasonable inferences are noted where appropriate. This chart makes it easier to move to drafting the analysis in a discussion.

Next, create a fact chart focusing on why the CNC Ana was asked to sign is overbroad and thus unreasonable by adding *Hanson* to the chart from Chapter 6:

Facts and Inferences to Support Why the CNC Is Unreasonable (Ana's Position)		
Facts of *Mats Transport* (unreasonable CNC)	**Facts of Ana's Case**	**Facts of *Hanson* (reasonable CNC)**
• CNC restricted competition throughout U.S. for 5 yrs.	• CNC covered 6 E.C. counties plus 2 towns in other counties for 3 yrs.	• CNC covered 12 states for 3 yrs.
• When sold, company had only 1 E.C. terminal with routes in E.C. and adjoining states, hauling infrequently across U.S.	• When sold, Harts owned 3 Centers in 3 counties named in the CNC but not in the remaining 3 counties or 2 towns listed in the CNC. ***Inference:*** *Centers existed in less than half the regions named in the CNC, so exceeds legitimate geographical scope and is thus unreasonable.*	• When business sold, company had up to 4 clients in states 1-9; 583 clients in states 10-11; and no clients in 1 state.
• Seller never expressed to buyer any intent to expand the business into any areas covered by the CNC.	• David & Ana had agreed to expand the business within the next 3 yrs. into 3 counties & 2 towns where Centers are not located but had taken no action to do so. ***Inference:*** *Discussion but no action taken to support intent to expand, supporting the CNC's being overbroad and unreasonable.*	• Sellers husband & wife knew buyer's plans to expand in other areas covered by CNC. No client in 12th state but buyer negotiating with major client at the time, known by seller husband.

Facts and Inferences to Support Why the CNC Is Unreasonable (Ana's Position)		
Facts of *Mats Transport* (unreasonable CNC)	**Facts of Ana's Case**	**Facts of *Hanson* (reasonable CNC)**
	• Prior CNCs signed by those selling clubs to Ana & David restricted sellers only to counties where sold clubs were located. ***Inference:*** *CNC that restricts territory to counties where Centers located at that time sufficient to protect David's interest.*	• Sellers husband & wife had successful relationship with their former clients, shown by clients' returning & referring friends to husband & wife. Company provided a service where the goodwill between owners & clients important to business.
	• Members usually use the club closest to their work or home. ***Inference:*** *Members will not travel great distances to go to another club; thus, unnecessary to have a broad territorial restriction, which is unreasonable.*	

Once again, notice that the facts in the three cases addressing the same points are set side-by-side in the chart. Additional facts that support Ana's position are also listed. Finally, reasonable inferences are noted where appropriate.

> **Note:** As stated in Chapter 6, the facts supporting Ana's position include some of the same facts that appeared when assessing David's position. Sometimes the same facts can be used to support both sides of an issue. In these instances, different inferences can be drawn from the facts, so long as those inferences are reasonable.

> **Note:** While assessing each position, be careful not to engage in speculation or otherwise consider situations that are not supported by the facts. When trying to find additional support for a client's case, there's the temptation to create circumstances that would help the client. However, don't "create" facts through speculation or imagination.

b. Using one or more cases to support the predicted conclusion and one or more new, additional cases to support the counteranalysis

Usually more than two cases will be helpful in analyzing a client's case. While there is no single template for structuring a legal analysis with multiple cases, strive (1) to ensure that the reader has a clear understanding of what the law says and how it has been interpreted and applied in each court opinion, and (2) to provide a complete and accurate analysis of the issue in the client's case by thoroughly exploring how to best support each party's position on each legal point.

When too few cases are used, the risk is to not be thorough; when too many cases are used, the risk is in not being clear. For example, if the writer begins a discussion of an issue by explaining five cases in a row, the reader will likely find it difficult to distinguish among so many cases in the analysis. To better ensure that the reader doesn't become lost, and the message and analysis is thorough and clear, consider discussing the key cases when supporting the predicted conclusion (which may also be used to support the counteranalysis), and then introduce, explain, and use additional cases when supporting the counteranalysis. Introducing new cases within the counteranalysis works only if those cases are more helpful in that analysis. As always, the overriding principle is to bring in information where it's most relevant to your reader. The structure might look like this:

- ***Conclusion*** (identifying the legal issue and the conclusion within factual context)
- ***Rule*** (and, where available, general explanations of the rule, such as definitions)
- ***Rule explanations*** (explanations of the cases used to support the predicted conclusion—key facts, holding, and reasoning—provided one case at a time), e.g., Case #1, Case #2, and Case #3
- ***Analysis/application*** of the law to the client's case
  - Assertion and support for the predicted conclusion
  - Inferences from client's facts and from case analogies and distinctions to support the predicted conclusion
  - Transition to the counteranalysis
  - Rule explanation(s) of additional case(s) used only to support the counteranalysis, e.g., Case #4
  - Inferences from client's facts, and case analogies and distinctions from newly introduced as well as previously introduced cases helpful to support the counteranalysis
- ***Conclusion*** addressing the predicted conclusion and the overall question(s) posed by the supervising attorney

c. Using a case parenthetical instead of the full explanation of a case

When many relevant cases are helpful, references to other supporting but less important cases may be provided through the use of a case parenthetical, which usually states only the court's factual holding in parentheses, following the citation to the case. Note, however, that not all the cases found *must* be used in the final written document; rather, provide only what's needed from the cited authority to give the reader a solid understanding of the relevant law and the arguments that can and likely will be made on behalf of both sides. Examples of providing an additional case and parenthetical to support the reasonableness of a CNC might look like the following:

> To be reasonable, a noncompetition clause must be limited in duration and geographic scope. *Hawkins Chem., Inc. v. McNea*, 321 N.W.2d 918, 920 (N.D. 1982) (limiting the enforcement of a noncompetition clause to one county); *Igoe v. Atlas Ready-Mix, Inc.*, 134 N.W.2d 511, 513 (N.D. 1965) (finding a noncompetition clause enforceable for the duration of ten years).[4]

> *See also, Mohanty v. St. John Heart Clinic*, 866 E.C.2d 85 (E.C. Ct. App. 2000) (CNC restricting the doctor from practicing within five-mile radius of Chicago for five years reasonable based on the right to freely contract, so long as it's not void for public policy reasons).[5]

If the last parenthetical were incorporated into the analysis of Ana's case, it might be included in the following way:

> In contrast, the court in *Hanson v. Albright* reviewed the contested first prong of the test for a valid CNC and found the CNC reasonable and enforceable. 539 S.E.2d 500, 502 (E.C. Ct. App. 1989). *See also, Mohanty v. St. John Heart Clinic*, 866 E.C.2d 85 (E.C. Ct. App. 2000) (CNC restricting doctor from practicing within five-mile radius of Chicago for five years reasonable based on the right to freely contract, so long as it's not void for public policy reasons).

d. Considering where to include public policy in a discussion of a fact-based issue

The final consideration is where to place any helpful public policy statements. As stated earlier, when addressing a fact-based issue such as the CNC issue, statements of public policy are used primarily to educate the reader as to why a rule exists and to provide additional support for the more important legal arguments based on the relevant law and facts of the case. Public policy statements are used primarily as the basis for analyzing law-based questions, where the focus is on how a rule should be interpreted or which rule of law

---

4. Eric P. Voigt, *Explanatory Parentheticals Can Pack a Persuasive Punch*, 45 McGeorge L. Rev. 269, 295-96 (2013).

5. Based on *Mohanty v. St. John Heart Clinic*, 866 N.E.2d 85 (Ill. 2000).

applies. When addressing a fact-based issue, statements of public policy are usually included in one or more of the following places:

(1) Within the explanation of the rule;
(2) Within the explanation of the case;
(3) In the analysis; or
(4) As part of the conclusion, to support why the predicted conclusion is stronger.

The sample discussion found in Chapter 6, with the addition of *Hanson*, is provided below. The language that has been added from *Hanson* is provided in **boldface type**. As you read this example, identify the different parts of the discussion, including:

(1) the predicted conclusion and topic sentences;
(2) the rules;
(3) the rule explanations (case facts, holdings, and reasonings);
(4) the factual analogies and distinctions, and the inferences drawn from those analogies and distinctions;
(5) any additional facts and inferences from the client's case;
(6) any public policy statements;
(7) the transitional words and phrases; and
(8) the overall conclusion.

Sample Discussion:

The covenant not to compete (CNC) that Ana Hart has been ordered by the court to sign as part of her divorce settlement is probably overbroad in its protection of David Hart's business interests and thus unreasonable and unenforceable. In East Carolina, courts use the following three-pronged test to determine whether a CNC related to the sale of a business is reasonable: "(1) the covenant must not be broader than necessary for the protection of the covenantee's legitimate business interest; (2) the covenant cannot have an adverse effect on the covenantor; and (3) the covenant cannot adversely affect the public interest." *Mats Transp. v. ABC Corp.*, 824 S.E.2d 1467, 1468 (E.C. Ct. App. 1992). A CNC is unreasonable "as a matter of law" if it fails any one of the prongs of the test. *Id.*

A CNC related to the sale of a business was found unreasonable as a matter of law because the CNC was broader than necessary to protect the buyer's legitimate business interest. *Mats Transport*, 824 S.E.2d at 1468. The CNC restricted the seller from competing with the buyer in the trucking business anywhere in the United States for five years when, at the time of the sale, the business included only one trucking terminal in East Carolina and hauled freight to adjoining states and infrequently to areas across the United States. After the sale of the business, the seller leased trucks to a former driver, who began operating a trucking business. The buyer alleged a CNC violation, and the seller filed a motion for summary judgment, which the trial court granted. *Id.*

The appellate court affirmed, finding the CNC overbroad because the territorial scope of the CNC exceeded the protection of the buyer's legitimate interests. *Id.* Both parties knew there was only one terminal and yet the CNC restrained the seller as if it was a national business. Since the first prong was not met, the CNC was unreasonable as a matter of law. *Id.*

In another case, however, the appellate court found the CNC was not overbroad. *Hanson v. Albright*, 539 S.E.2d 500, 502 (E.C. Ct. App. 1989). Since the other two prongs of the CNC test had also been met, the court found the CNC reasonable and enforceable, and the buyer's request for a permanent injunction was upheld. *Id.* The husband and wife sellers sold their pension consulting firm to a buyer, who then merged the sellers' firm with the buyer's other firms. The sellers signed a CNC covering twelve states and lasting three years. The sellers then became employees of the new company, also to last for three years. One year later the wife was fired, and her husband quit. The husband and wife sellers began a new consulting firm, soliciting their former clients. The sellers sued the buyer, alleging the twelve-state restriction in the CNC was broader than necessary to protect the buyer's interest since it extended to seven states where the buyer had only four customers and to one state where there were no customers. The buyer planned to expand to all twelve states, however, and was engaged in active negotiations with a prospective client in the state with no customers, which the sellers knew when they sold the business. The buyer filed a counterclaim, requesting an injunction that ordered the sellers to refrain from competing and to abide by the CNC.

In upholding the buyer's injunction, the court recognized that as a service business the consulting firm's good client relationships were essential. *Id.* at 501. Allowing the sellers to solicit former clients would destroy the goodwill the buyer purchased, especially since the former owners knew both the old and new clients. *Id.* Further, the sellers knew the buyer had been working to expand into all twelve states and had still agreed to the restricted states as part of the CNC, supporting its reasonableness. *Id.* at 502. The sellers received payment for this restriction and could not then later avoid it. *Id.* The goodwill of a business is an intangible asset that

may be transferred from seller to purchaser, and it becomes the buyer's right to expect that the firm's established customers will continue to patronize the purchased business. *Id.*

The CNC the court has ordered Ana to sign is likely unreasonable because it is overbroad in its protection of David's interest. The CNC restricts competition in three counties and two towns where the Harts own no Hart Fitness Centers, so the business has not developed relationships with customers in these areas. This is similar to *Mats Transport*, where the CNC was overbroad because it unreasonably restricted competition in every state, and the business operated in only one state with established trucking routes in the surrounding states. **Unlike in *Hanson*, where there were at least some clients in eleven of the twelve states restricted by the CNC and active negotiations to expand into the one remaining restricted state, the Harts neither maintained any Centers in the other restricted regions nor had any ongoing negotiations to establish clubs in those regions.**

Further, the seller husband in *Hanson* knew the buyer intended to expand to new areas where there were no clients at the time of the sale. More importantly, the sellers agreed to include in the CNC the state with no clients at that time. This is different from Ana's situation. Unlike in *Hanson* where the sellers voluntarily agreed to include all twelve states in the CNC, Ana made no such agreement and, in fact, is being forced to sign the CNC as part of her divorce settlement.

In addition, the CNC is unreasonable because it extends beyond the restrictions of the CNCs signed by sellers in prior sales of clubs to the Harts. Those previous CNCs restricted competition only to the county in which the purchased clubs were located. Both Harts considered this a reasonable restriction in those prior transactions. Therefore, in Ana's sale of her interest to David, a CNC restricting competition in locations where the Centers are not currently located exceeds what was considered reasonable in prior sales transactions.

Further support that the geographic restriction is too broad is that members usually use clubs that are closest to their homes or workplaces. Members probably will not travel great distances to go to another club; thus, it is not necessary to restrict competition over a geographic area that exceeds the present Center locations.

However, the CNC the court has ordered Ana to sign may be considered reasonable if more emphasis is placed on the planned expansion of the business, the nature of the business, and the importance of Ana's relationship with the members of the Hart Fitness Centers. Unlike the seller in *Mats Transport*, who never expressed to the buyer any planned expansion into other routes, Ana and David had planned to expand the business in the next three years into the three counties and two towns covered by the CNC. Further, the restriction covers only a limited geographic area in central East Carolina; this is more restrictive than the area covered by the CNC in *Mats Transport* that extended to every state, even though the business was located only in one state and operated only a limited number of routes in the surrounding states. **The Harts' planned expansion is similar to the buyer's planned expansion in *Hanson*, who had already taken steps to expand the business at the time of the purchase. David's planned expansion would also cover only a limited geographic area in central East Carolina, similar to the restricted areas in *Hanson*** and unlike the expanded restricted area covered by the CNC in *Mats Transport*.

The CNC the judge has ordered Ana to sign is broader than the one-county restriction contained in the CNCs signed by sellers in prior club purchases, but that broader restriction is necessary to adequately protect David's interest in the business. Those who sold their clubs to the Harts in the past did not have any relationship with the members of the Hart Fitness Centers prior to the sales. The past sellers are different from Ana, who presents a greater threat to the business of the Hart Fitness Centers because she has developed relationships with Center members. **Her relationships with members are similar to the sellers in *Hanson*, who had good relationships with their former clients and worked at the new company, enabling them to threaten the goodwill the buyer purchased if they tried to compete with the buyer.**

In addition, just as in *Hanson*, where the pension consulting firm was a service-oriented business, health and exercise clubs are also service-oriented businesses that rely heavily on the good relationship between members and the clubs for the continuing success of the business. Arguably, David needs to protect his interest in the business, and the CNC would ensure that Ana did not compete with the Centers and steal away members, which would lessen the value of the business. If Ana owned or worked in a club in the same county or town where members of the Centers live or work, members may quit the Centers, especially if her club is closer to their homes or workplaces.

Nevertheless, courts do not favor CNCs and strictly construe CNCs against the party seeking to enforce them because "they impede trade and distort the market mechanism which allows our economy to function." *Mats Transport*, 824 S.E.2d at 1467. Here, the CNC will be strictly construed against David. The geographic restriction in the CNC extends into counties and towns where the Harts do not currently operate any Centers or have any active ongoing negotiations to expand the business. Further, the geographic area exceeds the value of the goodwill Ana has in the current membership, which is what the CNC is meant to protect. Therefore, the CNC is likely overbroad for the protection of David's business interest and is unreasonable.

A sample checklist for an objective discussion is found in the Student Supplemental Materials for this book located on the publisher's website at http://www.aspenpublishing.com.

• Exercise 7-A

Read and brief *Schuler v. Baldwin*, found online in the Student Supplemental Materials for this book located on the publisher's website at http://www.aspenpublishing.com Revise your previous discussion drafted in Exercise 6-F by incorporating *Schuler* into the discussion of whether Ms. Broward will be barred from bringing an action against Dr. Warren for the return of her lost painting. This exercise provides you with an opportunity to apply the concepts presented in this chapter by drafting a single fact-based discussion using two cases.

• Exercise 7-B

Locate online *King v. Lennen*, 348 P.2d 98 (Cal. 1959), found in the Student Supplemental Materials for this book located on the publisher's website at http://www.aspenpublishing.com. Read and brief *King*. Revise your previous discussion drafted in Exercise 6-G by incorporating *King* into the discussion of whether the landowner Redwood Mobile Homes will be liable for the death of the child, Ricky Olson, because Redwood knew or should have known that a child like Ricky would not be able to appreciate the danger of the settlement tank, where he drowned.

CHAPTER SUMMARY

- When using multiple cases in the analysis of a single issue, the structure of the analysis will depend on whether the cases are helpful only in explaining the law, only in applying the law to the client's facts, or both.
- Choosing the best cases to *explain* the law will depend on each court's focus on the law and the court's explanation of any underlying policy that supports the law.
- Choosing the best cases to *apply* to the client's facts in the analysis depends on considerations such as the hierarchy and binding nature of the controlling authority; the similarity of the facts to the client's facts; the extent of the court's reasoning about the same legal issue; and the year the case was decided.
- Including relevant case law where most appropriate in the analysis will depend on where the information is most relevant and helpful to the legal reader.

CHAPTER

8

Synthesizing a Single Rule from Multiple Cases

A. Introduction

Common law rules develop over a period of time through numerous court decisions. It is the common thread existing in multiple cases where the same legal issue is being addressed that eventually develops into a common law rule. When a court is faced with a legal issue, it must review the relevant law in the controlling jurisdiction and decide the case in a way that is consistent with the binding case precedent. The facts of the current case before a court, however, are virtually never identical to the facts of the prior binding cases; it is because of the factual differences that common law rules often change as the rule developed in prior cases is applied to the facts in the new case. Consider the following three cases from the fictitious jurisdiction of East Carolina.[1]

B. Example of Synthesizing Three Case Holdings into a Single Rule

Sellers v. Johnson, 165 S.E. 470 (E.C. 1970)

James Osgood shot and killed his wife after she divorced him. Almost immediately thereafter, James Osgood died by suicide. The record included evidence that the

1. The summarized cases to show an example of an evolving common law rule are based on: *Shifanellia v. Wallace*, 315 A.2d 513 (Md. 1974); *Cordell v. Jenifer*, 150 A.2d 251 (Md. 1959); and *Sellers v. Hitaffer*, 165 A. 470 (Md. 1933). The internal case citations in each case have been omitted.

husband had previously threatened to kill his wife. The wife died without a Last Will and Testament (Will), which would make the statute of descent and distribution applicable in this case. The statute sets down who takes the assets of a person who dies without a Will. Under the language of the East Carolina statute of descent and distribution, the husband's relatives would be able to take one-half of the deceased wife's assets. The special probate court, a court that rules on matters related to a deceased's estate, held that because James Osgood killed his wife, the husband's relatives, or heirs, and their personal representatives could not share in the wife's estate. This decision was affirmed on appeal, and the losing parties now appeal to this highest court.

The East Carolina Legislature has not enacted a slayer statute in this state. A slayer statute prevents a person who kills another from benefitting from the victim's death. The specific requirements under the slayer statute vary from state to state. Since this specific issue has never before been addressed in East Carolina, we look to other jurisdictions, where two differing approaches are applied in resolving this issue. The first approach applies the common law principle of equity, providing that "no one shall be permitted to profit by his own fraud, to take advantage of his own wrong, to found any claim upon his own evil, or to acquire property by his own crime." *Madsen v. Jones*, 140 N.E.2d 23, 25 (Wisc. Ct. App. 1960). Under this approach, courts will interpret a Will, a life insurance policy, and a statute of descent and distribution in a way to prevent a killer from benefiting from the death of the victim. In reaching this decision, the court focuses on the universally recognized principles of justice and morality. *Id.* at 30.

The second approach recognizes the public policy of the common law but determines that this policy is outweighed by the public policy relied on when the Legislature enacts a statute governing how property is to be distributed when a deceased has no Will. *Adams v. Klein,* 154 A.2d 323, 326 (Fla. 1965). Since the Florida Legislature in its statute on descent and distribution has declared its public policy regarding who should take the assets of the deceased when there is no Will, the common law should not take priority over the legislative intent reflected in that statute. *Id.* Under this approach, if James was still alive, he would take from his wife's estate. Since he died by suicide, however, the portion that would otherwise be awarded to him would pass to his family.

We choose to follow the first approach, which prevents one who kills another from benefiting from the estate of the killer's victim. A person cannot lose what he never had; because of the husband's murderous act, he never gained a beneficial interest in any part of his wife's estate. This court will abide by the rule that "no one should be permitted to profit by his own fraud, to take advantage of his own wrong, to found any claim upon his own evil, or to acquire property by his own crime." *Madsen,* 140 N.E.2d at 25.

The court's decision in *Sellers* sets down the court's first ruling on this legal issue: "No one shall be permitted to profit by his own fraud, to take advantage of his own wrong, to found any claim upon his own evil, or to acquire property by his own crime." *Madsen v. Jones*, 140 N.E.2d 23, 25 (Wisc. Ct. App. 1960). In this case, the killer who would otherwise profit under the statute of descent and distribution from the estate of the killer's victim, since the victim had no Will, cannot share in the estate of the victim. This ruling extends to the family of the killer. Another court in East Carolina addressed the same issue twenty-six years later.

Cordell v. Roberts, 195 S.E.2d 251 (E.C. 1996)

This case presents the court with the question whether a wife can recover the proceeds of her husband's life insurance policy when she caused the husband's death. The relationship between this husband and wife had been unstable. The husband at times would drink too much alcohol, become intoxicated, and hit his wife with his hand or a weapon. At other times he would become intoxicated but not become violent. On this occasion, no evidence was introduced to show the husband possessed a weapon, although he did slap his wife and make threatening motions. In response, the wife picked up a knife and stabbed her husband, who later died. The wife was found guilty of manslaughter, not murder. The judge in the criminal court did not state whether the conviction was for voluntary or involuntary manslaughter.

Manslaughter is different from murder, only because murder requires that the killer plan the killing (premeditation); voluntary manslaughter is intentional, while involuntary manslaughter is not. The wife's representatives contend in this civil suit that when she stabbed her husband, she didn't intend to kill him. While her actions were unlawful and felonious, her representatives argued she should still receive her husband's insurance proceeds. We find that this killing was intentional, however, so the wife cannot receive the life insurance proceeds.

The court in *Sellers v. Johnson* sets out the basic rule in this state, which is that one who kills ordinarily may not profit by taking any portion of the estate of the one murdered. 165 S.E. 470, 474 (E.C. 1970). This policy is broad enough to cover not only when a victim dies without a Last Will and Testament (Will) but also, as in this case, where a victim dies with a life insurance policy.

This court does not distinguish between murder and manslaughter, because both are felonies and distinguished only by the presence or absence of malice aforethought. Malice aforethought occurs when one plans in advance to commit a wrong. Other courts have drawn a line, not between murder and manslaughter but between voluntary and involuntary manslaughter. We need not decide whether to draw the same line here because it is clear that the killing in this case was intentional. The wife neither acted in self-defense nor did she strike her husband by accident. She reacted to her husband's slap on the face with an excessive degree of force; she did not just act negligently or unintentionally. Where the killing is both felonious *and* intentional, the killer cannot benefit, and the lower court's ruling must be affirmed.

The court in *Cordell* expanded the rule set down in *Sellers*: First, the court found that, when determining whether a slayer can take assets from the victim, the same result should occur regardless of whether the assets are part of an estate where the deceased victim had no Will (the facts in *Sellers*) or are part of the proceeds of the deceased victim's insurance policy (the facts in *Cordell*). Second, the court found that a slayer can be prohibited from acquiring the assets of the deceased regardless of whether the deceased was convicted of murder or voluntary manslaughter. Both convictions require that the acts be felonious and intentional, which the court found occurred in *Cordell*. This adds to the East Carolina common law rule, since in *Sellers* there was no conviction because the husband died by suicide.

Finally, here is the most recent decision of the three Supreme Court of East Carolina cases addressing the same issue.

Turner v. Heinz, 315 S.E.2d 513 (E.C. 2010)

This appeal arises out of a dispute over the proceeds of a life insurance policy issued upon the life of Susan A. Heinz, now deceased. While Susan's husband, George Heinz, was cleaning his gun, he accidentally shot Susan, who died. Susan had named George as the sole beneficiary of her life insurance policy. John Turner, the attorney for Susan's estate, filed a suit in probate court on behalf of Susan's two minor children by a prior marriage. Turner argued that the proceeds of Susan's insurance policy should be paid to Susan's estate to benefit the children and not to George. The probate court disagreed and ruled that the proceeds be paid to the named beneficiary, George. We affirm.

The husband George in this case unintentionally killed his wife and was found guilty of gross negligence. Gross negligence occurs when an actor either does something in a conscious, voluntary manner or omits to do something in reckless disregard of a legal duty and the consequences to another party. In *Cordell v. Roberts*, 180 S.E.2d 251, 252 (E.C. 1996), we found that "[w]here the killing is both felonious and intentional, . . . the beneficiary cannot prevail. . . ." In *Cordell*, a wife was convicted of manslaughter for killing her husband, and the court found the killing intentional. *Id.* When someone kills another unintentionally, however, the majority of jurisdictions allow recovery from the deceased. Where there is no intent, the rule that no one should profit by his felony does not apply. Where the death is due to an accident or by the killer's gross negligence, resulting in a verdict based on <u>involuntary</u> manslaughter, the killer/beneficiary may still recover.

In *Turner* the court makes certain what could have been inferred from the reasoning in the former case: that if a killing is unintentional, the killer may still benefit from the victim's assets.

The synthesis of multiple court holdings into one single common law rule is a prime example of inductive reasoning. Inductive reasoning occurs when you reason from many specific ideas, such as multiple cases addressing the same legal issue, to one general principle, or a common law rule, as what occurs in this case. In contrast, deductive reasoning occurs when you reason from one general principle, such as a single statute, and apply it to specific situations, as in applying the statute to individual cases.

The resulting common law rule in this example, as developed through the three cases, becomes the following.[2]

> The common law rule of equity establishes that "no one should be permitted to profit by his own fraud, to take advantage of his own wrong, to found any claim upon his own evil, or to acquire property by his own crime." *Cordell v. Roberts*, 165 S.E.2d 270, 274 (E.C. 1996). In East Carolina, a person who kills another
>
> (1) *may not* share in the distribution of the decedent's estate as an heir by way of the statute of descent and distribution or as the beneficiary who collects the proceeds under a policy of insurance on the decedent's life when the homicide is both felonious and intentional;
>
> (2) *may* share in the distribution of the decedent's estate as an heir by way of the statute of descent and distribution, or as one who would otherwise take under the decedent's Will or life insurance policy when the homicide is unintentional, even though it is the result of such gross negligence as would render the killer criminally culpable of involuntary manslaughter.

> **Note:** Once the case holdings have been synthesized into a single common law rule, it would be inserted into a CREAC discussion in the same way that a statutory rule is addressed. Thus, once the topic and conclusion of your discussion is introduced, the complete rule or the relevant portion of the common law rule would be introduced and the key language quoted.

• Exercise 8-A

Read the *Sullivan* case facts, below, and answer the following:

(1) Would the court likely rule that Thomas should or should not take the proceeds of Jenny's life insurance policy? Explain.

(2) Based on your decision in (1), draft a common rule that adds to the rule, above, and now includes your decision in this case.

2. As set out in *Ford v. Ford*, 512 A.2d 389 (Md. 1986).

Facts in the *Sullivan* case:
Thomas and Jenny Sullivan live in Flora, East Carolina. For the last several years, Jenny has been fighting cancer. Recently her doctor told her nothing more could be done and she had only a few weeks to live. When asked about her condition during the upcoming weeks, the doctor reluctantly told her it would be difficult for her.

Once the doctor left the Sullivan home, Jenny asked her husband Thomas to buy some sleeping pills for her. She did not want to suffer anymore. Jenny and Thomas had been married for thirty years and were completely devoted to one another. Thomas went to the store, bought the pills, and went home. After spending some time together, Thomas gave the pills to Jenny, along with a glass of water. Jenny took the pills and passed away within the hour.

East Carolina does not have a law allowing assisted suicide. Thomas was arrested and convicted of voluntary manslaughter for Jenny's death. Jenny had a life insurance policy naming Thomas as the sole beneficiary. Jenny's siblings filed a lawsuit in the probate court, claiming Thomas should not benefit from Jenny's life insurance policy.

• Exercise 8-B

Read the following case excerpts and write the common law rule applied in each case in the fictitious state of East Carolina. Then write the common law rule that would apply in a future case in determining whether a landowner could be liable in negligence for injuries to a trespasser on the landowner's property. To complete this exercise, the rules applied in the cases must be synthesized into one single common law rule.

Case One: *McClain v. Painter*, 439 S.E.2d 555 (E.C. 1976)

On October 15, 1974, Sarah McClain was walking to school when she saw an apple tree on her neighbor's property, full of apples ready to be eaten. Since she didn't eat breakfast that day, she walked through the neighbor's gate, climbed the tree, and began shaking the limbs so apples would fall to the ground. As she was stretching out for some apples above her, the dead limb she was sitting on gave way, causing Sarah to fall to the ground, breaking her arm. Sarah's parents brought a negligence claim on behalf of Sarah against Jack Painter, owner of the property with the apple tree. Painter moved to dismiss the case, which was granted by the trial court and affirmed on appeal. We affirm the lower court's ruling.

It has been a long-standing rule that landowners owe no duty to trespassers. In this case there is no doubt that Sarah was not invited through the gate, up the tree, and onto the ground where she eventually landed. Sarah, as a trespasser, cannot recover from the landowner.

Case Two: *Sanders v. Kona Exports, Inc.*, 452 S.E.2d 1040 (E.C. 1982)

Kona Exports owns a coal mine in Salem, East Carolina. Seven-year-old Johnny Sanders lived in a housing development situated near the coal mine. Kona Exports left on its property equipment that was necessary to the mining business, including mining cars used to bring the coal out from the depths of the mine. The cars had brakes and locks that would disable the cars, preventing them from being moved. Unfortunately, the coal mine workers set the brakes but habitually failed to lock the cars at the end of each day.

Johnny and his friend, Tim Rider, would often go to the mine and play on the equipment left on the property. When the cars were locked, the boys would get inside a car and play around; on a couple of occasions, however, the children were there when the cars were unlocked, and they would take off the brake and push one another around. Mine supervisors saw the boys trespassing near the cars and other equipment; sometimes they told the boys to leave, and other times they did not.

On April 24, 1980, Johnny and his friends went onto the property and found the cars unlocked. Johnny climbed into one of the cars, and Tim Rider and some other friends rolled him around and into the mine. While they were inside, a mine wall collapsed, and Johnny died. Johnny's parents, Jim and Cady Sanders, filed a negligent wrongful death claim against the mine owners. The trial court dismissed the case, relying on the general rule that landowners owe no duty to trespassers. After the court of appeals affirmed the trial court's decision, the Sanders appealed.

Courts have long held that landowners are not liable to trespassers on their land. *McClain v. Painter*, 439 S.E.2d 555, 555 (E.C. 1976). However, Kona Exports keeps on its land machinery that is known to be dangerous and could be safeguarded. The landowner was also aware that children trespassed onto the land. Due to the nature of the condition and the knowledge by the landowner that children trespass on the land, a jury may find the landowner liable in negligence. The trial court's dismissal of this case is reversed, and the case is remanded for trial.

Case Three: *Vinson v. Hirokawa Imports*, 530 S.E.2d 12 (E.C. 2003)

Susie Vinson is fourteen years old and is of average intelligence for someone her age. She and her friends rode their skateboards onto a construction site of

Hirokawa Imports, located in Spring Valley, East Carolina. Hirokawa was building a warehouse to hold its goods. Workers neatly stacked the construction materials for the warehouse. Because some of the workers had seen children in the area before, the supervisor placed signs at multiple locations, instructing trespassers to stay off the construction site.

Susie decided to ride her skateboard across the top of some stacked construction materials. The construction materials were steel beams that were being used to build the main structure of the warehouse. The top of the stacked beams was approximately seven feet from the ground. Susie began climbing up the side of the stacked beams and had almost reached the top when they broke loose, falling down on top of Susie who was injured.

At trial the jury found for the plaintiff and awarded the Vinsons $100,000, which was affirmed by the court of appeals. We granted the appeal of Hirokawa Exports, Inc., and now reverse.

In this case the general rule that landowners owe no duty to those trespassing on their land applies. *McClain v. Painter*, 439 S.E.2d 555, 555 (E.C. 1976). A fourteen-year-old teenager who is of normal or above intelligence has the capacity to understand the danger that exists in going onto construction sites and playing on the materials left by the workers. These workers had no choice but to leave the materials on site, and they apparently tried to keep the materials stacked in an orderly manner. The supervisor also posted multiple "No trespassing" signs, which a fourteen-year-old of normal intelligence could easily read and understand. When a child is old enough and has sufficient intelligence to appreciate the danger on another's property, the landowner will not be held liable for the child trespasser's injuries. Reversed.

Case Four: *Jackson v. Wayne*, 560 S.E.2d 1224 (E.C. 2014)

Kenny Jackson, a five-year-old, often went with his parents to their next-door neighbors Waynes' swimming pool to swim. On June 23, 2013, Kenny was at home with his mother, Sylvia Jackson. Mrs. Jackson put Kenny down for a nap and went into another room to watch television. When Mrs. Jackson returned to the bedroom to check on Kenny, she found the bedroom window open and Kenny missing. Mrs. Jackson could see the swimming pool in the Waynes' yard from the open window; she also heard her neighbor, Maria Lopez, screaming. Mrs. Jackson ran next door and found Maria struggling to pull Kenny out of the pool; she seemed to have trouble getting Kenny up the steps. Eventually Kenny was rushed to the hospital for care. He survived but now suffers from brain damage.

In an affidavit, Ms. Lopez stated that she saw Kenny walk into the Waynes' open gate and toward the pool. She saw Kenny starting to walk down the pool steps but then slipped, causing him to fall and slide into the water. Ms. Lopez thought Kenny hit his head on the concrete steps. Upon inspection, the emergency workers found a slippery substance, later determined to be some kind of cleanser, at the top of the steps.

The Jacksons sued the Waynes and the judge granted the Waynes' motion for summary judgment, dismissing the case. The court of appeals affirmed, and the Jacksons have appealed.

There are conflicting policy reasons for allowing this case to go to trial. Courts used to hold that water was an open, apparent danger for which a landowner could not be held responsible. As the law has evolved, the rules have become less exact. Courts have more recently held that even if an injury occurs due to a water-related accident, if the landowner negligently maintains the water or the areas surrounding the water, the landowner may be held liable for the dangerous condition. *See, e.g., Chang v. Robinson*, 962 E.C. 43, 55 (E.C. 2007).

Courts also recognize, however, the need for parents to supervise their children, particularly those children of an age where they are unable to appreciate the potential dangerous consequences of their acts. At those times courts have found the parents and not the landowner responsible for the unfortunate injuries of their very young child. Although it's true that parents cannot supervise their children twenty-four hours a day, seven days a week, parents do have the responsibility to guide and protect those children, such as this five-year-old boy, who are too young to care for themselves.

In this case the facts were not clear as to whether the child's injuries were due to the water or the fall on the pool steps. There is also some question about whether the landowner negligently maintained the pool and whether the landowner knew or should have known about the dangerous condition near the pool. A landowner cannot be held liable for something of which they do not or should not know. Further, a jury must determine whether the parents' lack of supervision over their child prevents them from recovering from the landowner or at least reduces the damages awarded to the parents.

These cases must be decided on a case-by-case basis, carefully assessing the individual facts before the court. There are sufficient factual disputes in this case to warrant sending the case to trial. The lower court's decision is reversed, and the case is remanded.

• Exercise 8-C

Read the following case excerpts and write the common law rule applied in each case in the fictitious state of East Carolina. Then write the common law rule that would apply in a future case in determining who would keep an engagement ring after the engagement ends. Engagement rings are sometimes given to a future spouse in anticipation of marriage. To complete this exercise, the rules applied in the cases must be synthesized into one single common law rule.

Case One: *Smith v. Keener*, 754 S.E.2d 43 (E.C. Ct. App. 1998)

John Smith proposed to Sandy Keener and gave her an engagement ring. John and Sandy agreed that if something happened and they did not get married, Sandy would return the ring to John. Four months later, Sandy learned that John had been dating another woman. Sandy broke their engagement, and John then asked for the engagement ring back. Angry, Sandy refused to return the ring, and John brought a lawsuit to order its return. The trial court found that Sandy could keep the ring. John has appealed.

After a broken engagement, an explicit agreement made between the parties as to who will keep the ring should the engagement be broken will dictate ownership of the ring. It doesn't matter that John was unfaithful; Sandy must return the ring.

Reversed and remanded with instructions.

Case Two: *Jones v. Beck*, 782 S.E.2d 113 (E.C. Ct. App. 2001)

Sally Jones and Clint Clauson became engaged on February 14, 1998. They planned to be married on March 23, 1999; four weeks before the wedding Clint broke their engagement. After multiple efforts to get Sally to return the engagement ring, Clint sued. The lower court found for Clint and ordered Sally to return to Clint either the ring or its value. Sally now appeals.

Though jurisdictions address this issue in different ways, this court considers an engagement ring to be a conditional gift. When the condition—the engagement to be married—is broken, the ring must be returned to the donor, the one who gave the ring to the other.

Affirmed.

Case Three: *Singer v. Lansing*, 880 S.E.2d 409 (E.C. Ct. App. 2003)

Laura Lansing, a single twenty-five-year-old woman, began to date Jim Singer in the spring of 2001. At the time, Jim Singer was married to Nancy Singer. Jim promised Laura that he would get a divorce from his wife and marry Laura. To prove his commitment to Laura, he bought her an engagement ring. No wedding date was set, and, while he continued to express his love for Laura, Jim never took any steps to leaving his wife. After six months, Laura broke up with Jim, who then demanded that Laura return the engagement ring. When Laura refused, Jim sued. After Jim presented his case, the trial judge awarded Laura's motion for a directed verdict and dismissed the case, ruling that Jim had not sufficiently proved his case. Jim has appealed the trial court's decision.

Notions of equity dictate that the party seeking equitable relief (in this case the return of a ring) must come to court with "clean hands"; here the party seeking relief, Jim Singer, violated the bonds of marriage by engaging in an affair outside his own marriage. He did not, therefore, come to court with clean hands and is not in a position to ask a court to grant him any equitable relief.

Affirmed.

CHAPTER SUMMARY

- Common law rules are developed as multiple courts within the same jurisdiction apply the same legal principle set down in earlier binding cases to a new case addressing the same legal issue but with different case facts.
- To know what legal principle is relevant in a new case, a lawyer oftentimes must synthesize the holdings from multiple cases into a single rule.

CHAPTER

9

Beyond the Single CREAC: Structuring a Discussion of a Legal Issue Based on Its Applicable Test

A. Introduction

Analyzing legal issues would be easier if each analysis involved only a single question based on one simple CREAC organizational structure. This, however, is not the case. Legal tests may be created by a legislature in a statute or by an administrative agency required to establish rules based on a statute; the tests may also be created judicially through the development of the common law. A legal test that contains multiple requirements, all of which must be met to establish the test, is usually known as an elements analysis. A factors analysis, in contrast, has no specific requirements but weighs the strength of different factors to determine the outcome of a legal issue. In some instances, some factors, while not dispositive of the issue, may weigh more heavily than others. These are just two of the types of legal tests applied to determine the outcome of a legal issue.

Understanding the law and the tests the legislature or the courts have created is vital to an effective analysis and may create a different structure than in non-legal documents. This difference is due to how lawyers and judges solve problems when faced with litigation. In the broadest sense, lawyers and judges strive to resolve conflicts between parties. This definition is itself broad, however, because it includes non-lawyer problem solving such as what human resource professionals do. The more accurate definition of what lawyers and judges do is to try to solve conflicts between parties using the rules set by the legislature and the judiciary as the starting point.

The goal is to structure a legal analysis to reflect the approach courts in prior binding decisions have used in analyzing and answering a legal issue. If unsure how to structure a legal analysis, use the relevant court opinions as a guide. If the court separates its discussion of a legal test by elements or factors, for example, consider doing the same.

As stated in earlier chapters, one of the best guidelines to keep in mind is that legal writers bring in information only when it becomes most relevant to the legal reader. This is why CREAC serves as a logical checklist for an analysis. For example, when analyzing a rule of law that has both a general rule and one or more exceptions to the rule, logic dictates that you would address the general rule before analyzing any exceptions. Or, when analyzing a rule of law with its own multipart test, the multipart test creates the overall basic structure of the analysis. What follows are suggestions for the basic structure of an analysis, depending on the applicable legal test. The final structure will also depend on the cases chosen for the analysis, as well as whether any legal points are not in dispute.

B. Structuring an Elements Test

An elements analysis sets out specific requirements that must be met in order to satisfy a legal test. In Ana Hart's case addressing a covenant not to compete (CNC), the test to determine whether the CNC is reasonable is based on three elements (referred to in the case as "prongs"): "(1) the covenant cannot be broader than necessary for the protection of the buyer/covenantee in some legitimate interest, (2) the covenant cannot have an adverse effect on the seller, and (3) the covenant cannot have an adverse effect on the public interest." The basic structure of an elements analysis might initially look like the following.

(C) Conclusion	Predicted conclusion on the legal issue being addressed (within some factual context)
(R) Rule	Statement of the elements in the rule/legal test

At this point the overall rule and its requirements have been identified. If the definitions and explanations of all the cases relevant to the multiple requirements are explained next, the writer will likely confuse the reader because the writer is providing more information than the reader can grasp or remember. The writer, therefore, is not bringing in information where it is most helpful. Further, because the court must find either that *all* the requirements have been met to find the legal issue satisfied or, alternatively, that one of the requirements has *not* been met in order to find the legal issue is not satisfied, an element-by-element analysis is the most logical way to initially structure the objective analysis. The writer may decide later to move various sections around, but it is the most logical way to begin. The basic overall analysis of this legal issue with multiple requirements, therefore, is composed of the analysis of each legal requirement, each with its own CREAC checklist.

(A) Analysis/Application of the Law to the Facts

(1) conclusion:	Introduction and predicted conclusion regarding element #1
rule:	Any definition or explanation of element #1
explanation of rule:	Any case law relevant to explaining how the courts have analyzed and applied element #1 in different factual situations
analysis/application:	• Application of the law to the client's facts to support the predicted conclusion for element #1 • Transition to the application of the law to the client's facts to support the counteranalysis for element #1
conclusion:	Transition to the conclusion, explaining why the predicted conclusion is the court's likely outcome regarding element #1

(2) conclusion:	Introduction and predicted conclusion regarding element #2
rule:	Any definition or explanation of element #2
explanation of rule:	Any case law relevant to explaining how the courts have analyzed & applied element #2 in different factual situations
analysis/application:	• Application of the law to the client's facts to support the predicted conclusion for element #2 • Transition to the application of the law to the client's facts to support the counteranalysis for element #2
conclusion:	Transition to the conclusion, explaining why the predicted conclusion is the court's likely outcome regarding element #2

(3) conclusion:	Introduction and predicted conclusion regarding element #3
rule:	Any definition or explanation of element #3
explanation of rule:	Any case law relevant to explaining how the courts have analyzed & applied element #3 in different factual situations
analysis/application:	• Application of the law to the client's facts to support the predicted conclusion for element #3 • Transition to application of the law to the client's facts to support the counteranalysis for element #3
conclusion:	Transition to the conclusion, explaining why the predicted conclusion is the court's likely outcome regarding element #3

(C) Conclusion	Overall conclusion regarding the main legal issue, based on the conclusions regarding all three elements

Since finding that any one of the elements is not met will defeat a claim on that legal issue, again the most logical structure is to analyze each requirement separately from all other requirements. By following this structure, it's easier to understand the legal significance of the analysis.

> **Note:** One word of caution, however: If the predicted conclusion on the first element is that the element is likely *not* met, do not stop the analysis there. All three elements must be analyzed, since your supervising attorney or eventually a court might disagree with you and find that the first element has been met.

C. Structuring a Factors Test

The structure of a factors analysis often depends on the number and complexity of the factors used in determining the outcome of a legal issue. If a further breakdown of the factors is warranted, the structure of the factors analysis looks much like that of the elements analysis, with one additional component. After assessing the support for both positions on each factor, it is necessary to weigh the factors together to predict the likely outcome a court will reach regarding the legal issue. For example, many statutes covering residential burglary require that a burglary takes place in a dwelling. To determine whether a structure is considered a legal dwelling, courts consider factors such as (1) the composition or nature of the structure, (2) the use of the structure, and (3) the frequency of the use of the structure. Not all the factors need to be met in order to satisfy the dwelling requirement; instead, they are only considerations courts use to determine whether the building is considered a legal dwelling. One basic way to structure a factors analysis follows:

(C) Conclusion/Thesis:	Predicted conclusion on the legal issue provided within some factual context
(R) Rule:	Statement of the rule/legal test including relevant factors

(A) Analysis/Application of the Law to the Facts:

(1) conclusion:	Introduction to and predicted conclusion regarding which position factor #1 favors, if applicable
rule:	Any definition or explanation of factor #1, if applicable
explanation of rule:	Any case law relevant to explaining how the courts have analyzed & applied factor #1 in different factual situations
analysis/application:	• Application of the law to the client's facts to support the favored position for factor #1 • Transition to application of the law to the client's facts to support the counteranalysis for factor #1
conclusion:	Transition to explaining why the favored outcome is the court's likely outcome regarding factor #1, if applicable

(2) conclusion:	Introduction and predicted conclusion regarding which position factor #2 favors, if applicable
rule:	Any definition or explanation of factor #2, if applicable
explanation of rule:	Any case law relevant to explaining how the courts have analyzed & applied factor #2 in different factual situations
analysis/application:	• Application of the law to the client's facts to support the favored position for factor #2 • Transition to application of the law to the client's facts to support the counteranalysis for factor #2
conclusion:	Transition to explaining why the favored position is the court's likely outcome regarding factor #2, if applicable
(C) Conclusion:	Weighing/balancing factors #1 and #2 to determine whether, collectively, they support a finding that a court will likely find the legal test has or has not been met

Again, remember that the suggested organizational scheme above is not an absolute formula to be followed in all cases. Factors may be combined, or, if the number of factors is small and the analysis is straightforward, all factors might be analyzed together. One consideration in determining the structure is the actual factors at issue. If the factors are based on a fact rather than a legal term, it may be addressed fairly quickly. For example, when addressing a false imprisonment claim, one of the requirements is that the alleged victim be confined. One way to prove confinement is through a threat of physical force. To determine whether a threat of physical force existed, the court looks at factors such as (1) the actions of the defendant, (2) the relative size of the defendant compared to the size of the alleged victim, (3) the language and tone of the defendant's words, if applicable, and (4) the number of defendants compared to the number of alleged victims. These are all fact-based factors that can likely be addressed in a straightforward manner.

In contrast, factors are used to determine whether employees who normally are considered at-will employees who can be fired for any reason at any time have, in fact, elevated their status so they can be fired only for cause. The test is a factors test based on legal concepts. Those factors assess whether the employee (1) left permanent employment in the prior position, (2) was hired for permanent employment at the new position, and (3) was uniquely qualified for the position. All three of these factors require further defining, which means looking for definitions and case explanations to assist in understanding what permanent employment is and what constitutes being uniquely qualified. The discussion of these factors would require further explanation. Each factor could be addressed separately or both permanency factors could be analyzed together with a separate analysis for the "uniquely-qualified factor."

Determining the most logical structure is best achieved by reviewing the document from the reader's viewpoint. If upon review the draft is difficult to follow because factors have been combined, rewrite it, separating one or more factors. If, conversely, the review reveals that the factors are introduced separately in a way that makes the final weighing of the factors difficult to follow, rewrite it, combining one or more factors.

> **Note:** A good source when determining this structure is the relevant court opinions. If you find binding court decisions that tend to separate the factors in a consistent way, do that in your analysis as well. If, however, binding court opinions tend to group factors together, this is likely the best approach in your own analysis. The final decision may also depend on whether the factor is or is not in dispute. Chapter 10 addresses further how to include legal points that are relevant but not in dispute.

D. Structuring a Balancing Test

Some legal issues involve balancing the opposing parties' positions to determine which is stronger. This test is often used when assessing the validity of a constitutional claim. For example, let's say a citizen is prohibited from protesting on a courthouse lawn. To determine whether a citizen's First Amendment right to free speech under the U.S. Constitution has been violated, a court must weigh the government's interest in maintaining a peaceful and safe environment on public, governmental property against protesters' rights to express their political views. An example of the need to balance interests in a criminal case may occur when a police officer stops a suspect and searches the suspect's pockets, finding drugs. Since the police officer does not have a warrant to search the suspect, the defendant might move to suppress introducing the evidence of the drugs in court. The court must balance the governmental interest in bringing to justice criminals against the individual's right under the Fourth Amendment to be free from unwarranted governmental intrusions.

Balancing tests exist in state law issues as well. In a state nuisance action, for example, the court must weigh one family's complaint that the family's actions next door are intruding on the first family's right to peacefully enjoy their property against the neighbor family's right to use and enjoy their own property.

The structure of a balancing test might look like the following.

Conclusion/Thesis:	Predicted conclusion on legal issue, provided within some factual context
Rule:	Statement of the relevant balancing test
Explanation of Rule:	Description of relevant case law where courts applied the same balancing test in a similar factual situation (additional case law may also be introduced when the counteranalysis is introduced)

Analysis:	• Application of the law to the client's facts to support the predicted conclusion • Transition to the application of the law to the client's facts to support the counteranalysis
Conclusion:	Why, when weighing one party's interest against the other, the court is more likely to rule for the predicted conclusion

E. Structuring a Shifting Burdens of Proof Test

Sometimes deciding a legal issue includes both procedural and substantive components. For example, in a lawsuit where a female plaintiff who is fired sues her former employer for gender-based discrimination, the plaintiff employee bears the initial burden to show that the employer fired her for a discriminatory reason based on her gender. If the employee meets this initial burden, the burden then shifts to the defendant employer to prove a nondiscriminatory reason for firing the employee (such as tardiness or shoddy work). If the employer is able to meet that burden, the burden shifts again back to the employee, who then has an opportunity to prove that the employer's stated reason for firing the employee is really a pretext (or false reason) for the actual, discriminatory reason for being fired.[1] The structure of the analysis would follow the structure of the shifting burdens test, as follows.

(C) Conclusion:	Predicted conclusion regarding the legal test within some factual context
(R) Rule:	Statement of the shifting burdens of proof test (this example will cover two steps)

(A) Analysis/Application of the Law to the Facts:

conclusion	regarding the first burden of proof
rule:	any definitions or broad explanations of burden of proof #1
explanation	of any relevant cases where the court has applied the law to determine the outcome regarding burden of proof #1
analysis:	• application of the law to the client's facts to support the predicted conclusion • transition to the application of the law to the client's facts to support the counteranalysis
conclusion	regarding burden of proof #1, explaining why the court is likely to rule in favor of the predicted outcome

1. The burden of proof for indirect employment discrimination claims was established in *McDonnell Douglas Corp. v. Green*, 411 U.S. 792 (1973), and later clarified in *Tex. Dept. of Community Affairs v. Burdine*, 450 U.S. 248 (1981).

conclusion	regarding the second burden of proof
rule:	any definitions or broad explanations of burden of proof #2
explanation	of any relevant cases where the court has applied the law to determine the outcome regarding burden of proof #2
analysis:	• application of the law to the client's facts to support the predicted conclusion • transition to the application of the law to the client's facts to support the counteranalysis
conclusion	regarding burden of proof #2, explaining why the court is likely to rule in favor of the predicted outcome

(C) Conclusion: Overall predicted conclusion based on the conclusions on the two burdens of proof and answer to any question posed by the supervising attorney

Note: The above examples in the outlines refer only generally to the structure of an objective analysis based on the legal test. The examples do not include where to place specific information such as relevant public policy considerations. Placement of specific information depends on the specific questions raised and the extent of the relevant case law.

• Exercise 9-A

Each of the following cases sets down one or more legal tests that could be used as the basic structure for a legal analysis. Look up online and read each case, and determine:

(a) what legal test(s) the court applied in reaching its decision, noting where in the case you found each test; and
(b) how to outline the basic structure of each legal test.

1. *Mercury Vapor Processing Technologies, Inc. v. Village of Riverdale*, 545 F. Supp. 2d 783 (N.D. Ill. 2008)
2. *State v. Calmes*, 894 N.E.2d 199 (Ind. Ct. App. 2008)
3. *South/Southwest Ass'n of Realtors, Inc. v. Village of Evergreen Park*, 109 F. Supp. 2d 926 (N.D. Ill. 2006)
4. *Klunk v. County of St. Joseph*, 170 F.3d 772 (7th Cir. 1999)

F. Stipulations

Stipulations occur when opposing parties agree on the outcome of a legal point, eliminating the need to argue that point during the pretrial stage or at trial. For example, the statute of frauds' main provision requires that a sale of goods for more than $500 be in writing and signed by the party against whom enforcement is sought. If that provision is not met, however, an agreement might still be enforceable under the statute of frauds if one of the exceptions to the main provision is met, such as the exception that enforces an agreement if it involves specially manufactured goods that cannot be sold in the ordinary course of business and a substantial number of the goods have been completed. The parties might stipulate that the case involves goods that exceed $500 but not that there was a writing signed by the party against whom enforcement is sought. Or the parties might stipulate that the main provision of the statute of frauds has been met, focusing the dispute solely on whether the specially manufactured goods exception can be met. A fuller discussion of this statute of frauds exception is found in Chapter 10.

Stipulations may also take place when analyzing an elements test. For example, to prove that an enforceable contract exists, the plaintiff must prove there was (1) a valid offer, (2) a valid acceptance, and (3) consideration (the exchange of something of value between the parties). The parties might stipulate that there was a valid offer but dispute about the acceptance and consideration. Since this test comprises elements, stipulating that one element has been met does not defeat the claim. The defendant need only defeat one of the three elements to show there was no enforceable contract.

If a stipulation is reached on one of the parts of a legal test that's being analyzed, it still should be included in the discussion. Logically, once the main rule is presented, it's a good time to then set out any stipulations regarding any parts of that main rule. Be careful to not provide a stipulation *before* explaining the law, however; at that point the reader doesn't have any legal context for the stipulation and will likely not understand why the stipulation is legally relevant. For example, consider the following introduction:

Poor Example of the Placement of a Stipulation:

The covenant not to compete (CNC) that Ana Hart has been ordered by the court to sign as part of her divorce settlement is likely not to be enforced. David and Ana Hart own a series of Hart Fitness Centers. David petitioned for and the court ordered that David buy Ana's interest in the Centers at their fair market value and that Ana sell her interest in the Centers to David and sign a CNC. **Both parties agree that the sale of Ana's interest in the Centers does not affect the public interest.**

East Carolina courts apply a three-pronged test to determine whether a CNC signed as part of the sale of a business is unreasonable: "(1) the covenant must not be broader than necessary for the protection of the [buyer] covenantee's legitimate business interest; (2) the covenant cannot have an adverse effect on the [seller] covenantor; and (3) **the covenant cannot adversely affect the public interest.**" *Mats Transport v. ABC Corp.*, 824 S.E.2d 1467, 1468 (E.C. Ct. App. 1992).

If the reader does not know the law governing CNCs, the legal significance of the stipulation at the end of the first paragraph, "Both parties agree that the sale of the health club does not affect the public interest," will likely be confusing until the reader gets to the definition that includes the requirement that the covenant not "adversely affect the public interest." Since the information is provided out of order, the reader likely will have to go back and reread the earlier reference, so the facts are tied to the appropriate legal point. The better structure is to provide the stipulation immediately after providing the three-pronged test. Because the parties have stipulated that the third prong of the legal test has been met, an analysis of that prong is not required and the rest of the discussion and analysis can focus on the remaining two requirements. The more appropriate structure follows:

Good Example of the Placement of a Stipulation:

The covenant not to compete (CNC) that Ana Hart has been ordered by the court to sign as part of her divorce settlement is likely unenforceable. David and Ana Hart own a series of Hart Fitness Centers. David petitioned for and the court ordered that David buy Ana's interest in the Centers at their fair market value, and that Ana sell her interest in the Centers to David and sign a CNC.

East Carolina courts apply a three-pronged test to determine whether a CNC signed as part of the sale of a business is unreasonable: "(1) the covenant must not be broader than necessary for the protection of the [buyer] covenantee's legitimate business interest; (2) the covenant cannot have an adverse effect on the [seller] covenantor; and (3) **the covenant cannot adversely affect the public interest."** *Mats Transport v. ABC Corp.*, 824 S.E.2d 1467, 1468 (E.C. Ct. App. 1992). **Both parties agree that the sale of Ana's interest in the Centers does not affect the public interest.**

CHAPTER SUMMARY

- The structure of a legal analysis depends on the legal test used to resolve each legal issue.
- A legal test that requires an analysis of multiple elements, or requirements, is usually structured element by element.
- A legal test that requires an analysis of various factors, or considerations, is usually structured factor by factor, with the analyzed factors weighed together at the end to support the conclusion.
- A legal test that requires a balancing of the merits of each party's position is usually structured by first setting out the relevant law for each party and then

weighing one party's argument against the other to determine which position is stronger.

- Some legal tests require different parties to meet certain burdens of proof; once met, the burden then shifts to the opposing party to prove the next part of the legal test. The analysis tracks the shifting burdens of proof.
- Stipulations occur when parties agree on certain facts or a legal point, eliminating the need to establish those facts or legal points in the case.

CHAPTER

10

Analyzing the Law: Using Multiple Cases in Analyzing Multiple Issues

A. Introduction

Chapter 6 addresses how to analyze a single issue using a single case; Chapter 7 addresses how to analyze a single issue using multiple cases; and Chapter 9 addresses the various legal tests and basic outlines for each legal test. This chapter adds to the guidance from those chapters and focuses on how to analyze a client's case when it involves multiple issues and multiple cases. It also covers how to use one case in the analysis of multiple legal points.

To illustrate how to analyze a client's case when multiple issues and cases are involved, consider the following facts:

> James Eastridge, the president of Milton Hotels, with hotels worldwide, ordered special towels from Excel, Incorporated, for the women's locker rooms in the exercise clubs in his hotels. He placed this order with the president of Excel, Seong Li. Both corporations have offices in East Carolina. Excel manufactures and sells large quantities of towels to hotel chains such as Milton Hotels. Eastridge ordered 50,000

high-quality pink and purple towels, the colors used in the exercise clubs' women's locker rooms. The towels were to cost $500,000. The agreement was finalized through a series of email exchanges. One email followed a phone conversation and verified that Excel would add a stitched logo of a jogger on the lower left-hand corner of the towels. Following that conversation, Eastridge sent a quick email to Seong Li that said, "Good to talk with you today. I look forward to seeing what the jogger looks like!" Eastridge was later terminated from Milton Hotels for mismanagement of company funds. The new president, Carlton Warren, sent a fax to Excel, cancelling the contract. Excel tried for three months to sell the towels with the jogger logo, with no success. Since the cancellation, Excel has only been able to sell 1,000 of the 5,000 towels already manufactured by stitching over the jogger to make a large flower. Excel wants to sue Milton Hotels for breach of contract.

This contract is covered by the fictitious state of East Carolina's state law and specifically the East Carolina statute of frauds, which provides that "any contract (1) for the sale of goods that (2) exceeds $500 (3) must be in writing and (4) must be signed by the party against whom enforcement is sought."[1] This statute creates an elements analysis. If any one of the four elements of the statute of frauds is not met, another section of the statute of frauds creates an exception, stating that the contract may still be enforced if the manufacturer can prove the goods were specially manufactured for the buyer.

For the exception to the East Carolina statute of frauds to apply, the seller must prove three elements, that is, that "(1) the goods are to be manufactured specially for the buyer, (2) the goods are not suitable for sale to others in the ordinary course of the seller's business, and (3) the seller has made a substantial beginning of their manufacture prior to repudiation by the buyer."[2]

Thus, in *Excel*, the logical structure of a discussion section of an office memorandum would be to first analyze whether the main provision of the statute of frauds has been met, and then analyze whether, if the main provision of the statute has *not* been met, the contract can still be enforced under the specially manufactured goods exception, based on yet another elements analysis.

Analyzing both provisions requires addressing each of the three requirements for both the main provision and the exception to the statute of frauds separately. Even if the predicted conclusion is that one of the requirements is likely not met, all three requirements must be addressed in some way. This full analysis is necessary because a supervising attorney might disagree with the writer's predicted conclusion on one or more requirements.

1. E.C. STAT. § 26-1-2-201 (2010).
2. E.C. STAT. § 26-1-2-201(3)(a) (2010).

B. Using Multiple Cases to Analyze Multiple Legal Issues

This section discusses how to use case law where the opinion addresses more than one legal issue. For example, let's say the writer found three cases that are helpful in analyzing whether the client's case falls within the statute of frauds or, if not, meets the specially manufactured goods exception to the statute of frauds. Each of the courts in these three cases, however, did not address both rules or all the requirements within one of the rules. This might happen when a court finds that one of the elements is not met, so the court need not address the remaining elements. Alternatively, when certain points are obviously met in a case, a court might just state that conclusion with no reasoning.

Keeping in mind that information is best introduced only when it is most relevant to the reader, a good step is to chart the relevant case law within the legal test being analyzed. This chart will help reveal the overall structure of any legal test as well as which cases are relevant to each legal point within the legal test. First, read the following case excerpts:[3]

Case One: *Savilla Manufacturing v. American Crate Co.*, 778 S.E.2d 1045 (E.C. 1995)

Seller Savilla Manufacturing orally agreed to set up a cleat manufacturing plant in Honduras, in order to sell cleats to crate manufacturer American Crate Company. Cleats are the pieces of wood placed on the bottom of crates to raise the crate off the ground. In return, American Crate agreed to purchase all the cleats Savilla could produce from that plant. The only evidence of this oral agreement was a vague letter missing key terms that was written by Juan Carlos, president of Savilla, and signed by American Crate's president, Dave Dormand. About one year after Savilla began production, Dormand refused to purchase Savilla's entire output of cleats. After failing to find other purchasers, Savilla went out of business and sued American Crate Company and Dormand.

The lower court appropriately ruled that the signed letter was not a "contract for sale" and did not satisfy the writing requirement of the statute of frauds since it was missing key terms the two parties discussed orally but did not memorialize in writing. The only relevant exception to the writing requirement is the specially manufactured goods exception to the statute of frauds. The specially manufactured goods exception requires the seller to prove three elements, that is, that "(1) the goods are to be manufactured specially for the buyer, (2) the goods are not

3. The three hypothetical cases from the fictitious state of East Carolina are based on *Maderas Tropicales v. S. Crate & Veneer*, 588 F.2d 971 (5th Cir. 1979), *Bloom & Son, Inc. v. Kameyama, U.S.A., Inc.*, 1984 WL 560329 (R.I. Super. Ct. Dec. 4, 1984), and *Coca-Cola Co. v. Babyback's International, Inc.*, 841 N.E.2d 557 (Ind. 2006).

suitable for sale to others in the ordinary course of the seller's business, and (3) the seller has made a substantial beginning of their manufacture prior to repudiation by the buyer." E.C. § 26-1-2-201(3)(a) (2010).

The cleats were not so unusual as to qualify for this exception. The cleats were mere wooden sticks that form the frame of a crate. The crates were not so unusual or special that their manufacture would support the existence of a contract for their sale to a particular buyer without written proof, as required by the statute of frauds. The lower court also noted, and we agree, that the cleats were not manufactured specifically for American Crate, as evidenced by the fact that Savilla was able to sell one container of the 100 containers of cleats to a different crate company without altering them in any way. The lower court's ruling is affirmed.

Case Two: *By Special Order, Inc. (BSO) v. Hayakawa, Inc.*, 998 S.E.2d 587 (E.C. 2003)

This case involves the application of the specially manufactured goods exception to the statute of frauds. Apparently the manufacturer, By Special Order, Inc. (BSO), entered into an oral agreement with the buyer, Yuki Hayakawa, president of Hayakawa, Inc., to design, construct, and mass produce custom candle rack fixtures. BSO manufactures custom-designed retail store fixtures of all kinds. Hayakawa required BSO to first produce prototypes for Hayakawa's approval. Prototypes are original models designed and created prior to the mass production of the goods. On three occasions, the president of BSO, James Williams, informed Hayakawa over the phone that the construction of the prototype racks would be expensive. Williams on each occasion also said that if Hayakawa decided *not* to purchase a substantial number of the racks after the prototypes had been constructed, then Hayakawa would have to reimburse BSO for the cost of their construction. Hayakawa specified the desired dimensions of the racks to Williams, and Williams had sketches drafted of the prototypes, which were approved by Hayakawa's agent. Hayakawa then instructed Williams to continue with the construction of the prototypes, which cost $2,750. Hayakawa's representatives also approved the completed prototypes. After several weeks, Williams had still not received an order for the fixtures, so he mailed a bill to Hayakawa for $2,750 for the prototypes. Hayakawa refused to pay.

The lower court found the specially manufactured goods exception was met in this case, and we agree. The specially manufactured goods exception requires that the manufacturer prove three elements, that is, that "(1) the goods are to be manufactured specially for the buyer, (2) the goods are not suitable for sale to others in the ordinary course of the seller's business, and (3) the seller has made a substantial beginning of their manufacture prior to repudiation by the buyer." E.C. § 26-1-2-201(3)(a) (2010).

BSO would be unable to sell the prototypes to another purchaser in the ordinary course of its business. The very nature of its name, "By Special Order," suggests that the company was not in the candle fixture business and did not have any potential buyers for the prototypes. The crucial inquiry is whether the manufacturer could sell the goods in the ordinary course of its business to someone other than the original buyer. If with slight alterations the goods could be sold, then they are not considered specially manufactured. If, however, the goods could be sold only after the seller made essential changes to them, then the goods are considered specially manufactured and fall within the statute's exception. The prototypes for the candle racks were manufactured according to Hayakawa's design specifications and approved by the company's representatives, supporting their being specially manufactured. Further, the evidence supports that BSO could not have resold the prototypes in the ordinary course of business to any of its customers. The candle racks could not be altered for resale, even with significant alterations. Affirmed.

Case Three: *Sparkling Sodas, Inc. v. Hilliard Corp.*, 1029 S.E.2d 53 (E.C. 2010)

This case addresses whether a memo faxed from Sparkling Sodas to Hilliard, Incorporated, a restaurant chain, was sufficient to establish the existence of a contract or a memorandum describing a final contract; if not, it did not satisfy the statute of frauds. The statute of frauds, created to avoid any fraud in a transaction, requires that "any contract (1) for the sale of goods that (2) exceeds $500 (3) must be in writing and (4) must be signed by the party against whom enforcement is sought." E.C. § 26-1-2-201 (2010). The faxed memo in this case addressed the potential ongoing relationship between the two companies, including the phrase, "We have made further strides toward coming to an agreement," and referring to "the complexities that must be worked through."

There was no written contract signed by a representative of Hilliard, only the faxed memo. The faxed memo, though signed by Hilliard's representative, did not reflect a final contract that included the necessary essential terms; the language of the fax merely suggested that negotiations were still taking place and the agreement had not been finalized. Thus, the statute of frauds was not satisfied, and any agreement will only be enforced if the specially manufactured goods exception to the statute of frauds is met. The specially manufactured goods exception requires that the seller prove three elements, that is, that "(1) the goods are to be manufactured specially for the buyer, (2) the goods are not suitable for sale to others in the ordinary course of the seller's business, and (3) the seller has made a substantial beginning of their manufacture prior to repudiation by the buyer." E.C. § 26-1-2-201(3)(a) (2010).

The sale here involved the sale of a soda product. Soda products are not produced specially for any one buyer. Further, there is no reason why this product can't be resold easily in the company's ordinary course of business, since Sparkling Sodas is in the business of selling soda products. This product does not fall within the specially manufactured goods exception to the statute of frauds, and the lower court's ruling that no enforceable contract existed is affirmed.

C. *Including Case Explanations Where They Are Most Helpful*

When a single case is relevant to more than one legal requirement, as in this example, you must decide where to explain the relevant facts, holding, and reasoning of each case. If everything is explained about all three cases at the beginning of the discussion, including all the information from each case that is relevant to both the main provision and the statutory exception to the statute of frauds, the reader is likely to get overloaded with too much information. The reader may very well need to return to the case explanations at the beginning of the discussion when reading about a later requirement discussed in the same case, to determine which facts, and which parts of the court's holding and reasoning are relevant to that later requirement.

The preferred method is to explain any relevant case within the CREAC of each legal issue or requirement. When charting the cases for the statutory exception, for example, the key *facts*, the court's *holding*, and the court's *reasoning* (F/H/R) relevant to whether the goods are specially manufactured, the first requirement, will likely be different from the key *facts*, the court's *holding*, and the court's *reasoning* for whether the goods are suitable for sale in the ordinary course of business, and whether there has been a substantial beginning of manufacturing the goods prior to the buyer's repudiation.

Thus, the chart to show how each case could be used when analyzing the statutory exception might look like the following:

ELEMENTS → **AUTHORITY ↓**	**1. GOODS MUST HAVE BEEN SPECIALLY MANUFACTURED FOR BUYER**	**2. GOODS ARE NOT SUITABLE FOR SALE IN THE ORDINARY COURSE OF BUSINESS**	**3. SELLER UNDERWENT SUBSTANTIAL BEGINNING OF MANUFACTURE PRIOR TO REPUDIATION**
Savilla	F/H/R re: whether the goods were specially manufactured for the buyer	F/H/R re: whether the goods were suitable for sale in the ordinary course of business	
BSO	F/H/R re: whether the goods were specially manufactured for the buyer	F/H/R re: whether the goods were suitable for sale in the ordinary course of business	All protoypes were completed and worth $2,750
S. Sodas	F/H/R re: whether the goods were specially manufactured for the buyer	No question soda suitable for resale in the ordinary course of business	

Figure 10-1

When first explaining a case, provide not only the key facts, the court's holding, and the court's reasoning regarding the specific legal point you are addressing but also the overall holding in the case. For example, if you first explain *Savilla* when providing the CREAC for the requirement that the goods be "specially manufactured for the buyer," you would also include whether the court found that the specially manufactured goods exception to the statute of frauds was met. In addition, when first explaining a case, provide any background information necessary to put the case in the proper factual context so your reader understands the story.

D. Creating a Fact Chart When Analyzing a Fact-Based Issue

Creating a chart can also be helpful when determining which facts from the cited cases to compare or contrast to the facts of the client's case in the analysis. Charting was first introduced in Chapter 6 and again in Chapter 7. For example, let's say you are addressing whether in *Excel* the goods fall within the specially manufactured goods exception to the statute of frauds, introduced earlier in the chapter. Jim Eastridge asked that Excel manufacture pink and purple towels with a jogger logo on them.

When analyzing whether the pink and purple towels could be resold in the ordinary course of business (one of the requirements to prove the goods were specially manufactured), an example of a chart with the facts of *Excel* plus the three cases relevant for the analysis might look like the following:

Requirement 2 of the statutory exception: Whether the goods could be resold in the ordinary course of business

SAVILLA	**EXCEL (client)**	***BSO***
• Wooden cleats for crates (seller cleat manufacturer)	• **Pink & purple towels with jogger logo (seller towel manufacturer)**	• Prototypes of candle-rack fixtures (seller makes fixtures according to buyer specifications)
• Cleats not unusual or special	• **Oral evidence that buyer specifically requested colors & with jogger logo**	• Evidence that prototype designed to buyer's specification and with buyer's approval • Evidence that seller told buyer must pay for prototypes if substantial number of fixtures not purchased
• Seller was able to sell one container of cleats out of 100 to different crate company without alteration; could be resold in ordinary course of business	• **Excel sold 1,000 of 5,000 towels manufactured 3 months after stitching over jogger logo with a flower**	• Seller would be unable to sell prototypes in ordinary course of business without making significant changes

Figure 10-2

E. Preparing the Support for Each Party

For the analysis of each requirement, the same approach will apply as what was introduced in Chapters 6 and 7. That is, after explaining the relevant case(s), the writer will compare favorably the facts of any cited case to the facts of the client's case where the outcome favors a party's position and contrast the facts of any case from the facts of the client's case where the outcome favors the opposing party's position. For example, in the analysis section providing support for why Excel's towels *could* be resold in the ordinary course of business, the writer would compare favorably the relevant facts of the client's case to the relevant facts in *Savilla* and *Sparkling Sodas*, where the courts also found the goods could be resold in the ordinary course of business, and contrast or distinguish the relevant facts of the client's case from the relevant facts in *BSO*, where the court found the goods could not be resold.

Conversely, when providing support for why Excel's towels could *not* be resold in the ordinary course of business, the writer would compare favorably the relevant facts of the client's case to the relevant facts in *BSO*, and contrast or distinguish the relevant facts of the client's case from the relevant facts in *Savilla* and *Sparkling Sodas*, to support the argument that the towels could not be resold in the ordinary course of business.

F. Establishing the Basic Structure When Addressing Multiple Issues

When researching and drafting an objective discussion, always think about the basic structure of the document. In the example, where the applicable tests create an elements analysis, each element is analyzed in its entirety before moving to the next element. When discussing whether the agreement meets the main provision of the statute of frauds as well as the requirements of the specially manufactured goods exception, the requirements would be introduced with a roadmap in the introduction followed by a separate discussion (as much of a CREAC checklist as is necessary) of each of the requirements for each provision. Only after this complete analysis can the predicted conclusion be reached.

The large-scale structure for the issues raised in *Excel, Inc. v. Milton Hotels* would be:

I. Does the sale of the towels by Excel to Milton Hotels meet the statute of frauds?

(1) Must be a sale of goods;
(2) The sale must exceed $500;
(3) The agreement must be in writing; and

(4) The writing must be signed by the party against whom enforcement is sought.

II. If the main provision of the statute of frauds is not met, is the agreement enforceable under the specially manufactured goods exception to the statute of frauds?

(1) The goods must be specially manufactured for the buyer;

(2) The goods must not be suitable for sale in the company's ordinary course of business; and

(3) The manufacturer/seller must have made a substantial beginning of the manufacture of the goods prior to repudiation by the buyer.

G. Providing Roadmaps When Addressing Multiple Issues

Prior chapters discuss what to provide in a roadmap. The decision about *where* to provide information in the discussion of an office memorandum becomes more complex when addressing multiple legal issues or subissues. If addressing whether there's an enforceable contract under the statute of frauds, for example, the introductory roadmap will introduce the statute of frauds as well as the specially manufactured goods exception without including the requirements for each rule. Instead, at the beginning of the CREAC of each of the rules, the specific requirements of each rule will be presented, providing a roadmap of what's to follow.

When addressing multiple legal points, such as separate requirements, provide a CREAC checklist for each point separately. Further, wait to explain the case law relevant to each requirement within the CREAC of that requirement. In conclusion, if addressing more than one issue, and each issue has its own subissues, such as requirements, include multiple roadmaps: one in the main introduction and additional roadmaps at the beginning of each legal issue discussed.

An example of a roadmap in the overall introduction of *Excel, Inc. v. Milton Hotels* follows:

> A court is likely to find the agreement between Excel, Inc., and Milton Hotels enforceable under East Carolina's statute of frauds. The president of Milton Hotels ordered from Excel, Inc., special towels for the exercise clubs in his chain of hotels. The request for the towels, including their pink and purple color and a jogger logo, was made through a series of email exchanges. When Milton Hotels canceled the order, Excel had completed 5,000 of the 50,000 towels ordered. Enforceability under the statute of frauds is likely. While the writings likely do not meet the main rule of the statute of frauds, the agreement falls within an exception to the statute of frauds because the towels would be considered specially manufactured goods.

H. Addressing Requirements Not in Dispute

Analyzing a legal rule that includes its own requirements might disclose that not all parts of the legal rule are in dispute. However, if the indisputable point is a requirement that must be satisfied, it must also be established in the discussion of the office memorandum. The guideline is to provide as much of the CREAC checklist as is necessary. To do so when addressing an indisputable legal point:

- **(C)** State the conclusion on the requirement;
- **(R)** If applicable and necessary, provide any relevant rule, including any relevant definitions or explanations of the rule;
- **(E)** If applicable and necessary, provide any case explanations relevant to the rule;
- **(A)** Apply the rule to the facts in the client's case to support what is the obvious (not just predicted) conclusion; and
- **(C)** if necessary, again conclude. If establishing this indisputable point is short, it's likely a second conclusion is not needed.

For example, the main provision of the statute of frauds requires that (1) the agreement involves a sale of goods, (2) the goods cost more than $500, (3) the agreement includes a writing sufficient to indicate that a contract for sale has been made between the parties, and (4) the writing be signed by the party against whom enforcement is sought.[4] Establishing in *Excel* that the agreement for the sale of the exercise club towels involves (1) a sale of goods that (2) exceeds $500 is quite easy. Since they are both requirements, however, each requirement must be established as part of the analysis. The writer would need only set out the statute of frauds language and then match the legal requirements (sale of goods over $500) with the facts of the client's case (towels to be sold for $500,000).

Some indisputable legal points require a more extensive discussion. The extent of the discussion of an indisputable issue depends on the point being addressed. For example, in another statute of frauds case, if Grantham Carpet Company not only sold carpet but also provided the installation of that carpet, any subsequent dispute would involve not only the sale of goods but also the performance of services. Research reveals that in the controlling jurisdiction a supreme court case ruled that when both sales and services are involved in a contract dispute, the agreement falls within the statute of frauds, and the statute of frauds must be satisfied as though the entire agreement involved only a sale of goods.[5] The requirement that the agreement in dispute involves a sale of goods is now not so clear but is still not in dispute, based on the supreme

---

4. E.C. STAT. § 26-1-2-201 (2010).
5. *See Colo. Carpet Installation, Inc. v. Palermo*, 668 P.2d 1384 (Colo. 1983).

court case. To establish this indisputable issue, the supreme court case must be explained, to show that even though the Grantham Carpet case involves both sales and services, it falls within the statute of frauds.

After setting out the rule explaining the main provision of the statute of frauds, the CREAC checklist for the Grantham Carpet case on this point would look like the following:

> **C**—Does a contract involving both sales of goods and services fall within the statute of frauds requirement that the contract involve a sale of goods?
>
> **RE**—Rule explanation (F/H/R) of the supreme court case establishing that an agreement involving both a sale of goods and a sale of services falls within the statute of frauds as a sale of goods.
>
> **A**—Grantham Carpet's case involves a combination of a sale of goods and a sale of services, as in the controlling supreme court case.
>
> **C**—Therefore, as a sale of goods the contract falls within the statute of frauds.

I. Setting the Final Structure of the Document

A legal test provides the basic structure of a legal analysis. However, the discussion of the test may change depending on the facts of a client's case, which parts of the legal test are in dispute, and which parts are not in dispute.

First and foremost, if the law dictates a certain structure, follow it. For example, threshold issues must be discussed first. In a statute of frauds case, the writer would first address whether the main provision of the statute of frauds has been met before addressing whether the specially manufactured goods exception to the statute of frauds is met. In another example, focusing on a contracts case, the questions in the case might be (1) whether the statute of limitations period to file a lawsuit has passed, and (2) if not, whether the contract is enforceable.[6] If a judge determines the statute of limitations has passed, the case will not proceed, the contract dispute is irrelevant, and the judge will dismiss the case. Logic, therefore, dictates that the procedural statute of limitations question is addressed before analyzing the substantive issues in the contracts claim.

Should the court decide the statute of limitations had not passed, and the breach of contract claim is addressed, there are three requirements that must be met to enforce the contract. There must be (1) a valid offer, (2) a valid acceptance, and (3) consideration.[7] It would make the most sense to follow

6. The statute of limitations period for most contract actions is two years.

7. Consideration is an agreement to exchange performances or promises between two or more parties that requires the parties to act, forbear from acting, or give up a present or future right. *See* RESTATEMENT (SECOND) OF CONTRACTS § 71.

chronological order, if applicable, addressing the valid offer requirement before addressing whether the seller validly accepted that offer. The placement of the consideration requirement, however, is not dictated by logic in the same way and may be introduced either before or after the analysis of the offer and acceptance requirements.

One last example of a legal issue that might logically dictate an order for the analysis occurs when the law in the jurisdiction is not settled. The initial question the court must answer, therefore, is which rule of law to apply to the client's case. Only after that decision is made can the court apply the correct rule of law to the particular facts of the client's case to determine the outcome.

If the structure of an analysis is not dictated by the law or by logic, consider using one of the following organizational patterns:

- Present the indisputable points first, followed by the disputable points; or
- Present the legal points in the order in which they are provided in the legal test, regardless of whether they are disputable or indisputable.

What follows is an annotated sample discussion of an office memorandum for the potential statute of frauds case between Excel, Incorporated and Milton Hotels.

A court is likely to find the agreement for Excel, Incorporated, to sell 50,000 towels to Milton Hotels enforceable under East Carolina's statute of frauds. Through a series of email exchanges, the president of Milton Hotels, James Eastridge, communicated with Seong Li, the president of Excel, about selling 50,000 towels to Eastridge for his hotels. The high-quality towels were to be pink and purple with a jogger logo. Enforceability under the statute of frauds is likely because (1) while the writings between the two parties do not meet the main provision of the statute of frauds, (2) the agreement falls within the specially manufactured goods exception to the statute of frauds.

> This paragraph begins with the conclusion, introduces the parties, and provides a roadmap to the two issues that are to follow.

I. The Main Provision of the Statute of Frauds

The series of exchanges between the two company presidents were insufficient to satisfy the statute of frauds, which requires that "any *contract* (1) for the sale of goods that (2) exceeds $500 (3) be in writing and (4) must be signed by the party against whom enforcement is sought." (*Emphasis added.*) E.C. Code § 26-1-2-201(3) (2010). *See Sparkling Sodas, Inc. v. Hilliard Corporation*, 1029 S.E.2d 53, 53 (E.C. 2010). There's no question that the agreement

> The two issues are identified with headings. The first sentence provides the conclusion on the first issue, followed by the rule. The rest of the paragraph establishes the first three requirements that are not in dispute.

between Excel and Milton Hotels involved a sale of goods, towels, and that the price for the towels exceeded $500, since the price discussed was $500,000. Further, the terms were written in a series of emails, satisfying the writing requirement. However, the content of the emails exchanged between Excel and Milton Hotels do not support a final agreement between the parties.

A formal, signed letter isn't always required to prove the statute of frauds has been met when the agreement, as in this case, is between merchants. *Sparkling Sodas*, 1029 S.E.2d at 54. Key is that the parties' actions reflect their intent to enter into an agreement. *Id.* The court in *Sparkling Sodas* found a faxed memo from the president of a restaurant to the seller, the president of a soda company, insufficient evidence of such an agreement. *Id.* The two presidents had discussed engaging in a long-term relationship where the soda company would provide the buyer with a continuous supply of sodas. The faxed memo from the restaurant's president included language about the two companies' potential ongoing relationship, including the phrase, "We have made further progress towards coming to an agreement," and referring to "the complexities that must be worked through." *Id.* The court affirmed the lower court's ruling that the main provision of the statute of frauds had not been met, finding in part that the faxed memo, though signed by the restaurant's president, only reflected ongoing negotiations between the parties and did not support an intent to enter a final agreement. *Id. See also*, *Savilla Manufacturing v. American Crate Co.*, 778 S.E.2d 1045 (E.C. 1995) (finding a vague letter that did not include key terms the parties previously discussed orally insufficient to support a final agreement).

This paragraph further explains the main provision and explains *Sparkling Sodas* (F/H/R). It ends with a parenthetical to a second case, *Savilla*.

The mail exchanges between Milton Hotels and Excel also did not satisfy the main provision of the statute of frauds. In both *Sparkling Sodas* and this case the exchanged correspondence never included language reflecting agreed-upon final terms. Just like the faxed memo in *Sparkling Sodas* that included only phrases to support ongoing negotiations, including making further progress toward coming to an agreement, Eastridge, in his last email to Seong Li, stated, "I look forward to seeing what the jogger looks like!" This reference infers that Eastridge was looking forward to seeing the jogger logo sometime in the future, not that he agreed ahead of time to whatever logo Excel produced.

This paragraph provides the analysis for the predicted conclusion, by comparing this case to the facts in *Sparkling Sodas*. This is treated as an issue that's also not in dispute but requires further analysis than the other requirements, above.

The only way a court might find the statute of frauds was met would be if there was evidence that these two companies' relationship was such that Eastridge would, indeed, trust that Excel would create a logo that he would approve without seeing the final product. However, this seems highly unlikely. Without more information, there's no evidence in this case to support that the exchanged emails between the two presidents reflected a final agreement. Therefore, this agreement will be enforced only if it meets the specially manufactured goods exception to the statute of frauds.

This last paragraph concludes the issue by stating that, without more evidence, the main provision is not met, transitioning to the statutory exception.

II. The Specially Manufactured Goods Exception to the Statute of Frauds

This agreement likely falls within the specially manufactured goods exception to the statute of frauds. To prove the exception applies, the seller must prove that "(1) the goods are manufactured specially for the buyer, (2) the goods are not suitable for sale to others in the ordinary course of the seller's business, and (3) the seller has made a substantial beginning of their manufacture prior to repudiation by the buyer." E.C. Code § 26-1-2-201(3)(a) (2010).

This paragraph provides the predicted conclusion for the exception and the rule.

The high-quality pink and purple towels with a jogger logo ordered were made specially, according to Milton Hotels specifications as relayed by Eastridge, establishing the first requirement. Further, Excel made a substantial beginning in manufacturing the towels prior to the repudiation, satisfying the third requirement. The percentage of towels ordered that were completed may be considered relatively low, that is, 5,000 towels, or ten percent of the 50,000 towels ordered, but the sale price of the 5,000 high-quality towels at $10.00 each is $50,000. In *BSO*, the candle-rack prototypes were completed, but the cost was much lower, at $2,750. While not all the special towels were produced, as were the prototypes in *BSO*, a $50,000 investment would be considered a substantial beginning toward fulfilling the order. Therefore, the specially manufactured exception will be met if a court finds the towels could not be resold in the ordinary course of business.

This paragraph establishes the 2 requirements that are not in dispute, transitioning to the requirement in dispute.

The court is likely to find the towels Milton Hotels ordered could not be resold in the ordinary course of business. The test to determine whether goods can be resold is the degree to which alterations must be made to make the product marketable. *By Special Order, Inc. (BSO) v. Hayakawa, Inc.*, 998 S.E.2d 587, 588 (E.C. 2003). If "with

This paragraph begins with the predicted conclusion and explains the disputable requirement.

slight alterations the goods could be sold, then they are not considered specially manufactured." *Id.* However, if it was necessary to make "essential changes" to the goods, then they would fall within the statutory exception. *Id.*

The specially manufactured goods exception to the statute of frauds is met when, as in *BSO,* the produced goods are so specialized that no alteration would make them marketable. *Id.* at 589. In *BSO*, the presidents of two companies agreed orally that the manufacturer would "design, construct, and mass produce" custom candle-rack fixtures. *Id.* The manufacturer custom-designed store fixtures for retail businesses. The candle company's president requested that prototype racks be produced for his approval. Prototypes are original models designed and created prior to any mass production of the goods. The manufacturer agreed but emphasized multiple times to the candle company's president that the prototypes would be costly; as a result, the candle company would be obligated to pay $2,750 for the prototypes if it did not subsequently order a substantial number of the racks. The prototypes were produced according to the candle company's specifications after the president or his representatives approved not only the sketches of the prototypes but later the actual prototypes. After several weeks without an order, the manufacturer's president billed the candle company for $2,750. The candle company's president refused to pay. The court found that due to the special nature of the prototypes, coupled with the specialized nature of the company, which was to build fixtures for each individual customer, the manufacturer would be unable to sell any of the prototypes to its customers, and any change necessary to sell the models would require significant alterations. *Id.* Therefore, the exception to the statute of frauds applied. *Id.*

This paragraph provides a case explanation (F/H/R) of *BSO.*

In contrast, manufactured cleats, small pieces of wood used underneath crates to elevate them off the ground, did not fall within the specially manufactured goods exception. *Savilla,* 778 S.E.2d at 1047. The court found the cleats were not "so special or unusual that their manufacture supported the existence of a contract for sale to a particular buyer without written proof, as required by the statute of frauds." *Id.* Further, the cleat manufacturer had been able to sell one of the 100 containers manufactured for the crate company without making any changes, supporting the conclusion that they could be resold in the ordinary course of business. *Id.*

This paragraph provides a case explanation (F/H/R) of *Savilla.*

While towels would usually be considered a product that could be easily resold in the ordinary course of business, similar to the sodas in *Sparkling Sodas* and the cleats in *Savilla*, the high-quality towels Milton Hotels ordered and the 5,000 towels Excel produced could not be resold as is in the ordinary course of Excel's business, in contrast to the sodas in *Sparkling Sodas* and the cleats in *Savilla*, which could be resold without alteration. Unlike in *Savilla*, where the goods were mere sticks of wood, and in *Sparkling Soda*, where the goods were sodas, here the high-quality towels for Milton Hotel were produced according to the specifications of Milton Hotel's president, that is, in purple and pink colors, the colors used in the women's dressing rooms in the exercise clubs, with a jogger in the lower corner of each towel. The high-quality nature of the towels, along with the colors and the specific jogger logo, severely limited the number of Excel's customers that might be willing to purchase the towels as is. In fact, none of the towels were sold in their original form, and only 1,000 of the 5,000 could be sold after stitching over the jogger logo to make a flower. Excel's situation is more similar to that in *BSO*. The time and expense for the extra stitching of the 5,000 towels could arguably be considered an "essential change," similar to the candle rack prototypes in *BSO*, which were produced according to the buyer's specifications, and, as the court found, could not be sold without "significant alterations." *BSO*, 998 S.E.2d at 588.

This paragraph begins with the predicted conclusion and then provides support by contrasting *Excel*'s facts from those in *Savilla* and comparing them to the facts in *BSO*. *Note:* No cite is needed when comparing/contrasting facts, only when referring to what the court found.

However, a court might find the towels could be resold in the ordinary course of business if it focuses on the business of Excel and the nature of the goods. In *BSO*, the nature of the company's business was to produce special orders for retail displays, which is reflected in the name of the company, "By Special Order." In fact, the candle company was the first to request from BSO prototypes specifically for candle-rack fixtures. This is arguably different from *Excel*, where the nature of Excel's business is to manufacture towels, which is what the hotel chain ordered, similar to the manufacturer in *Savilla*, where the business was to manufacture wooden cleats, which is what the crate manufacturer ordered, and in *Sparkling Sodas*, where the business was to produce the requested sodas.

This paragraph transitions to the counteranalysis, here by contrasting *Excel*'s facts from those in *BSO* and comparing them to the facts in *Savilla* and *Sparkling Sodas*. Notice the use of "Excel," a party in the client's case, and the generic term "candle company," a party in a cited case.

Further, the court in *Savilla* considered cleats a product that could easily be resold, since it had resold one of the 100 containers produced for the crate company without any alteration. *Savilla*, 778 S.E.2d at 1046. A court might find that stitching the flower over the jogger is only a slight alteration, unlike the significant alteration of the candle racks required in *BSO*. The alteration affected only the lower left corner of the towel, and in that condition could be resold, evidenced by Excel's selling 1,000 of the 5,000 completed towels, once altered. In fact, while in *Savilla* the company resold only ten percent of the cleats, Excel was able, arguably with slight alterations, to resell twenty percent of those towels produced, supporting Excel's ability to resell the towels in the ordinary course of business.

This paragraph provides further support for the counteranalysis.

Nevertheless, the court in *BSO* required only that the manufacturer try to resell its product to *its customers*. *BSO*, 998 S.E.2d at 587. The court stated in its opinion, "The evidence suggests [the manufacturer] could not have resold the prototypes to any of *its customers*. . . ." (*Emphasis added*.) *Id*. This suggests that the manufacturer is not obligated to explore more options than with its present customers, which severely restricts the marketability of the goods. Not only was Excel unable to resell *any* of the towels in their original condition, the alteration to the towels was arguably more than slight. Therefore, a court is likely to find that the towels could not be resold in the ordinary course of business, and the specially manufactured goods exception to the statute of frauds has been met, resulting in an enforceable agreement.

This paragraph transitions back to the conclusion on this requirement, explaining the key reasons for the predicted conclusion.

A general checklist that can be used when analyzing multiple issues using multiple cases is online with the Student Supplemental Materials for this book located on the publisher's website at http://www.aspenpublishing.com.

CHAPTER SUMMARY

- When writing a structured discussion with multiple issues or subissues, address each legal point separately.
- When a single case is relevant to more than one legal point, explain the key facts, the court's holding, and the court's reasoning as it becomes relevant to each legal point.

- Separate the parts of a legal test, and create a chart or outline of the legal test as soon as possible, placing relevant information from the case law where appropriate in your chart or outline.
- When addressing a fact-based issue, creating a chart of each legal point that includes both the client's facts and the facts from the relevant cases better ensures that your analysis is accurate and complete.
- When analyzing a rule with elements, or requirements, you must address all the elements, even those not in dispute in your client's case.
- When writing an objective discussion, let logic guide your choices about the order in which to place the multiple issues.

CHAPTER

11

Using Policy to Support a Legal Analysis

A. Public Policy Generally

Public policy underlies the creation or application of most U.S. law, whether it is constitutional law, common law, or statutory law. Public policy has been defined as "that principle of the law which holds that no [citizen] can lawfully do that which has a tendency to be injurious to the public, or against the public good. . . ."[1] Public policy is not static and unchanging. What one individual or group considers injurious to the public or against the public good may not necessarily be considered so by another individual or group. Also, public policy can change over time as the general public's attitudes and ideas change.

The term "public policy" should not be interpreted to mean that this policy reflects an agreement among the populace or even a majority opinion as to what is injurious to the public or against the public good. Those who make the laws—legislators and judges—can make public policy determinations. When legislators create law, and judges create or apply the law, they may be trying to remedy what they identify as detrimental to society or trying to promote what they perceive is in the public good.

1. *Porterfield v. Mascari II, Inc.*, 823 A.2d 590, 602 (Md. 2003) (quoting *Eagerton v. Brownlow*, 4 H.L. (House of Lords) Cas. 1, 196 (1853)).

B. Public Policy Reflected in the Law

Federal and state constitutions can reflect public policy. And, amendments to the constitutions can be made, though changes are infrequent, to reflect perceived changes in public policy. For example, the 1919 ratification of the Nineteenth Amendment to the U.S. Constitution gave women the right to vote, arguably representing a change from the nation's prior public policy that allowing women to vote would potentially harm the public good or the democratic process because women were somehow considered not sufficiently qualified.

Public policy can also be reflected in federal and state statutes. Legislatures often identify public policy or express public policy reasons for enacting a statute when stating the statute's purpose. For example, many states have slayer statutes that prohibit a murderer from inheriting any portion of their victim's estate. The policy behind this statute is that an individual cannot benefit from their own wrongdoing.[2] The policy is not always expressly stated in a statute[3] but may be construed through other means, such as reviewing the legislative history (if available)[4] behind the statute's enactment. As with constitutional provisions, statutes may be amended or revoked by legislatures when perceived public policy has changed from the time of the original statute's enactment.

C. How Public Policy Affects Court Decisions

Public policy can serve as a powerful tool of the courts. It can be used to support the continued use of precedent or a break from precedent when public policy considerations have changed.

When constitutions and statutes are silent on an area of law, courts have the power to step in and articulate principles of public policy to support a common law decision. Thus, in a state where there is no slayer statute, a court still may prohibit a beneficiary from inheriting from an estate if they killed the deceased. The court could base its decision on policy identical or similar

---

2. *See Cook v. Grierson*, 845 A.2d 1231, 1233 (Md. 2004).

3. *But see, e.g.*, Idaho's slayer statute, which states, "This section shall not be considered penal in nature, but shall be construed broadly in order to effect the policy of this state that no person shall be allowed to profit by his own wrong, wherever committed." Idaho Code Ann. §15-2-803(n).

4. Legislative history comprises actions by a legislative body (e.g., hearings and debates) and legislative documents (e.g., committee reports) that relate to a bill (a proposal for a statute), beginning with the bill's introduction to the legislative body and ending with the legislature's enacting the bill into law (as a statute). The federal government publishes legislative histories (such as committee reports, floor debates, and histories of actions taken) for enacted federal statutes, but few states publish legislative histories for enacted state statutes.

to the policy considerations of legislatures passing slayer statutes—that is, a person should not benefit from their own wrongdoing.[5]

Sometimes, though, a court may be reluctant to establish new principles of public policy. The court may prefer the legislature take the lead role in identifying public policy. Legislatures are composed of members elected by the public to represent the interests of their constituents. And so, courts may consider legislators to be in a better position to identify public policy on the basis that legislators arguably express the will of the people. For this reason, courts sometimes defer to the legislature on matters involving public policy.[6]

D. How Lawyers Use Public Policy

Lawyers may rely on public policy to advance a client's position. A court will sometimes explicitly mention in a decision the public policy for creating or applying a rule. Other times the public policy used by a court will merely be implied in the decision. Lawyers would welcome a case decision where a court explicitly mentioned the public policy behind the common law and applied that public policy to the facts in the cited case to reach an outcome favorable to their client's position.

Public policy arguments can also be used to persuade a court to depart from precedent because of a perceived change in the concept of what is injurious to the public. In this regard, lawyers may consider using persuasive law, such as scholarly writings, or common law or statutory trends from other jurisdictions, to convince a court to adopt a new rule that reflects current public policy.

A legal analysis may include public policy supporting a party's position. As mentioned in Chapter 6, lawyers typically consider using three sources to support a client's position: (1) the relevant law, (2) the client's facts, and (3) the policy considerations underlying the law. Because it is bound by precedent, a court is most interested in whether precedent applies to the facts before the court. Therefore, a legal writer typically begins a fact-based analysis of a party's position by presenting any factual similarities[7] and distinctions[8] between prior case decisions and the facts of the client's case, as well as any additional

---

5. *See, e.g.*, *Ford v. Ford*, 512 A.2d 389, 391 (Md. 1986).

6. *See, e.g.*, *Kendall v. Starnes*, 548 So. 2d 775, 777 (Fla. Dist. Ct. App. 1989) (court rejected the argument that the state's public policy would extend the state's slayer statute to children of the murderer who were natural or statutory beneficiaries under the victims' estates, finding that "[i]f there is to be declared in Florida such a public policy . . . , it must be accomplished by a legislative amendment to the Slayer Statute and not by a pronouncement of this court.").

7. *Comparison*, *analogy*, *similarity*, and the various forms of these nouns are synonymous when discussing how facts of a client's case are similar to the case facts.

8. *Contrast*, *distinction*, *differences*, and the various forms of these nouns are synonymous when discussing how facts of a client's case are different from the case facts.

facts of the client's case that support the party's position but are not comparable to facts in prior case decisions. Public policy may be inserted, where logical, to give additional support to the reasonable inferences drawn from the factual comparisons and the other facts of the client's case.

Recall in Chapter 6 the analysis of Ana's case discussing the reasonableness of a covenant not to compete (CNC). The public policy expressed in *Mats Transport* may be added to the rebuttal of David's position that the CNC is not broader than necessary to protect his interests. Below, the last paragraph of that discussion has been revised to reflect the added policy considerations, which are highlighted in boldface:

> Nevertheless, **courts do not favor CNCs and strictly construe CNCs against the party seeking to enforce them because "they impede trade and distort the market mechanism which allows our economy to function."** *Mats Transport*, 824 S.E.2d at 1467. Here, the CNC will be strictly construed against David. The geographic restriction in the CNC extends into counties and towns where Hart Fitness Center does not currently operate health and exercise clubs. **Allowing the CNC to extend beyond the present locations of the clubs will limit the availability of health and exercise clubs to the public and limit competition; doing so would negatively affect service and value to the public.** Further, the geographic area exceeds the value of the goodwill Ana has in the current membership, which is what the CNC is meant to protect. Therefore, the CNC is likely overbroad for the protection of David's business interest and is unreasonable.

• Exercise 11-A

Add to your analysis of Ms. Broward's case from the exercises in Chapter 6 the public policy expressed in *Everett* to support one or both parties' positions regarding the return of Ms. Broward's painting, even though the statute of limitations period had passed.

CHAPTER SUMMARY

- Public policy is a principle of law that promotes the protection of the public's well-being, which may include, for example, public health and safety.
- Public policy can change over time as legislators or judges perceive a change in the general public's ideas and attitudes.
- When deciding issues of law, judges can be guided by public policy reflected in relevant constitutional provisions and statutes.

- If the constitution or statutory law is silent on public policy as it relates to certain issues, judges may articulate public policy to support the common law for these issues.
- Public policy should be used, where appropriate, in the legal analysis of an issue and to support a client's position in an argument before the court.

CHAPTER

12

An Introduction to Statutory Interpretation and Analysis of a Law-Based Issue

A. Introduction

Previous chapters have focused on analyzing fact-based issues when applying a statute or common law rule. When analyzing a fact-based issue, the parties are not disputing which statute, rule, or principle is applicable to the legal issue raised and are not disputing the facts of the case. A law-based issue requires the court to determine (1) whether a statute, rule, or principle applies to the case; or (2) which legal principle applies when more than one relevant applicable legal principle exists.

For analysis of law-based issues, lawyers should have an understanding of how courts engage in statutory interpretation. After all, statutes are a primary source of law in the United States, both at the state and federal levels. Courts are often faced with the task of interpreting statutes. Lawyers may need to interpret and apply statutes in their analysis for predictive documents for clients.

This chapter briefly introduces commonly used statutory interpretation tools and theories.[1] It then provides an overview of how to write the analysis of a law-based issue.

B. Why Is Statutory Interpretation Necessary? What Is the Role of Courts in Interpreting Statutes?

The U.S. Congress and state legislatures write and enact statutes. At the time statutes become law, the statute may be abundantly clear to all who have worked to bring it into being.

However, a statute is not always clear, or, even if clear at inception, may grow unclear over time. Even after a diligent effort to do otherwise, legislators may create an ambiguous statute. An ambiguous statute means that the statute is capable of at least two reasonable but possibly contradictory meanings. Even one comma can make an otherwise clear statute an ambiguous one. A single word that can have more than one meaning might have been left undefined. Also, at the time of enacting a statute, the legislature may not have anticipated future circumstances, like changes in technology or culture.

In deciding a case, courts may need to interpret and apply ambiguous statutes. A statute can be ambiguous "on its face" or "as applied." Clerical errors in the drafting of the legislation can create an ambiguity "on the face" of the statute, meaning that the ambiguity is evident to anyone reading the statute. When a statute is used and applied by lawyers and the general public, legislation that by its wording appeared to be clear during the drafting stage might become ambiguous. Legislators can't foresee every instance where a statute might apply and thus may fail to address the statute's applicability to

1. A law student interested in learning more about statutory interpretation theory and related discussions will have no shortage of sources to consult. *See, e.g.*, James J. Brudney & Corey Ditslear, *Canons of Construction and the Elusive Quest for Neutral Reasoning*, 58 VAND. L. REV. 1 (2005); Larry Eig, *Statutory Interpretation: General Principles and Recent Trends*, Congressional Research Service (Sept. 24, 2014), https://sgp.fas.org/crs/misc/97-589.pdf; Abbe R. Gluck & Lisa Schultz Bressman, *Statutory Interpretation from the Inside—An Empirical Study of Congressional Drafting, Delegation, and the Canons: Part I*, 65 STAN. L. REV. 901 (2013); Anita S. Krishnakumar, *Backdoor Purposivism*, 69 DUKE L.J. 1275, 1331 (2020); Christopher J. Walker, *Inside Agency Statutory Interpretation*, 67 STAN. L. REV. 999 (2015).

an unanticipated situation. When a statute is ambiguous either as applied or on its face, a court must determine the statute's true meaning.

A court may also need to interpret statutes that are incomplete. The court may need to fill in gaps. Sometimes legislatures enact laws that intentionally leave gaps in the law. For example, legislators may leave gaps in the law for political convenience. They may rush to pass legislation before the end of a legislative session, and, perhaps because of disagreement among the lawmakers, they are unable to fill in the details of the legislation before enactment. At other times, unable to predict evolving circumstances in areas like technology and culture, the legislature unintentionally leaves gaps in a statute.

Whenever a legislature intentionally or unintentionally leaves gaps in a statute, a court may attempt to fill in the gaps. Not all judges and lawyers agree on the extent or method of gap-filling that should be undertaken by a court. Providing one view of a federal court's gap-filling duties, U.S. Supreme Court Justice John Paul Stevens once wrote in a concurring opinion:

> For example, [w]hen a federal statute creates a new right but fails to specify whether plaintiffs may or may not recover damages or attorney's fees, we must fill the gap in the statute's text by examining all relevant evidence that sheds light on the intent of the enacting Congress. The inquiry varies from statute to statute. Sometimes the question is whether, despite its silence, Congress intended us to recognize an implied cause of action.... Sometimes we ask whether, despite its silence, Congress intended us to enforce the pre-existing remedy provided in [the statute].... And still other times, despite Congress' inclusion of specific clauses designed specifically to preserve the pre-existing remedies, we have nevertheless concluded that Congress impliedly foreclosed the [statute's] remedy.... Whenever we perform this gap-filling task, it is appropriate not only to study the text and structure of the statutory scheme, but also to examine its legislative history.[2]

C. Tools of Statutory Interpretation

This section describes the tools commonly used by courts when interpreting a statute. A court usually begins by reviewing the statute's text to determine

2. *City of Rancho Palos Verdes v. Abrams*, 544 U.S. 113, 129 (2005) (Stevens, J., concurring) (citations omitted).

"Legislative history" comprises actions by a legislative body (e.g., hearings and debates) and legislative documents (e.g., committee reports) that relate to a "bill" (a proposal for a statute), beginning with the bill's introduction to the legislative body and ending with the legislature enacting the bill into law. The federal government publishes legislative histories (such as committee reports, floor debates, and histories of actions taken) for enacted federal statutes, but few states publish legislative histories for enacted state statutes.

its plain meaning. If the statute's meaning still remains ambiguous, courts may review outside sources to determine the legislature's intent in enacting the statute or the statute's purpose.

A court may decide to refer to outside sources to uncover the legislature's intent, the statute's purpose, or the meaning of the words. Or it may not. How broadly or narrowly a court interprets a statute can depend on the statutory interpretation tools employed and the court's approach and purpose in using them.[3]

1. *Plain meaning*

When interpreting a statute, a court begins by looking at the language of the statute to determine its plain meaning. In other words, the court reads the statute to see if the language is clear and understandable without need for exploring beyond the statute. For example, the Federal Arbitration Act (the "Arbitration Act")[4] requires courts to enforce written arbitration agreements. Section 1 of the Arbitration Act excludes from coverage "contracts of employment of seamen, railroad employees, or any other class of workers engaged in foreign or interstate commerce."[5] Let's say an employee working in a retail store brings an employment discrimination action against their employer in court. When the retail employee was hired, however, they signed an agreement to settle all disputes arising out of their employment by arbitration. Because of this agreement, the employer responds to the employee's complaint by seeking to dismiss the action and compel arbitration of the employee's claims as required under the Arbitration Act.[6]

Typically, a court first considers commonly accepted principles of English grammar, syntax, and punctuation to determine the meaning of a statute's words as understood by a reasonable person.[7]

---

3. The statutory codes of all states and the District of Columbia provide general rules of interpretation for reading their statutes. *See, e.g.,* Nicholas Quinn Rosenkranz, *Federal Rules of Statutory Interpretation,* 115 HARV. L. REV. 2085, 2089 n.10 (2002) (listing examples of state "interpretive codes"). These interpretive rules usually appear at the beginning of the statutory code. Few courts, though, directly rely on or even cite these rules when interpreting statutes.

4. 9 U.S.C. §§ 1-16.

5. 9 U.S.C. § 1.

6. This problem is based on the facts of *Circuit City Stores, Inc. v. Adams,* 532 U.S. 105 (2001).

7. *See, e.g., Tenn. Valley Auth. v. Hill,* 437 U.S. 153 (1978) (Court used the plain meaning rule when interpreting the Endangered Species Act of 1973 to uphold the U.S. Secretary of Interior's decision to stop construction of a dam, almost completed at an expense of $100 million, because it would destroy the only known habitat of the snail darter, a species of perch).

> One would be hard pressed to find a statutory provision whose terms were any plainer than those in § 7 of the Endangered Species Act. Its very words affirmatively command all federal agencies "*to insure* that actions *authorized, funded,* or *carried out* by them do not *jeopardize* the continued existence" of an endangered species or "*result* in the destruction or modification of habitat of such species. . . ." 16 U.S.C. § 1536 (1976 ed.) (Emphasis added.)

When using this approach, the court does not refer to outside sources, not even a dictionary, to help ascertain the meaning of the words. Such a restrictive approach to statutory interpretation, however, rarely yields the meaning of an ambiguous statute.

A court attempting to determine whether the plain language of section 1 of the Arbitration Act applies to the retail employee's dispute could construe the provision to exclude all "contracts of employment of . . . any other class of workers engaged in foreign or interstate commerce." This reading would exclude the retail employee's agreement with their employer. On the other hand, the statute makes an explicit reference to "seamen" and "railroad employees" directly preceding what may be considered the residual clause, "any other class of workers." Arguably, if Congress had intended to exclude all employment agreements from the Arbitration Act, it would not have specifically included employment agreements of seamen and railroad employees before the residual clause in section 1. Because the two arguments present reasonable but conflicting interpretations of the statute's plain meaning, a court might use selected canons of construction, discussed next, to help with its interpretation of the statute.

2. *Canons of construction*

At any stage in interpreting a statute, a court may pick among a variety of canons of construction to help determine the meaning of a statute. Canons of construction are persuasive—not mandatory—rules or principles used by courts to help give meaning to ambiguous statutory language.[8] As noted by the United States Supreme Court, "canons of construction are no more than rules of thumb that help courts determine the meaning of legislation."[9]

The canons can be divided into the textual, or linguistic, and the substantive.[10]

a. Textual canons

Textual, or linguistic, canons guide the interpreting court in determining the meaning of statutory words or phrases. These canons focus on the legislature's choice of words in the statute, the syntax used, or the relationship of the words

---

> This language admits of no exception. Nonetheless, petitioner urges, as do the dissenters, that the Act cannot reasonably be interpreted as applying to a federal project which was well under way when Congress passed the Endangered Species Act of 1973. To sustain that position, however, we would be forced to ignore the ordinary meaning of plain language.

Tenn. Valley Auth., 437 U.S. at 173 (citations omitted).

8. "Canons are not mandatory rules. They are guides 'that need not be conclusive.'" *Chickasaw Nation v. United States*, 534 U.S. 84, 94 (2001) (quoting *Circuit City*, 532 U.S. at 115).

9. *Conn. Nat'l Bank v. Germain*, 503 U.S. 249, 253 (1992).

10. *See* James J. Brudney & Corey Ditslear, *Canons of Construction and the Elusive Quest for Neutral Reasoning*, 58 VAND. L. REV. 1, 12-13 (2005).

or phrases in question to words or phrases found in other provisions of the same statute or in those found in similar statutes.[11]

Examples of textual canons include the following.

- "[T]erms connected by a disjunctive [word must] be given separate meanings, unless the context dictates otherwise."[12] The word "or" is a common disjunctive word.
- Words shall be given "their ordinary, contemporary common meaning," unless otherwise specifically defined.[13]
- *Shall* imposes a mandatory duty; *may* is permissive.[14]
- Words shall be read so that their meaning is consistent with other provisions of the same statute or other statutes.[15]
- *Ejusdem generis*: General words following specifically listed words include only those items "similar in nature" to the listed words.[16]
- *Expressio unius est exclusio alterius*: Mentioning one or more items of a class implies the exclusion of other items.[17]
- *Noscitur a sociis*: The meaning of a word or phrase may be known from "the words immediately surrounding it."[18]

For an example applying a textual canon of construction, let's return to the problem of whether a retail employee's agreement to arbitrate disputes with their employer is excluded from the Arbitration Act by its section 1. The court may use the canon of *ejusdem generis* to help uncover the statute's meaning. Applying this canon, the meaning of the general phrase in section 1, "any other class of workers engaged in . . . commerce," includes "only objects similar in nature to those objects enumerated by the preceding specific words."[19] In section 1, "seamen" and "railroad workers" preceded the general phrase.

---

11. *See* James J. Brudney & Corey Ditslear, *Canons of Construction and the Elusive Quest for Neutral Reasoning*, 58 Vand. L. Rev. 1, 12-13 (2005).

12. *Reiter v. Sonotone Corp.*, 442 U.S. 330, 339 (1979).

13. *Perrin v. United States*, 444 U.S. 37, 42 (1979).

14. *See, e.g., Weinstein v. Albright*, 261 F.3d 127, 137 (2d Cir. 2001).

15. *See United States v. Jones*, 527 F.2d 817, 829 n.13 (D.C. Cir. 1975).

16. *Circuit City*, 532 U.S. at 114-15.

17. *See, e.g., Barnhart v. Peabody Coal Co.*, 537 U.S. 149, 168 (2003) (quoting *United States v. Vonn*, 535 U.S. 55, 65 (2002)) ("the canon *expressio unius est exclusio alterius* does not apply to every statutory listing or grouping; it has force only when the items expressed are members of an 'associated group or series,' justifying the inference that items not mentioned were excluded by deliberate choice, not inadvertence.")

18. *Noscitur a sociis*, Black's Law Dictionary (11th ed. 2019). *See, e.g., Gutierrez v. Ada*, 528 U.S. 250, 255 (2000) (quoting *Jarecki v. G.D. Searle & Co.*, 367 U.S. 303, 307 (1961)) ("The maxim *noscitur a sociis*, . . . while not an inescapable rule, is often wisely applied where a word is capable of many meanings in order to avoid the giving of unintended breadth to the Acts of Congress.").

19. *Circuit City*, 532 U.S. at 114-15 (quoting 2A N. Singer, Sutherland on Statutes and Statutory Construction § 47.17 (5th ed. 1991)). Using the canon of *ejusdem generis*, the Supreme Court found that the phrase excluding "contracts of employment of seaman, railroad workers, or any other class of workers engaged in foreign or interstate commerce" from the coverage of the Federal Arbitration Act, 9 U.S.C. § 1, was limited to workers engaged in enterprises similar to "seamen" and "railroad workers." *Id.*

These types of workers have transportation jobs. Therefore, if the canon of *ejusdem generis* is applied, the phrase "any other class of workers engaged in . . . commerce" refers only to employment agreements of transportation workers. The employee in our problem worked in a retail store; therefore, under this interpretation, the employee's agreement would not be subject to the Arbitration Act.

If the meaning of a statute is determined by reviewing the words of the statute and its statutory scheme, an interpreting court usually will stop there.[20] But in instances where the logical meaning remains ambiguous even after a plain reading of the statute, a court may review legislative history.

For instance, in determining whether the retail employee's agreement with his employer is subject to the Arbitration Act, a court may review the legislative history of section 1 of the Act to find out whether Congress intended to exclude only the employment agreements of transportation employees from the Arbitration Act.[21] This may include examining published committee reports of House or Senate committees, congressional hearings, bills, and transcripts of floor debates.

b. Substantive canons

If the meaning of a statute cannot be determined using textual or linguistic canons, a court may turn to substantive canons. These canons do not focus on the meaning of the text or what the legislature intended when it drafted the text. Rather, substantive canons relate to matters such as constitutional concerns, the common law prior to the statute's enactment, and specific statutory policies.[22] For example, the principle that a statute must be interpreted to avoid unconstitutional results is a substantive canon, as is the policy that an ambiguous criminal statute should be interpreted in favor of the defendant.

D. Theories of Statutory Interpretation

Different courts and different judges through the years have varied in their focus when interpreting statutes. Some courts, pointing to the supremacy of

---

20. *See, e.g., Circuit City*, 532 U.S. at 119 (Court did not review legislative history because the meaning of the statute could be determined from the text of the statute).

21. The majority in *Circuit City* did not resort to legislative history, noting that available history on section 1 was "sparse," because the meaning of the statute was made clear by interpreting the statute using the canon of *ejusdem generis*. *Circuit City*, 532 U.S. at 119. Even so, the dissenting opinion criticized the majority for overlooking abundant legislative history that supported Congress's intent to exclude all employment agreements from the Arbitration Act. *Id.* at 123-28 (Stevens, Ginsburg, and Breyer, JJ., dissenting).

22. *See, e.g.*, James J. Brudney & Corey Ditslear, *Canons of Construction and the Elusive Quest for Neutral Reasoning*, 58 VAND. L. REV. 1, 12-13 (2005).

the legislature, exercise judicial restraint when interpreting statutes by focusing on the meaning of the statute's words. Other courts are more interested in the meaning of the statute as intended by the legislature or the meaning of the statute in furthering the purpose of the legislation.

A helpful starting point for studying and understanding theories of statutory interpretation is consideration of textualism and intentionalism. A textualism approach to statutory interpretation generally discourages consulting legislative history and other sources, and encourages courts to make great efforts to interpret a statute by closely reviewing the statute's plain language. Textualists embrace plain meaning and textual canons of construction. Textualists may still look at legislative history to determine the meaning of the statutory words when there is "genuine ambiguity in the statute"[23] or when reading the statute according to its plain meaning causes an absurd or unconstitutional outcome.[24]

Although there are various schools of thought on intentionalism, a goal is to "effectuat[e] the collective intent of the enacting legislature."[25] The intentionalist looks to the words of a statute as an expression of the legislature's intent that can be clarified through the use of outside sources.[26] The intentionalist may refer to legislative history, agency determinations, previous cases determining legislative intent, and legislatively created purpose statements. If the discovered legislative intent conflicts with the plain meaning of the statute, the intentionalist's paramount concern is giving effect to the intent of the legislators who passed the statute as opposed to a plain reading of the text, which might create a result not intended by the legislature.[27]

• Exercise 12-A

A Russian brewer (a manufacturer of beer) and a New York beer wholesaler entered into a written agreement in which the brewer agreed to supply the wholesaler with beer. Under the terms of the agreement, the brewer transferred the beer to the wholesaler's possession at the Russian brewer's place of business. There is no indication that there was an "offer to sell" the beer in New York.

The agreement permitted either party to unilaterally terminate the agreement. On January 1 of this year, the brewer refused to fill the wholesaler's most recent order and advised that it would not fill any future orders. The wholesaler claims that New York law, which governs the agreement between the parties, prohibits brewers from terminating agreements with wholesalers

23. *See, e.g., Bd. of Trade v. SEC*, 187 F.3d 713, 720 (7th Cir. 1999) (Easterbrook, J.).

24. *See, e.g., Green v. Bock Laundry Mach. Co.*, 490 U.S. 504, 527 (1989) (Scalia, J., dissenting).

25. David A. Forkner & Kent M. Koska, *Unanimously Weaving a Tangled Web: Walters, Robinson, Title VII, and the Need for Holistic Statutory Interpretation*, 36 HARV. J. ON LEGIS. 161, 178 (1999).

26. Carlos E. González, *Reinterpreting Statutory Interpretation*, 74 N.C. L. REV. 585, 606 (1996).

27. Forkner & Koska, *supra* n.25, at 179. *See, e.g., Pub. Citizen v. U.S. Dep't of Justice*, 491 U.S. 440 (1989).

unless the termination occurs for "good cause." New York Alcoholic Beverage Control Law section 55-c(4)(a) states: "No brewer may cancel, fail to renew, or terminate an agreement unless the party intending such action has good cause for such cancellation, failure to renew, or termination. . . ." N.Y. Alcoh. Bev. Control L. § 55-c(4)(a).

The brewer does not contend that it terminated the agreement for "good cause." Rather, the brewer argues that the New York statute applies only to sales or offers to sell that occur in New York. The brewer contends further that the business deal between the wholesaler and brewer occurred outside of New York.

The wholesaler contends that the statute applies to any transaction entered into with a New York wholesaler no matter where the deal took place.

Both parties base their arguments on New York Alcoholic Beverage Control Law § 55-c(2)(b), which states:

> "Brewer" means any person or entity engaged primarily in business as a brewer, manufacturer of alcoholic beverages, importer, marketer, broker or agent of any of the foregoing who sells or offers to sell beer to a beer wholesaler *in this state* or any successor to a brewer.

N.Y. Alcoh. Bev. Control L. § 55-c(2)(b).

There is no published legislative history for this statute. However, the policy statement specifically addressing agreements between brewers and beer wholesalers states:

> It is hereby declared to be the policy of this state, that the sale and delivery of beer by brewers to beer wholesalers shall be pursuant to a written agreement. That further, the regulation of business relations between brewers and beer wholesalers is necessary and appropriate to the general economy and tax base of this state and in the public interest.

New York Alcoholic Beverage Control law § 55-c(1).

Other sections of the New York Alcoholic Beverage Control Law also may assist in determining the application of section 55-c(4)(a). The general policy statement for all sections of the New York Alcoholic Beverage Control Law provides:

> It is hereby declared as the policy of the state that it is necessary to regulate and control the manufacture, sale and distribution within the state of alcoholic beverages for the purpose of fostering and promoting temperance in their consumption and respect for an obedience to law. . . .

N.Y. Alcoh. Bev. Control L. § 2.

Section 3(28) of the New York Alcoholic Beverage Control Law provides:

> "To sell" includes to solicit or receive an order for, to keep or expose for sale, and to keep with intent to sell and shall include the delivery of any alcoholic beverage in the state.

N.Y. Alcoh. Bev. Control L. § 3(28).

Using the statutory interpretation tools discussed in this chapter, draft an argument that supports the brewer's position that the statute applies only to sales or offers to sell in New York. Then, draft an argument that supports the wholesaler's position that the statute applies to any transaction entered into with a New York wholesaler no matter where the deal took place.

E. *Writing an Objective Analysis of a Law-Based Issue Involving Statutory Interpretation*

An attorney may not realize an issue requires interpretation of a statute until after beginning research. Recall the divorce of Ana and David Hart introduced in Chapter 6. Let's say Ana has told a senior attorney in the law firm she has hired that during their marriage David became suspicious that Ana was having an extramarital affair with a friend, John Sweeney. To find evidence of this, David purchased a telephone recording device at a local electronics store and secretly attached the device to a telephone—not a mobile phone—in the couple's home. Without Ana's knowledge, David taped several conversations between Ana and her friend, John. Ana is outraged that her soon-to-be ex-husband taped her telephone conversations with John without her knowledge or consent. She wonders whether she has a cause of action against David for his actions. The senior partner in the firm has assigned a junior attorney to look into the matter and write an objective discussion of the issue.

1. *Pre-drafting process*

The junior attorney begins the pre-drafting process by following the steps introduced in Chapter 4 and further discussed in Chapter 6. After collecting and analyzing the facts, the junior attorney collects the relevant law and analyzes it. In their research of federal statutory law, the junior attorney discovers 18 U.S.C. §§ 2510-2523 (the "Wiretap Act"). Section 2511(a) of the Wiretap Act generally prohibits interceptions of telephone conversations without the knowledge or consent of the parties talking on the telephone:

> Except as otherwise specifically provided in this chapter any person who—(a) intentionally intercepts, endeavors to intercept, or procures any other person to intercept or endeavor to intercept any wire, oral, or electronic communication . . . shall be punished . . . or shall be subject to suit. . . .

David intercepted Ana and John's conversations by making recordings of their conversations without their knowledge or consent. Although the Wiretap Act does not explicitly state that it prohibits a spouse's wiretapping of a partner's conversation with a third party ("interspousal wiretapping"), the Wiretap Act's broad, general prohibition language seems to include this situation.

Consider that, during research, the lawyer discovers that sections 2511 and 2520 of the Wiretap Act permit a lawsuit against those who violate the Act and allow for the recovery of damages. If Ana can show that the Wiretap Act prohibits interspousal wiretapping, she can bring a legal action against David.

When analyzing a statutory interpretation issue, a lawyer must be mindful of the interpreting court's role and be able to respond to the court's concerns. As noted earlier in this chapter, some courts take a strict view of statutory interpretation, focusing on the plain meaning of a statute and using textual canons of construction, turning to sources outside the statute itself only if the statute's meaning remains ambiguous, or if applying the plain meaning of the statute would create an absurd result. Other courts, however, more readily refer to sources other than the statute itself to determine the legislative intent or the legislative purpose behind a statute.

A lawyer can never be sure what tools of statutory interpretation the court will use when construing a statute or how the court will use these tools in reaching its decision. Therefore, a lawyer should perform diligent research beyond the mere text of the statute. For instance, a lawyer should explore the legislative history of the statute, where available; the statutory scheme surrounding the statute; any related statutes in the code; and any administrative regulations that may have been promulgated under the statute. The lawyer's goal is not only to determine the plain meaning of the statute but also to move beyond the statute's plain meaning to determine, if possible, the legislative intent and legislative purpose for the statute. The lawyer should consider as well what other canons of construction might be helpful or relevant to uncovering the meaning of the statute.

Returning to Ana's case, section 2511(a) states that there are exceptions to the Wiretap Act's prohibition. The junior attorney's review of the Wiretap Act's exception provision discloses that none of the exceptions expressly apply to Ana's case. So far, this is good for Ana.

The plain meaning of section 2511(1)(a) apparently prohibits interspousal wiretapping because it applies to all persons except those specifically exempt from the statute's reach. But the junior attorney anticipates that David's attorney will argue that section 2511(1)(a) is ambiguous and that the Wiretap Act impliedly exempts interspousal wiretapping. David's attorney may try to persuade the court that the statutory scheme of the Wiretap Act supports their argument. Therefore, the junior attorney must look at all parts of the Wiretap Act, as well as sections surrounding the Wiretap Act, to see if anything might support David's position. The junior attorney becomes a little concerned when they discover that the Wiretap Act is part of an Act entitled the "Omnibus Crime Control and Safe Streets Act of 1968." This title might suggest that the purpose of the Wiretap Act is to focus solely on crimes that do not involve a domestic dispute between two people married to each other. Moreover, federal courts are reluctant to address matters that are typically addressed in state courts, such as domestic disputes. Congress may not have intended the Wiretap Act, a federal law, to govern domestic wiretapping issues. Although the language of section 2511(1)(a) seems clear as written (on its face), an interpreting court might find it ambiguous as applied to Ana's case.

The junior attorney anticipates that a court might look beyond a plain reading of the Wiretap Act to the legislative intent or the legislative purpose to clarify the scope of section 2511(1)(a)'s prohibition. Therefore, the junior attorney researches the legislative history of the Wiretap Act to ensure that the legislative intent and the legislative purpose support a plain reading that section 2511(1)(a) prohibits interspousal wiretapping. Because the federal government publishes legislative history for its federal legislation, the junior attorney locates committee reports, transcripts of legislative hearings, and debates on the Wiretap Act. The junior attorney finds that some of the legislative history seems to support Ana's position that the congressional intent and statutory purpose of the Wiretap Act were to prohibit interspousal wiretapping. Still other excerpts from legislative history seem to support David's position that interspousal wiretapping is an implied exception to the Wiretap Act.

In an effort to obtain more clarification, the junior attorney researches case law in the federal jurisdiction of the Thirteenth Circuit (which includes East Carolina)[28] to determine how prior courts have construed section 2511(1)(a). Research reveals that no court in this jurisdiction has addressed the issue of whether interspousal wiretapping is prohibited by section 2511(1)(a). The junior attorney expands the research of case law to cases decided by courts outside the Thirteenth Circuit. They discover that courts in other jurisdictions are divided on the issue of whether interspousal wiretapping is prohibited under the Wiretap Act.

Once the initial research is completed, the junior attorney organizing the research notes whether each court used a plain reading interpretation of the statute or explored legislative intent, the purpose of the statute, or public policy concerns. At this point, the junior attorney considers any additional canons of construction or public policy concerns that courts have not used. Now the junior attorney is ready to begin drafting the analysis of the law-based issue.

2. *Structuring an objective legal analysis of a statutory interpretation issue*

Just as in an analysis of a fact-based issue, the writer should keep in mind the purpose of the writing and the audience. In an objective analysis of a statutory interpretation issue, the writer should focus on informing the reader of the law and legislative history surrounding the statute in question and predicting how the court will interpret the statute. If there is more than one

28. The Thirteenth Circuit is a fictitious federal jurisdiction, and East Carolina is a fictitious state created solely for purposes of this case problem.

reasonable interpretation of the statute, the writer should inform the reader of the different interpretations and explain the support for these positions. The writer must carefully weigh the respective interpretations of the statute to decide which interpretation the court will likely adopt. The writer's goal is to provide a complete, accurate, and concise analysis of the law that is readily understandable to the reader.

a. Roadmap paragraph

Begin the objective discussion with a roadmap paragraph. The roadmap paragraph for a statutory interpretation issue that raises two different interpretations of a statute usually includes

(1) a conclusion sentence,
(2) a quote of the pertinent language of the statute in question,
(3) a statement that the issue is one of first impression in the jurisdiction (so that the reader will understand why you are not using authority from the governing jurisdiction), and
(4) a statement that courts outside the governing jurisdiction are divided on the issue (if this is, indeed, the case).

b. Analysis of a statutory interpretation issue

Similar to the basic organizational structure of a fact-based analysis, begin the discussion of a statutory interpretation issue with analysis supporting the predicted conclusion. The predicted conclusion is the interpretation of the statute the legal writer has determined the court will likely adopt. After completing the support for the predicted conclusion, the writer should transition to and present the counteranalysis. The counteranalysis supports the interpretation of the statute that the court will likely reject. The writer should finish the analysis with a conclusion that includes an explanation of pivotal reasons for the predicted conclusion.

While the basic organizational structure of a discussion of a statutory interpretation analysis is similar to the organizational structure of a discussion of a fact-based issue, the substantive focus of the discussion is different. Recall that in a fact-based analysis, the substantive focus is in applying the relevant law to the specific facts of the client's case. Such an analysis draws relevant analogies and distinctions between the client's case facts and the facts in the relevant case law. In contrast, the substantive focus in a statutory interpretation analysis is on the text of the statute and interpreting that statute using the tools of statutory interpretation discussed earlier in this chapter. The law used in the analysis of a statutory interpretation issue, including the counteranalysis, may include any or all of the following:

- The language of the statute in question;
- The statutory scheme of the statute in question (including statutory definitions of terms used in it, preambles to it, and other statutory sections related to it);

- Any administrative regulations that may have been created under the statute in question;
- Canons of construction;
- Legislative history of the statute in question (including committee reports, hearings, bills, and floor debates);
- Case decisions where courts have interpreted the statute in question or a similar statute;
- Scholarly treatises or articles that have discussed possible interpretations of the statute in question; and
- Public policy concerns.

Case decisions, as noted above, are persuasive only, for example, to show that other courts have adopted a similar view. When using a case in interpreting a statute, the rule explanation of the case takes a slightly different focus than in a fact-based analysis, where the facts of the cited case are of great importance. In a rule explanation for a statutory interpretation analysis, include only enough facts to show that the situation in the cited case raised an interpretation issue similar to the one addressed in the lawyer's client's case. The legal writer's primary focus is on the cited court's holding and reasoning, including its use of legislative tools and its goal in using these tools. These aspects of the cited case are discussed in detail in the rule explanation.

An annotated sample of an objective statutory interpretation analysis of Ana's issue regarding whether interspousal wiretapping is exempt from the Wiretap Act follows.

The purpose of this discussion is to address whether David Hart's recording of several telephone conversations between his wife and our client, Ana Hart, and her friend, John Sweeney, without their knowledge or consent is prohibited under Title III of the Omnibus Crime Control and Safe Streets Act of 1968 (the "Wiretap Act"). 18 U.S.C. §§ 2510-2522 (2012). If David's recordings violate the Wiretap Act, then he will be subject to civil remedies authorized under 18 U.S.C. § 2520 (2012). This is a case of first impression in the Thirteenth Circuit.

Statement introducing the purpose of the discussion.

Statement advising reader that this is a case of first impression in the reviewing court's jurisdiction.

Courts in other federal circuits have considered whether interspousal wiretapping is within the scope of the Wiretap Act and are divided on the issue. Several courts have found that interspousal wiretapping is prohibited by the Wiretap Act. *See, e.g., Glazner v. Glazner*, 347 F.3d 1212, 1215-16 (11th Cir. 2003); *Heggy v. Heggy*, 944 F.2d 1537, 1541 (10th Cir. 1991); *Kempf v. Kempf*, 868 F.2d 970, 973 (8th Cir. 1989); *Pritchard v. Pritchard*, 732 F.2d 372, 374 (4th Cir. 1984); *U.S. v. Jones*, 542 F.2d 661, 673 (6th Cir. 1976); *Kratz v. Kratz*, 477 F. Supp. 463, 472 (E.D. Pa. 1979); *People v. Otto*, 831 P.2d

Statement advising that courts are divided on the issue.

1178, 1190 (Cal. 1992). Other courts, however, have found that interspousal wiretapping is impliedly exempt from the Wiretap Act. *See, e.g., Anonymous v. Anonymous*, 558 F.2d 677, 679 (2d Cir. 1977); *Simpson v. Simpson*, 490 F.2d 803, 810 (5th Cir. 1974); *Lizza v. Lizza*, 631 F. Supp. 529, 532-33 (E.D.N.Y. 1986); *Stewart v. Stewart*, 645 So. 2d 1319, 1321 (Miss. 1994); *Baumrind v. Ewing*, 279 S.E.2d 359, 353 (S.C. 1981).

A court in the Thirteenth Circuit will probably find that the Wiretap Act applies to interspousal wiretapping. The Wiretap Act mandates that "[e]xcept as otherwise specifically provided in this chapter *any person* who—(a) intentionally intercepts, endeavors to intercept, or procures any other person to intercept or endeavor to intercept *any wire, oral, or electronic communication* ... shall be punished ... or shall be subject to suit...." 18 U.S.C. § 2511(1)(a) (2012) (*emphasis added*). David is "any person" within the meaning of section 2511(1)(a). *Id.* Also, his recording of telephone conversations between Ana and John using a device he purchased and attached to a telephone within the Harts' home fits the description of "intentionally intercept[ing] ... any wire, oral, or electronic communication...." *Id.* Therefore, under the plain meaning of section 2511(1)(a), David's recording of Ana and John's conversations violated the Wiretap Act. "The language of [the Wiretap Act] demonstrates that Congress decided that one spouse should not be permitted to record, without consent, electronically transmitted conversations between the other spouse and third parties." *Glazner*, 347 F.3d at 1215 (overruling the decision of *Simpson* as precedent in the Eleventh Circuit[29] and holding that interspousal wiretapping is not an exception to the Wiretap Act). The meaning of the statute is unambiguous. *See id.* Furthermore, the application of the Wiretap Act to David and his recordings is clear and does not lead to an absurd result. *See id.*

Thesis statement beginning the analysis supporting the predicted conclusion.

The writer quotes the relevant language of the statute.

Writer applies the plain meaning of the statute to the facts of the client's case.

29. In 1981, the Fifth Circuit Court of Appeals split into two circuits. The states of Louisiana, Mississippi, and Texas remained in the Fifth Circuit; Alabama, Florida, and Georgia formed the new Eleventh Circuit Court of Appeals. Although the Eleventh Circuit was not required to follow previous decisions of the Fifth Circuit Court of Appeals, it was thought that starting anew, with no binding precedent, was too daunting for the courts. Consequently, the Eleventh Circuit Court of Appeals in *Bonner v. City of Pritchard*, 661 F.2d 1207, 1209 (11th Cir. 1981) (en banc), decided to "adopt" the Fifth Circuit Court of Appeals' decisions existing on September 30, 1981, as precedent for the Eleventh Circuit.

Although the Eleventh Circuit Court of Appeals in *Glazner* overruled *Simpson*, the holding in *Simpson* that interspousal wiretapping is an implied exception from the Wiretap Act is still binding precedent in the Fifth Circuit.

Although a court usually will not refer to legislative history when a statute is "clear on its face," legislative history nevertheless reveals that Congress intended the Wiretap Act to apply to interspousal wiretapping. *Jones*, 542 F.2d at 667. Professor Robert Blakey, the author of the Wiretap Act, testified before the Subcommittee on Administrative Practice and Procedure of the Senate Judiciary Committee. In his testimony, Professor Blakey stated that wiretapping in a marital dispute was one of the two main reasons for the Wiretap Act: "[P]rivate bugging in this country can be divided into two broad categories, commercial espionage and marital litigation." Sen. Subcomm. on Admin. Prac. & Proc. of the Sen. Jud. Comm., *The Right to Privacy Act of 1967*, 90th Cong. 413 (1967), *quoted in Jones*, 542 F.2d at 669.

Passages from legislative history showing legislative intent.

A co-sponsor of the Wiretap Act, Senator Hruska, joined by Senators Dirksen, Scott, and Thurmond, stated: "A broad prohibition is imposed on private use of electronic surveillance, particularly in domestic relations and industrial espionage situations." Sen. Rpt. 90-1097 (Apr. 29, 1968) (*reprinted in* 1968 U.S.C.C.A.N. 2112, 2274). Additionally, the chairman of the Subcommittee on Administrative Practice and Procedure, Senator Long, identified divorce cases as one of three areas "where private electronic surveillance was widespread." *Jones*, 542 F.2d at 668 n.12. The Sixth Circuit Court of Appeals relied, in part, on these comments to conclude that section 2511(1)(a) "establishes a broad prohibition on all private electronic surveillance and that a principal area of congressional concern was electronic surveillance for the purposes of marital litigation." *Id.* at 669 (reversing a district court's dismissal of a criminal indictment of a husband for recording telephone conversations between his estranged wife and a third party in the estranged wife's home in violation of the Wiretap Act).

Parenthetical explanation briefly stating court's holding under the case facts.

Furthermore, the legislative purpose of the Wiretap Act supports the conclusion that interspousal wiretapping is prohibited. The Senate Report on the Wiretap Act stated:

Legislative purpose supporting the plain meaning of the statute.

> [The Wiretap Act] has a dual purpose (1) protecting the privacy of wire and oral communications, and (2) delineating on a uniform basis the circumstances and conditions under which the interception of wire and oral communications may be authorized. To assure the privacy of oral and wire communications, [the Wiretap Act] prohibits all wiretapping and electronic surveillance by persons other than duly authorized law enforcement officers. . . ."

Sen. Rpt. 90-1097 (*reprinted in* 1968 U.S.C.C.A.N. at 2153). Reviewing this passage from the Senate Report, the Sixth Circuit Court of Appeals concluded, "[T]he Senate Report makes it clear that the purpose of the bill was to establish an across-the-board prohibition on all unauthorized electronic surveillance." *Jones*, 542 F.2d at 668.

Reporting the Sixth Circuit court's reliance on the statute's purpose to support its holding.

Finally, an individual's right to privacy is a fundamental right in our society. A spouse's taping of a telephone conversation between the targeted spouse and a third party, without either party's knowledge or consent, is a violation not only of the spouse's privacy but also the third party's privacy. *See id.* at 670.

Public policy supporting the plain meaning of the statute.

Although the majority of federal and state courts have concluded that the Wiretap Act is applicable to interspousal wiretapping, *see Glazner*, 347 F.3d at 1215, a minority of federal courts and two state courts have found that interspousal wiretapping is impliedly excepted from the Wiretap Act. *Anonymous v. Anonymous*, 558 F.2d at 679; *Simpson v. Simpson*, 490 F.2d at 810; *Lizza v. Lizza*, 631 F. Supp. at 532-533; *Stewart v. Stewart*, 645 So. 2d at 1321; *Baumrind v. Ewing*, 279 S.E.2d at 353. The Fifth Circuit Court of Appeals found that, although "the naked language" of the Wiretap Act seemingly applies to interspousal wiretapping, "Congress did not intend such a [far-reaching] result." *Simpson*, 490 F.2d at 805.

Transition to the counteranalysis.

In *Simpson*, the court concluded that a husband's actions were impliedly excepted from the Wiretap Act when he purchased a recording device and attached it to a telephone within the marital home to record conversations between his wife and a third party. *Id.* at 810. Reviewing Senate Report 90-1097, the court found that most of the report focused on "electric surveillance by law enforcement officials" and "contain[ed] no clear indication that Congress intended to intrude into the marital relation within the marital home." *Id.* at 807. Reviewing transcripts of several congressional hearings on the Wiretap Act, the court found sparse references to private surveillance within the marital home, most of which were "directed towards the involvement of private investigators in marital conflicts." *Id.* at 807-09. Based on the court's findings, it would seem that the Wiretap Act would apply only to those domestic situations where a third party, such as a private investigator, was responsible for attaching a recording device and recording the telephone conversations.

Reporting the Fifth Circuit court's reasoning for its interpretation of the statute, which focuses on its review of legislative history to ascertain legislative intent.

Lending further support to the assertion that there is an implied exception in the Wiretap Act for interspousal wiretapping, at least one court has pointed to the comment of

Professor Herman Schwartz, who appeared at a hearing before the House Judiciary Committee: "I take it nobody wants to make it a crime for a father to listen in on his teenage daughter or some such related problem." H.R. Jud. Comm., *The Anti-Crime Program Before Subcom. 5*, 90th Cong. 901 (1967), *quoted in Lizza*, 631 F. Supp. at 532. In *Lizza*, the District Court for the Eastern District of New York deduced that "if nobody wants to make it a crime for a husband to record conversations between his wife and his daughter. . ., a husband's recording of conversations between his wife and a third party should [not] be viewed any differently." *Lizza*, 631 F. Supp. at 533 (citing *Anonymous*, 558 F.2d at 679). In *Lizza*, the court held that interspousal wiretapping is impliedly excepted by the Wiretap Act, dismissing a complaint filed by a wife and third party against her husband for recording conversations on the telephone within the marital home without the parties' knowledge or consent.

Additional legislative history that a district court used to concur with the Fifth Circuit in its interpretation of the statute.

Brief explanation of the facts and holding in the district court case.

Courts finding an implied exception for interspousal wiretapping also have noted that the Wiretap Act is a part of the Omnibus Crime Control and Safe Streets Act of 1968, which is a crime control act. *See Simpson*, 490 F.2d at 806. According to Senate Report 90-1097, "[t]he major purpose of [the Wiretap Act] is to combat organized crime." Sen. Rpt. 90-1097, *reprinted in* 1968 U.S.C.C.A.N. at 2157. Consequently, in addition to providing civil remedies, the Wiretap Act "prescribes criminal sanctions for its violators." *Simpson*, 490 F.2d at 809. Thus, if spouses violate the Wiretap Act for taping conversations between their partners and third parties, the spouses will be "subject to severe criminal penalties, assuming of course that the prosecution could meet the higher standards of proof required for criminal convictions." *Id.* Because of this possibility, the court in *Simpson* stated that a court construing the Wiretap Act should be "bound by the principle that criminal statutes must be strictly construed." *Id.*

Purpose of the statute based on the statutory scheme.

Substantive canon of construction.

Further, if the Wiretap Act were to apply to interspousal wiretapping, it arguably "would have serious ramifications as to the degree of federal control over actions by family members within their own homes." *Lizza*, 631 F. Supp. at 533. Domestic conflict within a marital home is an area "normally left to states" to handle. *Simpson*, 490 F.2d at 805. The court in *Simpson* noted that finding interspousal wiretapping subject to the prohibition of the Wiretap Act would "override the interspousal immunity for personal torts accorded by the majority of states." *Id.* at 805 n.7. "Given the novelty of a federal remedy for persons aggrieved by the personal acts of their spouses within the marital home, and given the severity of the remedy seemingly provided by [the Wiretap Act]," *id.* at 805 (footnote omitted), and absent a clear indication from the statute's language or legislative history, the courts in *Simpson* and *Lizza* refused to find that the Wiretap Act applied to interspousal wiretapping. *Simpson*, 490 F.2d at 10; *Lizza*, 631 F. Supp. at 533.

Nevertheless, although Congress amended the Wiretap Act in 1986 extensively by the Electronics Communications Privacy Act, 18 U.S.C. §§ 2510-2522 (2012), it did not revise the language of section 2511(1)(a) or other sections of the Wiretap Act to provide an express exception for interspousal tapping. Since the *Simpson* decision, the "overwhelming majority of federal circuit and district courts, as well as state courts, addressing the issue have refused to imply an exception to [the Wiretap Act] liability for interspousal wiretapping." *Glazner*, 347 F.3d at 1215. In light of this strong trend in the courts, it would seem that, if Congress had intended to provide an interspousal exception to the Wiretap Act, it would have expressly done so when amending the Wiretap Act for other reasons. The Wiretap Act very likely prohibits interspousal wiretapping. Therefore, David will probably be subject to civil penalties, as well as criminal sanctions, for his recording of the telephone conversations between Ana and John. *See* 18 U.S.C. §§ 2511, 2520 (2012).

Transition to the conclusion.

A canon of construction, commonly known as "the dog didn't bark" canon.

Conclusion statement.

F. Overview: An Objective Analysis of a Law-Based Issue Addressing Alternative Rules or Principles

In addition to a statutory interpretation issue, another type of purely legal question arises when a court must determine which of more than one competing rules or principles should govern the resolution of a dispute. The result will vary depending on which rules or principles are ultimately applied.

Sometimes courts within a jurisdiction may be divided as to which rules or principles should apply. For example, there might be a split within a state's intermediate appellate courts as to which rules or principles are appropriate to apply to resolve an issue. Let's say an attorney in East Carolina represents a man who has recently broken an engagement for marriage with a woman. The client had given his ex-fiancée an expensive ring, symbolizing their commitment to each other (commonly referred to as an engagement ring), at the beginning of the engagement. In light of the broken engagement, the client wants his ex-fiancée to return the ring, but she refuses. While researching the issue of whether the ex-fiancée must return the ring, the lawyer finds that the intermediate appellate courts in East Carolina are divided as to which rule to apply when determining whether an engagement ring should be returned. Of the three state districts, the First Circuit Court of Appeals for East Carolina has applied a "fault" rule, mandating that unless the parties mutually agree to end the engagement, the party who unjustifiably broke the engagement should not receive the ring. Conversely, the Third Circuit Court of Appeals for East Carolina has applied the "no fault" rule, providing that the ring should be returned to the person who gave it, regardless of who is at fault, emphasizing that the ring was a gift conditioned on their getting married. The client and his ex-fiancée reside in the jurisdiction of the Second Circuit Court of Appeals, which has not yet addressed this issue. Therefore, the lawyer will need to determine whether the Second Circuit court will apply the "fault" rule or the "no-fault" rule.

Another situation where a court must choose between competing rules is when the controlling jurisdiction has not addressed the issue but courts in other jurisdictions have. In this instance, the reviewing court may look to jurisdictions outside the reviewing court's jurisdiction ("foreign courts") that have addressed the issue to determine how those jurisdictions resolved the issue. Sometimes the foreign courts are divided on how to resolve the issue, and the reviewing court must determine the rules or principles it will adopt to resolve the present dispute.

Recall again the divorce of Ana and David Hart introduced in Chapter 6. The trial court in that scenario ordered as part of the property settlement that Ana sell her interest in a health club business owned by the couple and sign a covenant not to compete (CNC) with the business in exchange for David's payment of the fair market value of Ana's interest in the business. The fact-based issue in Chapter 6 focused on whether the terms of the CNC imposed by the trial court were reasonable.

Consider this scenario: A junior attorney is asked by a senior attorney in their firm to research that issue. While researching the issue, the junior attorney discovers there may be an additional issue — that is, whether the trial court exceeded its judicial power when ordering Ana to enter into the CNC. Although no East Carolina court and no East Carolina statute has addressed this issue, the junior attorney found that state courts outside of East Carolina have considered the issue and are divided on whether a trial court has exceeded its judicial authority by ordering a spouse to enter into a CNC as part of a divorce property settlement. The junior attorney reports this finding to the senior attorney, and the junior attorney is asked to look further into this issue.

When an issue is one of first impression, as in East Carolina in Ana's case, it is helpful to learn how other state jurisdictions have resolved the issue. It is also helpful to determine whether the existing law and public policies in the controlling court's jurisdiction would support the adoption of certain rules or principles.

The alternative rules or principles in light of the controlling jurisdiction's existing laws and policies will then be used in analyzing whether the reviewing court is likely to adopt any of the new rules or principles. In Ana's case, if she appeals the trial court's order requiring her to sign a CNC and the appeals court finds that the trial court abused its judicial power, then the trial court's order would be reversed. If this occurs, Ana would not be forced to sign the CNC, regardless of whether the terms of the CNC are reasonable.

1. Roadmap paragraph

An objective analysis of a law-based issue addressing alternative rules or principles begins with a roadmap paragraph that usually includes

(1) a conclusion statement,
(2) a statement that the issue is one of first impression within the jurisdiction of the deciding court, and
(3) a brief introduction to the alternative rules or principles that may be adopted by the deciding court.

Using the law-based issue raised in Ana's case as an example, the attorney might begin the discussion as follows.

Conclusion statement and introduction to alternative rules

The trial court probably abused its judicial discretion when it ordered Ana to execute the CNC in return for David's payment of one-half of the fair market value of her interest in Hart Fitness Center. Whether a court can order a spouse to sign a CNC as part of a property settlement in a divorce proceeding is a case of first impression in East Carolina. Jurisdictions, including Oklahoma and Texas, have ruled that it is an abuse of the trial court's discretion to order a spouse to sign a CNC as part of a property settlement because the interest protected by the CNC is an involuntary agreement that restricts trade and represents the spouse's future earning capacity, which is not marital property subject to division upon divorce. *Favell v. Favell*, 957 P.2d 556, 561 (Okla. Civ. App. 1997); *Ulmer v. Ulmer*, 717 S.W.2d 665, 667-68 (Tex. App. 1986). Other jurisdictions, such as Idaho and Maine, permit courts to order a spouse to sign a CNC as part of a property settlement, identifying the interest protected by the CNC as the goodwill of the business, which is subject to division upon divorce. *Carr v. Carr*, 701 P.2d 304, 309-10 (Idaho Ct. App. 1985); *Lord v. Lord*, 454 A.2d 830, 834-35 (Me. 1983).

Conclusion statement.

Statement advising this is an issue of first impression so that the reader understands why decisions of foreign courts are being used.

Statement advising that foreign courts are divided on whether a judge may order a spouse to execute a CNC in the marital business upon dissolution of a marriage. Reserve any further explanation or elaboration of these conflicting rules for the analysis.

2. Analysis

Next, the analysis would include a discussion of each rule or principle. If logical, you should begin with the analysis of the rules or principles that you predict the reviewing court will ultimately adopt. Open with a conclusion sentence that signals the beginning of the analysis supporting the predicted conclusion. If necessary, define the rules or principles, and then follow with an explanation of the primary decision(s) where the foreign court(s) adopted the rules or principles. Similar to a rule explanation for a fact-based issue discussion, the rule explanation for a law-based issue discussion contains

(1) the facts of the case relevant to the issue being analyzed,
(2) the foreign court's holding on the issue being analyzed, and
(3) the foreign court's reasoning for its holding on the issue being analyzed.

The rule explanation in a discussion of a law-based issue, however, does not emphasize the case facts as in a discussion of a fact-based issue; rather, the rule explanation in a law-based issue emphasizes the court's reasoning for adopting the rule or principle and shows how the rule was applied in that case. The court's reasoning is of utmost importance because the law and policies relied on by that court will be used as a basis to determine whether the reviewing court in the present instance will adopt that rule.

Example of a rule explanation supporting the predicted conclusion in Ana's case

An East Carolina appeals court will most likely follow the court in *Favell* and find that the trial court abused its discretion when it ordered Ana to sign the CNC. In *Favell*, the husband and wife were majority stockholders in nine corporations created or acquired after the couple's marriage. In return for awarding the husband a portion of the corporate assets, the trial court imposed a CNC on the husband, preventing him from competing with the corporations awarded to the wife. The appellate court reversed the trial court's decision, holding that the court could not impose a CNC upon the husband. *Favell*, 957 P.2d at 561. *See also Ulmer*, 717 S.W.2d at 667 (trial

Sentence introduces the analysis of the rule that the writer predicts the reviewing court will adopt.

The writer briefly states the facts so that the reader understands the situation is similar to the client's issue. The holding follows.

court erred in ordering a husband not to compete with the janitorial business awarded to the wife because an individual's ability to practice his profession is not property subject to division in a divorce proceeding). The court in *Favell* reasoned that the imposition of the CNC was contrary to Oklahoma policy expressed in statutory law, which limited restraints on trade to specific situations where the seller of the goodwill of a business or where the parties dissolving a business agree to "refrain from carrying on a business within geographically specified (and statutorily limited) parameters." *Favell*, 957 P.2d at 560-61 (citing Okla. Stat. tit. 15, §§ 217-219 (1989)). The court in *Favell* also reasoned that the CNC "violated another general principle" that future earning capacity is not recognized in Oklahoma as marital property subject to division upon divorce; *Id.* (citing *Mocnik v. Mocnik*, 838 P.2d 500 (Okla. 1992)). The CNC in *Favell* infringed on the "[h]usband's right to pursue his chosen line of work, i.e., his future earning capacity." *Id.* "By including in the marital estate the value directly attributable to a restriction on [the h]usband's future earning ability, the trial court [impermissibly] treated at least a portion of [the h]usband's future earning capacity as marital property and awarded a portion of the value of that capacity to [the w]ife." *Id.*

[The writer continues with the analysis, presenting an analogy between Oklahoma statutory law and East Carolina statutory law and explaining further the state of the common law in East Carolina. The writer describes an East Carolina decision that explains two different types of goodwill (enterprise goodwill, a business asset that outlives any person's involvement in a business, and professional goodwill, a personal asset that depends on a particular person's involvement) and whether they are subject to property division upon divorce. The writer then applies the rules to the facts of Ana's case, leading up to the predicted conclusion.]

Because *Ulmer* does not add any new principle to the analysis, the writer does not provide a rule explanation but only cites it with a parenthetical explanation showing that the *Ulmer* court ruled similarly. Because the writer provides a rule explanation only of *Favell*, the analysis focuses only on that decision.

The court's reasoning focused on public policy as reflected in Oklahoma statutes.

The second part of the court's reasoning relied on another general principle applicable to divorces in Oklahoma as expressed in the state's common law.

After completing the analysis supporting the predicted conclusion, the lawyer should transition to the counteranalysis. In the counteranalysis, the lawyer should present the rules or principles that the court will be less likely to adopt. Similar to the analysis supporting the predicted conclusion, the counteranalysis usually includes

- any necessary definitions of the rules or principles the court will be less likely to adopt;
- an explanation of the primary decision(s) in which foreign court(s) adopted the rules or principles; and
- an analysis of the likelihood that the rules or principles followed by the foreign court will be adopted by the reviewing court, which may include
    - current law and public policy in the reviewing court's jurisdiction that may support the reviewing court's adoption of these new rules or principles;
    - where necessary, analogies or distinctions between the current laws or policies, or both, in the reviewing court's jurisdiction and the laws and policies existing at the time of the foreign court's decision to determine whether the two jurisdictions have similar law and public policy interests; and
    - if appropriate, an application of the rules or principles to the facts of the client's case.

3. *Conclusion*

After a thorough analysis supporting the predicted conclusion, followed by the counteranalysis, the writer must state the conclusion and the reasons for the conclusion, including the pivotal reason why the court is more likely to reach the predicted conclusion instead of the one discussed in the counteranalysis.

Example of a conclusion paragraph for Ana's issue

Nevertheless, East Carolina is more likely to find that it was an abuse of discretion for the trial court to order Ana to sign the CNC. East Carolina is careful to separate professional goodwill from enterprise goodwill, and an East Carolina court would probably find that there was professional goodwill directly attributable to Ana in the valuation of the business because of her name recognition and dedicated clientele. Because there was professional goodwill, which represents future earning capacity that is not marital property, and because public policy in East Carolina does not favor agreements in restraint of trade, an East Carolina appeals court is likely to determine that the trial court abused its discretion in ordering Ana to sign the CNC.

Conclusion to the law-based issue.

Reasons supporting the conclusion.

G. *Organizing a Document That Addresses Both a Law-Based Issue and a Fact-Based Issue*

If a lawyer were to address the law-based issue analysis for Ana's case (whether the trial court exceeded its judicial powers in ordering Ana to sign the CNC) in the same document as the fact-based issue analysis for Ana's case (whether the terms of the court-ordered CNC are reasonable), the lawyer would need to determine whether the law-based issue or fact-based issue should be presented first. In Ana's case, the threshold issue is the law-based issue. If the appellate court found the trial court exceeded its judicial powers in ordering Ana to sign the CNC (as was the conclusion in the foregoing discussion), then the appellate court would not need to address whether the terms of the CNC are reasonable. But because the lawyer is only *predicting* what a court is likely to conclude and the goal is to inform the reader on all the issues relevant to the case, the lawyer would still provide a complete discussion of whether the terms of the CNC were reasonable.

A document containing both discussions should begin with an overall introduction presenting the two issues to be addressed, followed by the entire law-based discussion. An example of an overall introduction in Ana's case might look like the following paragraph.

> This discussion addresses whether the trial court abused its judicial discretion when it ordered Ana to execute a CNC in return for David's paying her one-half of the fair market value of their health club business. This discussion will further address whether, if the trial court did not abuse its discretion, the CNC is unenforceable because it is overbroad in its protection of David's business interests.
>
> [The law-based issue discussion of whether the trial court exceeded its judicial powers when it ordered Ana to execute the CNC would be inserted here.]

Immediately following the law-based issue discussion in the predictive document would be the fact-based issue discussion of whether the terms of the CNC are reasonable, as covered in Chapters 6 and 7. The second issue would begin with an appropriate transitional statement:

> In the event the appeals court finds that the trial court did not exceed its authority when it ordered Ana to sign the CNC, the appeals court will likely find that the CNC that Ana has been ordered to sign is overbroad in its protection of David's business interests and is therefore unreasonable and unenforceable.
>
> [The fact-based discussion of whether the provisions of the CNC are reasonable would be inserted here.]

The document would end with an overall conclusion that summarizes the conclusions reached under the law-based issue and fact-based issue:

> The appeals court will probably find that the trial court exceeded its discretion when it ordered Ana to sign the CNC because the CNC represents a protection against the professional goodwill of Ana. The value of professional goodwill is tied to future earning capacity, which is not an asset subject to division upon divorce. Even if the court should find that the trial court did not abuse its discretion, the court will probably find the CNC unenforceable because the territorial restriction is overbroad for the protection of David's business interests.

CHAPTER SUMMARY

- Courts interpret and apply statutes to legal disputes.
- When interpreting ambiguous statutes, courts use tools of statutory interpretation such as the "plain meaning" rule, canons of construction, and legislative histories.
- Courts may use different approaches to interpret a statute—for example, the "textualist" approach or the "intentionalist" approach.
- A law-based issue requires a court to determine (1) whether a statute, rule, or principle applies to a dispute; or (2) which legal principle applies when more than one relevant applicable legal principle exists.
- An objective discussion of an issue involving statutory interpretation informs the reader of the law and legislative history, where available, surrounding the statute in question and, using the tools of statutory interpretation, predicts how the court will likely interpret the statute.
- An objective discussion of competing rules or principles includes a thorough discussion of the rules and whether the law and policies in the reviewing court's jurisdiction favor the adoption of one rule over another.

CHAPTER

13

Beyond the Objective Discussion of a Legal Issue: Other Elements of the Office Memorandum

A. Introduction

Chapter 6 introduced the Discussion section as part of a more formal document, the office memorandum. The office memorandum is usually written for a supervising attorney. The goal of the office memorandum is to present an objective discussion and analysis of the arguments for both parties in a dispute, as a way to assess the strength of the client's case. The writer both (1) *educates* the supervising attorney about the relevant law, facts, and policy in the client's case, and (2) *predicts* a likely outcome in the case. The objective analysis addressed earlier in this book reflects what would be included in the Discussion section. This chapter explains the other sections of a formal office memorandum, including the Questions Presented, Brief Answers, Statement of Facts, and Overall Conclusion, in that order.

> **Note:** This order and the sections of a formal office memorandum are suggestions only. Many practicing lawyers use a different order and may eliminate some of the sections discussed in this chapter (such as the Questions Presented, Brief Answers, or the Conclusion section). If writing a document for a supervising attorney, always follow that attorney's guidance.

Consider again Ana's case where she and her husband David are divorcing. During the divorce proceeding, the court ordered that (1) David buy Ana's interest in their health clubs (the Hart Fitness Centers), and (2) in exchange for this sum, Ana sell to David her one-half interest in the business and sign a covenant not to complete (CNC). In the CNC, Ana was required "not to engage either directly or indirectly, on her own or in the employ of another, in the health and exercise club business in any form for a period of five years in the counties of Hamilton, Hancock, Boone, Marion, Johnson, and Hendricks, plus the towns of Arcadia and Bloomtown, East Carolina." Ana does not want to sign the CNC or abide by the terms of the CNC.

B. Question(s) Presented

The goal in drafting questions is to disclose early what's in dispute in the case. Since this is the first section of an office memorandum, each question must make sense if read independently of all other sections. The structure used in drafting a substantive issue statement when writing a case brief, introduced in Chapter 3, is the same structure followed when drafting a question for an office memorandum. The substance of each question, however, will vary depending on whether the question reflects a fact-based issue or a law-based issue.

1. Writing a single, fact-based question

When drafting a fact-based legal question, consider the following steps:

Step One: Provide a legal question that reveals an issue in dispute.

Step Two: Provide the specific facts relevant to that legal question.

Since the goal is to write a question so the reader understands why a dispute about the law exists, a helpful question provides sufficient relevant facts to show why the parties disagree. A writer, faced with this client's situation, might begin by drafting the following legal question:

Legal question:	Under East Carolina law, is a CNC a wife is being forced to sign in connection with the sale to her husband of their health and exercise clubs as part of their property settlement in a divorce proceeding enforceable

The legal question tells the reader in which jurisdiction this issue arose. If a question is particularly long, the broad legal language may be eliminated ("Under East Carolina law"). This section also provides the specific legal question, that is, whether the CNC is enforceable.

Note also the use of generic, neutral references (husband and wife) rather than personal names (Ana and David Hart) to refer to the parties. Proper names are not necessary in understanding the legal issues and relevant facts in the case. Generic names better focus the reader on the relationship of the parties in the case.

The facts in the question may be the most difficult section to write. The writer must decide which specific facts supporting each party to include. Including all the facts relevant to each question may be too cumbersome. Instead, focus on those facts that are absolutely essential to understanding what's in dispute. A sample set of specific facts included in the Question Presented section follows.

Specific facts relevant to the legal question:	(1) the CNC prohibits the wife from engaging in the same health club business in cities and counties where the health clubs being sold are not currently located, though the couple had planned to expand to those cities and counties in the next three years, and (2) when the couple purchased other health clubs in the past, the CNCs required were limited to only the counties in which those health clubs were located at the time of the sale.

The CNC Ana is being required to sign extends beyond the cities and counties where the Hart Fitness Centers are presently located, unlike the CNCs the Harts had required when purchasing other health clubs in the past. This fact supports Ana's position. However, the Harts had planned to expand their business to those cities and counties in the future, which supports her husband David's position. Together, these facts in the question reveal the dispute in the case.

Sample Single Fact-Based Question Presented

Under East Carolina contract law, is a CNC a wife is being forced to sign in connection with the sale to her husband of their health and exercise clubs as part of the property settlement in their divorce proceeding enforceable when (1) the CNC prohibits the wife from engaging in the same health club business in cities and counties where the health clubs being sold are not currently located, though the couple had planned to expand to those cities and counties in the next three years, and (2) when the couple purchased other health clubs in the past, the CNCs required were limited to only the counties in which those health clubs were located at the time of the sale?

Notice that the question, though long, is one sentence only. Each question should be written, when possible, as a single sentence. A question may be easier to follow, especially when there are numerous facts, by numbering the facts, as above.

While the formal Questions Presented section is usually the first section found in a formal office memorandum, the formal version of the questions is often not written until after drafting the Discussion section of the office memorandum. It is oftentimes difficult to know which facts are most legally significant until after working through the analysis and completing the discussion.

Finally, when you include only one question, do not give it a number, letter, or roman numeral.

2. *Writing a single law-based question*

A law-based question requires the same two steps as provided above. The inclusion of the facts, however, is different.

Law-based questions focus more on the legal test rather than the law's application to a particular set of facts. For that reason, the facts are usually limited to the general story, or the factual category. Let's say the assigning attorney added a law-based issue to the office memorandum, asking whether a judge has the discretion to order a spouse in a divorce case to sign a CNC as part of a property settlement. Since this issue had not yet been addressed in East Carolina, it's a case of first impression, requiring the appellate court to decide as a matter of law whether requiring Ana to sign the CNC as part of her property settlement is allowed. Other states have reached countervailing decisions on this question, so the focus in answering the question is on the court's reasoning for adopting or not adopting the rule or principle based on the law and public policies relied on by courts in other jurisdictions. The question on the law-based issue might be:

> In a case of first impression in East Carolina, after agreeing in a property settlement in a divorce proceeding to split the value of a number of health clubs, does a judge have the discretion to order a spouse to sign a CNC as part of the settlement agreement

This first-half of the question tells the reader the jurisdiction is East Carolina and the relevant law is the judge's ability to require that a CNC be signed as part of a property settlement in a divorce. Added to this would be the countervailing public policy arguments, as follows:

> that (1) arguably restricts the wife's ability to practice in her profession and may limit her future earning capacity but (2) may be considered business goodwill, which is marital property, rather than personal goodwill, and is divisible and arguably necessary to protect the value of the goodwill for which the husband is paying?

Note the lack of factual detail in the above example. The facts are in the question only to set up the law-based question.

Sample Single Law-Based Question and Fact-Based Question

In a case of first impression in East Carolina, after agreeing in a property settlement in a divorce proceeding to split the value of a number of health clubs, does a judge have the discretion to order the wife to sign a CNC as part of the settlement agreement that (1) arguably restricts the wife's ability to practice in her profession and may limit her future earning capacity but (2) may be considered business goodwill, which is marital property, rather than personal goodwill, and is divisible and arguably necessary to protect the value of the goodwill for which the husband is paying?

3. *Writing multiple questions*

Sometimes the office memorandum will include more than one question. The Questions Presented section in the Harts' case now reflects one law-based question and one fact-based question. The law-based question, whether a judge can order a spouse to sign a CNC as part of a property settlement in a divorce, must be analyzed first in the discussion, because the answer to the law-based question determines whether the fact-based question becomes an issue. This order is also reflected in the questions.

Sample Separated Law-Based and Fact-Based Questions

I. In a case of first impression in East Carolina, after agreeing in a property settlement in a divorce proceeding to split the value of a number of health clubs, does a judge have the discretion to order the wife to sign a CNC as part of the settlement agreement that (1) arguably restricts the wife's ability to practice in her profession and may limit her future earning capacity but (2) may be considered business goodwill, which is marital property, rather than personal goodwill, and is divisible and arguably necessary to protect the value of the goodwill for which the husband is paying?

II. If a judge does have the discretion to order the wife to sign the CNC, is the CNC enforceable when (1) the CNC prohibits the wife from engaging in the same health club business in cities and counties where the health clubs being sold are not currently located, though the couple had planned to expand to those cities and counties in the next three years, and (2) when the couple purchased other health clubs in the past, the CNCs required were limited to only the counties in which those health clubs were located at the time of the sale?

Notice that the second question has been revised due to the content of the first question. If a court would decide that a judge in East Carolina could not order a spouse to sign a CNC as part of a property settlement agreement in a divorce, then the court would not address the second issue reflected in II, above. However, the memo writer must still include the analysis of the fact-based issue in case the court does recognize that judicial authority. The transition used in II, "If a judge does have the discretion to order the wife to sign the CNC," alerts the reader of the relationship between the questions in I and II.

In some instances, the legal test being analyzed includes multiple sub-issues, creating a new challenge when writing the questions. For example, if in the CNC case, more than one of the prongs required to make the CNC enforceable were at issue in the case, the most likely structure of the question would be to write one broad legal question that introduces the legal issue regarding the enforceability of the CNC, and then to write two subquestions, each one reflecting the two requirements in dispute that must be met in order to make the CNC enforceable.

Sample Broad Fact-Based Question with Two Sub-Questions

In a divorce settlement, is a CNC a wife is being forced to sign in connection with the sale of the couple's health and exercise clubs overbroad and unenforceable?

I. Is the CNC broader than necessary for the protection of the seller's business interest when (1) the CNC prohibits the wife from engaging in the same health club business in cities and counties where the club being sold is not currently located, but the couple had planned to expand to those cities and counties in the next three years, and (2) the couple purchased other health clubs in the past, the CNCs required were limited to only the counties in which those health clubs were located at the time of the sale?

II. While the CNC does not adversely affect the public interest, does the CNC have an adverse effect on the seller when ... [and the facts in dispute would be presented here]?

Notice that the broad single question does not have a number, letter, or roman numeral. Also note that questions I and II are written to reflect the two issues in dispute. Since there are actually three prongs or requirements in the test for enforceability of a CNC, the third prong, that the "covenant cannot adversely affect the public interest," is subsumed in the question framed in II. It will be mentioned in the Discussion as a requirement that is obviously met in this case. Further, the question above is written as though the fact-based question was the only question raised in the memorandum, leaving out the law-based question. If the law-based question was included, the structure of the Questions Presented would look like the following:

Sample Law-Based Question, Then a Fact-Based Question with Sub-Questions

I. In a case of first impression in East Carolina, after agreeing in a property settlement in a divorce proceeding to split the value of a number of health clubs, does a judge have the discretion to order the wife to sign a CNC as part of the settlement agreement that (1) arguably restricts the wife's ability to practice in her profession and may limit her future earning capacity but (2) may be considered business goodwill, which is marital property, rather than personal goodwill, and is divisible and arguably necessary to protect the value of the goodwill for which the husband is paying?

II. If a judge does have the discretion to order the wife to sign the CNC, is the CNC unenforceable?

A. Is the CNC broader than necessary for the protection of the seller's business interest when (1) the CNC prohibits the wife from engaging in the same health club business in cities and counties where the club being sold is not currently located, but the couple had planned to expand to those cities and counties in the next three years, and (2) the couple purchased other health clubs in the past, the CNCs required were limited to only the counties in which those health clubs were located at the time of the sale?

B. While the CNC does not adversely affect the public interest, does the CNC have an adverse effect on the seller when . . . [and facts in dispute would be presented here]?

To summarize, keep the following guidelines in mind when drafting the Questions Presented section:

- Frame each separate legal point in dispute in a separate question.
- Provide questions that address only issues in dispute.
- Aim to write each question as one sentence only.
- Exclude any legal conclusions.
- Refer to the parties using generic, or neutral names, rather than proper names.
- If an office memorandum addresses only a single question, do not number that question. If there are multiple questions, number each question, using the formal outlining process. The same outline designation will be provided at the beginning of the Brief Answer and Discussion sections of the office memorandum, discussed below.
- If providing several facts in a question, consider numbering them to make the question easier to understand.

• Exercise 13-A

(1) Draft a Questions Presented section that reflects the issue(s) raised in Edina Broward's case. The facts are found in Chapter 1 and the case continues in the exercises in Chapters 6 and 7 regarding whether she can recover her lost painting after the statute of limitations has expired. The case authority is found in the Student Supplemental Materials for this book located on the publisher's website at http://www.aspenpublishing.com.

(2) Draft a Questions Presented section that reflects the issue raised in the exercises in Chapters 6 and 7 regarding whether the landowner Redwood Mobile Homes can be held liable for the drowning of the child Ricky Olson in Redwood's settlement tank. The case authority is found in the Student Supplemental Materials for this book located on the publisher's website at http://www.aspenpublishing.com.

C. Brief Answer(s)

The Brief Answer section is as it is described—it is a quick answer to each question raised in the Questions Presented section with a brief explanation of the answer, based on the applicable law and facts.

First answer the question directly, using terms such as the following:

Yes.
No.
Probably.
Probably not.
Likely.
Likely not.

After each direct answer, briefly explain that answer, including references to both the relevant law and the client's facts. Avoid citing to authority, unless a reference is absolutely essential to answering the question. Again, use generic references to refer to the parties.

Sample Brief Answers Section for the Law-Based Question and the Fact-Based Question in the CNC Case:

I. Likely yes. The appellate court is more likely to find the trial judge does not have the discretion to order the wife to sign the CNC. East Carolina separates professional goodwill from enterprise goodwill, and the court would probably find there was professional goodwill directly attributable to the wife in the valuation of the business because of her name recognition and dedicated clientele. Further, professional goodwill represents future earning capacity that is not marital property; since public policy in East Carolina does not favor agreements in restraint of trade, an appeals court is likely to find the trial court abused its discretion in ordering the wife to sign the CNC.

II. Likely yes. The CNC extends into counties and towns where no health clubs currently operate and no active steps have been taken to expand into those areas. Thus, the CNC is probably overbroad for the protection of the husband's business interest and is unreasonable and unenforceable.

• Exercise 13-B

(1) Draft a Brief Answer section for a memorandum that answers and briefly explains whether Edina Broward can recover her lost painting after the statute of limitations has expired. The case authority is found in the Student Supplemental Materials for this book located on the publisher's website at http://www.aspenpublishing.com.

(2) Draft a Brief Answer section that answers and explains whether the landowner Redwood Mobile Homes can be held liable for the drowning of the child Ricky Olson in Redwood's settlement tank. The case authority is found in the Student Supplemental Materials for this book located on the publisher's website at http://www.aspenpublishing.com.

D. Statement of the Facts

The legal reader may know something about the legal issues raised in a client's case; however, the client's story—the narrative—is the one part of the case that is unique and what the reader may not know or know only generally. It is essential, therefore, to completely and accurately convey the facts necessary to understand the legal issues in dispute. Consider the following guidelines:

1. ***Tell the story in chronological order, unless there's a reason to do otherwise.*** Stories are normally told in the same order as the story unfolds, and readers expect this. Alter the order of the story only if there is a legitimate reason to do so, such as when one group of facts relates to one event with its own legal issue and another group of facts relates to a different event with a different legal issue. If so, it may be more helpful to the legal reader to group the facts by legal significance rather than chronologically.

2. ***In the first sentence or two, introduce the key parties, providing their status or relationship in the case and briefly explaining the basis for the case.*** Unlike in the Questions Presented and Brief Answer sections, in this Statement of Facts section it's important to use the proper names of the parties and companies involved in the case. Thus, in the CNC case, the parties would be identified as Ana Hart as the client/potential plaintiff/wife, and David Hart as the potential defendant/husband, who are divorcing.

3. ***Provide the legally significant facts as well as any background facts necessary for the story to make sense.*** The best way to determine whether a fact is legally significant is to write the discussion first. Any fact included in the discussion because it's legally significant *must* be included in the Statement of Facts section. Background facts are not legally significant but help the reader follow the story. An example of a background fact in Ana's case is that Ana and David met at a weightlifting competition. As with the questions, the legally significant facts will include those facts that support both the client's position as well as the opposing party's position. Both are vital to understanding the conflict between the parties. In addition, provide in the fact statement where and when the event(s) took place. The location of the event is important in determining which court has proper jurisdiction over the case, in the event the client chooses to file a lawsuit. The dates could be important in determining whether the statute of limitations for the cause of action has passed, prohibiting the filing of the suit unless an exception applies.

4. *Omit any legal conclusions.* The Statement of Facts section should contain facts only, without references to any opinions or conclusions about those facts. For example, a legal conclusion for the facts in Ana's case would be, "The overbroad restriction in the CNC prevented Ana from working in any health club business located in cities and counties where the Hart Fitness Center didn't presently operate." This example states a legal conclusion, that the CNC is overbroad, which is one of the requirements the memo writer will analyze and conclude on in the discussion.

5. *Be careful to omit any adverbs and adjectives unless part of a quote.* Use strong nouns and verbs instead of adverbs and adjectives, unless they are a part of a quote. If providing testimony by one of the parties, and that testimony is relevant to the legal analysis, provide the key language word-for-word and in quotes. Even if quoting testimony is not necessary, always indicate the source of the information provided in the fact statement, for example, by explaining which party relayed which facts.

> **Note:** Consider doing a side-by-side reading of the Discussion section and the Statement of Facts section. Every fact contained in the discussion must also be included in the fact statement. All specific detail should be included in both sections. Do not rely on the Statement of Facts section to provide the specific facts and then refer only generally to those facts in the Discussion section.

Sample Statement of Facts

Ana Hart and her husband, David Hart, are divorcing. David petitioned the court to award him ownership of the couple's Hart Fitness Centers. After a hearing on David's petition, the court ordered that (1) David buy Ana's interest in the business, and (2) in exchange for this sum, Ana sell to David her one-half interest in the business and sign a covenant not to complete (CNC). In the CNC, Ana must promise "not to engage either directly or indirectly, on her own or in the employ of another, in the health and exercise club business in any form for a period of five years in the counties of Hamilton, Hancock, Boone, Marion, Johnson, and Hendricks, plus the towns of Arcadia and Bloomtown, East Carolina." Ana does not want to sign the CNC or abide by the terms of the CNC.

Ana and David live in Flora, East Carolina. Flora is located in Marion County. They met while both were competing in weightlifting competitions. Shortly after their marriage, they started the health and exercise club in Flora under the name of their business partnership, "Hart Fitness Center" (Center). Both are active partners in the business. The business thrived, and the Harts later purchased two other health and exercise clubs, one in Hamilton County and one in Johnson County. The sellers of these clubs did not have any connection with members of Hart Fitness Center prior to the sale. The purchase agreements for these clubs included CNCs that restricted the sellers, for a period of five years, from engaging in any health and exercise club business in the counties where the purchased clubs were located. The Harts do not own any Centers in Boone, Hancock, or Hendricks counties, or in the towns of Arcadia or Bloomtown, though the couple had planned to expand into these areas within the next three years. The counties border Flora. Bloomtown is located approximately forty-five miles south of Flora, and Arcadia is located approximately fifty miles northwest of Flora. At the time of the divorce, the membership in the Centers totaled 5,200 clients. A recent survey of Center members showed that, although members may use any of the Centers, they usually use the Center closest to their homes or workplaces.

- **Exercise 13-C**

  (1) Draft a Statement of Facts for Edina Broward's case regarding the return of her lost painting after the statute of limitations period had passed, introduced at the end of Chapter 1 and continued in the exercises in Chapters 6 and 7.

  (2) Draft a Statement of Facts for the *Ricky Olson* case regarding whether Redwood Mobile Homes can be held liable for the drowning of the child Ricky in Redwood's settlement tank, discussed in Chapters 6 and 7.

E. Conclusion

The final conclusion may seem much like the Brief Answer section, and in some office memoranda the Conclusion or the Brief Answer section is omitted. The Conclusion section usually includes the pivotal reasons for the predicted conclusion and, if necessary, why those reasons support the predicted conclusion. Do not add new information in this section.[1] If information is important, include it in the Discussion section. Make sure, however, that you are answering any questions posed by the supervising attorney. A sample Conclusion section for the CNC would simply summarize the conclusions reached in the law-based and fact-based issues.

1. The one exception to this rule is when citing public policy. In particular, if you are analyzing a fact-based issue and public policy can be used to bolster that analysis, you may choose to wait and discuss the policy in the Conclusion section, to show why you favored the stronger position.

Sample Conclusion

The court is likely to find the trial judge did not have the judicial discretion to order Ana Hart to sign a CNC as part of a property settlement in the Harts' divorce proceeding. The CNC included Ana's professional goodwill that is not considered marital property, and the CNC restricted Ana's ability to pursue her profession in locations beyond where the couple owned any health clubs. East Carolina does not favor agreements in restraint of trade. *Mats Transport*, 824 S.E.2d at 1468. However, should the court determine that a trial judge can order a spouse to sign a CNC as part of a property settlement, because the CNC extends into counties and towns where no health clubs currently operate, and the couple never took any active steps to expand into those areas, the CNC is probably overbroad for the protection of David Hart's business interest and is therefore unreasonable and unenforceable.

A checklist covering the sections of an office memorandum is found in the Student Supplemental Materials for this book located on the publisher's website at http://www.aspenpublishing.com.

• Exercise 13-D

(1) Draft an overall Conclusion section that summarizes and answers whether the statute of limitations will be tolled, so Edina Broward's lost painting can be returned to her. The case authority is found in the Student Supplemental Materials for this book located on the publisher's website at http://www.aspenpublishing.com.

(2) Draft an overall Conclusion section that summarizes and answers whether the landowner Redwood Mobile Homes can be held liable for the drowning of the child Ricky Olson in Redwood's settlement tank. The case authority is found in the Student Supplemental Materials for this book located on the publisher's website at http://www.aspenpublishing.com.

CHAPTER SUMMARY

- A formal office memorandum includes, in addition to the Discussion section, sections on Questions Presented, Brief Answers, Statement of Facts, and an overall Conclusion.
- The Questions Presented section focuses the reader on the legal issues that will be analyzed in the memorandum.
- The Brief Answers section provides the answer to each of the questions and briefly explains the reasons for those answers, based on both the relevant law and facts of the case.

- The Statement of Facts section provides the story of the case and includes all legally significant facts as well as any background facts necessary for an understandable story.
- The overall Conclusion, similar to the Brief Answers section, includes a summary of the key legal points addressed in the discussion, along with the main reason(s) supporting the conclusion and answers the question(s) posed by the supervising attorney.

CHAPTER

14

Writing Letters and Electronic Communications

A. Introduction

This chapter focuses on expository writings and, specifically, on letters and common electronic communications written by attorneys in the United States. Most law students have experienced and are comfortable writing letters, either formally or in an email. When writing letters or communicating via email about a case or legal issue, however, a lawyer must exercise particular caution. In the United States, lawyers should consider any written product as potential evidence to be used in court and should write even email communications with this understanding.

The two main types of letters still being written by many attorneys in the United States are client letters and demand letters. Always consider the cultural differences among legal employers that may influence the approach to these types of writings. For example, this chapter covers some of the recommended techniques to use when communicating a disappointing message to a client; lawyers in other countries, however, may be more direct than what is advised in this chapter. When any lawyer writes letters to someone in another country, the writer should understand the customs lawyers in that country follow. This knowledge can only enhance any lawyer's credibility in their international practice.

The chapter concludes with guidelines for writing electronic communications, including emails and the more informal version of a formal office memorandum, the e-memo. Lawyers in the United States frequently use emails and e-memos in their practice.

B. *Writing Letters to Clients*

As with any written document, first consider (1) the purpose in writing the letter; (2) the appropriate tone for the letter; and (3) the audience or individual who will receive the letter.

1. *The purpose*

Client letters may be written for any one or more of the following reasons:

- To verify information received from the client.
- To answer questions posed by the client.
- To inform the client of progress in the case.
- To inform the client of the analysis of the legal issues in the case.
- To ask the client for additional or clarifying information.
- To predict how the case might proceed.
- To make recommendations to the client.

Knowing the purpose of the letter allows the writer to include only the content that satisfies that purpose. With this clear direction, the final product will be more complete and focused.

2. The tone and the audience

The appropriate tone of a letter written by an attorney in the United States depends on the person receiving the letter (the audience). If, for example, the client is a friend or someone the lawyer knows well, a more informal, friendly tone may be appropriate. If, however, the lawyer does not know the client well, or does know the client and knows that client prefers a more formal style of writing, then choose a more formal tone.

Consider also the client's background and experience. A predominant goal is to write a letter the client can easily understand. If the client is also a lawyer or otherwise has a legal background, the lawyer writing the document may feel comfortable using legal terminology and being more specific, for example, about the source of the law and the analysis. If, however, the client has had little experience reading legal materials, avoid legal terminology wherever possible and use language that can explain the message and be easily understood. The goal is to satisfy the client's needs; to achieve this goal, pay particular attention to the use of language.

The guidelines below include examples of a client letter that might have been written to Ana Hart, the client who does not want the CNC ordered by the judge during a divorce proceeding enforced.

3. What to include in a client letter

In the United States, letters from attorneys to clients usually contain the following sections:

a. Heading
b. Salutation
c. Introduction
d. Statement restating the facts about the case
e. Statement of the conclusion, if applicable, and the reasoning behind the conclusion and how it might affect the client's case
f. Recommendations and any follow-up questions summarized, if applicable and not included in the introduction
g. Offer to meet or talk further with the client and the lawyer's contact information
h. Closing

a. Heading

A letter to the client begins with a heading that includes the lawyer's address, the client's address, and the date. Usually a reference to the case is also included, using a "Regarding" or "Re:" line.

The heading in our sample letter about Ana Hart's case would look like:

Smith, Jones, & Brown, P.C.
Attorneys at Law
532 Main Street
Flora, East Carolina 57235
May 12, 20xx

Ana Hart
1030 Meadowlark Lane
Flora, East Carolina 57235

Re: Enforceability of the Covenant Not to Compete (CNC).

b. Salutation

Next, provide a salutation. In the above example, the salutation would be "Dear Ms. Hart," or, if the lawyer knows her well, "Dear Ana."

A sample salutation would be:

Dear Ms. Hart,

c. Introduction

The introduction must state the purpose of the letter and, if answering a specific question or request by the client, an explicit reference to the question or to the request to which the lawyer is responding. The lawyer might also refer to the last time they talked, either in person, by phone, or through written communication.

The letter's introduction might read as follows.

Thank you for meeting with me on Wednesday, May 10, regarding your divorce and the CNC the judge is requiring you to sign as part of the property settlement agreement. I will be happy to help you in any way I can. My recommendation is to take steps to avoid signing the CNC, explained below.

In this first paragraph the writer reconnects with the client and states the specific purpose for writing. The writer also answers the question raised regarding signing the CNC.

d. A restatement of the facts

Sometimes the story the client meant to convey and the story the lawyer heard in the initial meeting are not the same. In addition, clients may omit facts, oftentimes not realizing that those facts might be important. These facts may be helpful to the client's position or helpful to the opposing party's position. The goal is to gather as many legally significant facts as possible when interviewing the client. Even if during a meeting the lawyer repeats the facts orally to the client, it is always advisable to put the story and legally significant facts in a follow-up letter to the client. This gives the client an opportunity to clarify any misunderstanding or to provide missing facts. Once the facts as understood are presented in the letter, ask the client to respond if there are any additions or corrections. Potential clients, for example, may relay only those facts that are helpful to their position. However, it's important to hear all the important facts, even those that support the opposing party's case.

Sample facts for the letter to Ana Hart follow.

> Below I provide my understanding of the facts you shared with me. Please advise me if my understanding of the facts is inaccurate in any way, or if any facts are missing, as I have based my analysis and recommendations on the facts in this letter.
>
> I understand that David wants ownership of the Hart Fitness Centers, which the two of you own and operate in Hamilton, Johnson, and Marion counties. He is offering to pay you for one-half the fair market value of the business and the CNC. In exchange for this sum, David wants you to sell to him your interest in the business and sign a CNC, which the judge in the divorce proceeding agreed to require. In the CNC, you must promise "not to engage either directly or indirectly, on her own or in the employ of another, in the health and exercise club business in any form for a period of five years in the counties of Hamilton, Hancock, Boone, Marion, Johnson, and Hendricks, plus the towns of Arcadia and Bloomtown, East Carolina."
>
> Previously you and David purchased health clubs from sellers who signed CNCs that restricted competition only in the county in which the purchased clubs were located. Further, you planned to expand your business into those counties and towns listed in the CNC where you presently have no Centers, but you and David never took any action toward that end. David, however, has told you the inclusion of those locations in the CNC is appropriate since the Centers are service-oriented and you have personal relationships with many of the Centers' clients.
>
> Again, my recommendations are based on my understanding of the facts obtained during our meeting. Let me know if any facts are missing or stated inaccurately.

Above, the lawyer provides the key facts relied on in reaching the conclusion. The lawyer also emphasizes the need to reach out should any facts be inaccurate or missing.

e. Statement of the conclusion and reasoning behind the conclusion

If the lawyer's conclusion regarding the case has not been included in the introduction, it should be provided here. Answer the client's question or request explicitly. After the conclusion, explain the reasons for that conclusion. This requires laying out the reasoning step by step, so it's clear to the client. State completely any advice or recommendation for action, including the facts relevant to that advice or recommendation. This thoroughness will allow the client to assess whether the lawyer is acting on complete and accurate information.

It may be necessary to convey that the client's position is not as strong as the opposing party's position. To make that clear, include the support for both the client as well as the opposing party; doing so may help convince the client that any stated conclusion or recommendation is valid. Strive to explain this information in more general terms, if those general references suffice; omit any detailed information if not necessary to explain the conclusion or recommendation. For example, instead of quoting the CNC language and citing a source in the text of the letter, consider explaining what's key to the client's case and then provide a footnote to the quoted language and a citation to the rule. Unless the reader is an attorney or business client who wants the specific information about the law, this level of detail is not necessary and may be confusing. Another suggestion would be to attach to the letter, or offer to provide, any key statutes or cases, in case the client is interested.

This section of the sample letter follows.

> Based on my research and my understanding of the facts as we discussed in our meeting, David's proposed CNC is likely too broad because it gives more protection to David's interests than is reasonable. The CNC restricts competition in three counties and two towns where you do not operate any Hart Fitness Centers. As a result, the business has not developed any relationships with customers in those areas. In addition, the CNC is unreasonable because it extends beyond the one-county restriction of the CNCs signed by those who previously sold their health clubs to you and David.
>
> The agreement with the previous sellers included CNCs that restricted competition only in the county in which the purchased clubs were located. Your and David's purchase of those clubs under the limited terms in the CNCs reflects an understanding that a one-county restriction in those sales was reasonable. These past CNCs, more limited in scope than the CNC you have been ordered to sign, supports the position that a CNC restricting competition in locations beyond where the Centers are currently located is broader than necessary and unenforceable.

A single-county restriction also reflects the practice that members usually attend clubs that are closest to their homes and work. Members probably will not travel great distances to go to another club, so it's not necessary to restrict competition over a geographic area that exceeds the present Hart Fitness Center locations.

I realize that David claims this extensive coverage in the CNC is reasonable because the two of you had planned to extend the business into these new areas. David also feels it's reasonable because of your personal relationship with many of the present clients, which he believes creates a greater threat to this service-oriented business. However, courts do not favor CNCs. In your situation, the two of you never took any definitive action to expand the business into the areas where you do not currently operate any Centers. Allowing the CNC to extend beyond the present locations of the Centers might limit the availability of health and exercise clubs to the public and limit competition, which encourages better service and value to the public.

Further, the geographic area in the CNC exceeds the value of the goodwill David has in the current membership, which is what a CNC is meant to protect. Therefore, the CNC is likely overbroad for the protection of David's business interest and is unreasonable and unenforceable.

The first sentence, above, states the writer's conclusion and the main reason for the conclusion; the writer then explains in more detail how that conclusion was reached. In this section the writer recognizes the position of the opposing party — here the husband — and explains why that position will not change the outcome.

f. Recommendation

Based on the analysis of the client's case, recommend to the client a certain course of action. That recommendation may be to negotiate, settle, or proceed with or provide a defense of a claim. When putting anything down in writing, remember that written communications are sometimes later introduced as evidence in court, unless it's privileged communication of an attorney's work product. Strive to inform the client fully but do so in a way that avoids as many future problems as possible. This can occur only by thoroughly explaining the reasons for any conclusions as well as any concerns that exist regarding the case.

Sometimes the recommendation must be that the client cannot do what was initially requested. Whenever possible, make this bad news easier for the client to receive by, if possible, offering alternatives that might fulfill the same or a similar objective. The recommendation may be, for example, that a lawsuit is financially impractical, but a negotiation may bring about some of the client's desired results. Where appropriate, provide exact time schedules, costs, or other important information related to the recommendations you make in a client letter. If certain information is not available when the letter is written, let the client know and provide some idea as to when that information will become available.

A recommendation in Ana's case might look like the following.

> I recommend we first send a letter to David's attorney requesting a change in the CNC language. At a minimum, a fair amendment would be to restrict the CNC to those counties and towns only where Hart Fitness Centers are located. In the letter, I will require a response from David's attorney by the end of the day three weeks after the date on the letter. If David does not agree to the CNC terms, we may need to raise this issue in court. This would involve additional time and expense, but if you plan to continue in the health club business, you may consider this a valid issue to pursue.

Often, an attorney in the United States may want to communicate recommendations more quickly, either during a virtual meeting, over the phone, or by email. By conveying the information in a virtual meeting or over the phone, the client's money is likely saved, and the suit can proceed more quickly without the delay of mail correspondence. Whether a discussion takes place in person, over the phone, or on a virtual platform, however, always document in writing, by email or letter, any decisions reached between the lawyer and the client.

g. Offer to meet or talk further and closing

It is essential to invite the client to talk further, preferably by phone or perhaps in a meeting. This is especially important when the news is bad; without that invitation, the client may feel unimportant and not treated fairly. It is essential to offer to help the client work through the reasons why the case is weak or lacks merit.

The following paragraph from the letter to Ms. Hart makes this offer.

> I know you are anxious to get your divorce finalized, and I will make every effort to proceed as quickly as possible. Please let me know by May 19 how you would like to proceed. Again, let me know whether my version of the facts provided at the beginning of this letter are complete and accurate. My analysis and recommendation are based on the facts as I understand them.
>
> If you would like to talk further, you may call me at (222) 547-9975, or you may email me at dsmith@smithjones.com. I would also be happy to speak with you over the Internet or personally, if you prefer. If you would like to set up an Internet call or a personal meeting, please contact my assistant, Jerry Jameson, at the above phone number to schedule an appointment. I look forward to hearing from you.

h. Closing

Include a respectful closing, such as "Regards," "Sincerely," or "Respectfully."

> With best regards,
> Daniel A. Smith
> Attorney at Law

The final version of the sample letter appears below.

> Smith, Jones, & Brown, P.C.
> Attorneys at Law
> 532 Main Street
> Flora, East Carolina 57235
>
> May 12, 20xx
>
> Ana Hart
> 1030 Meadowlark Lane
> Flora, East Carolina 57235
>
> Re: Enforceability of the Covenant not to Compete (CNC).
>
> Dear Ms. Hart,
>
> Thank you for meeting with me on Wednesday, May 10, regarding your divorce and the CNC the judge is requiring you to sign as part of the property settlement agreement. I will be happy to help you in any way I can. My recommendation is to take steps to avoid signing the CNC, explained below.
>
> Below I provide my understanding of the facts you shared with me. Please advise me if my understanding of the facts is inaccurate in any way, or if any facts are missing, as I have based my analysis and recommendations on the facts provided in this letter.
>
> I understand that David wants ownership of the Hart Fitness Centers, which the two of you own and operate in Hamilton, Johnson, and Marion counties. He is offering to pay you for one-half the fair market value of the business and the CNC. In exchange for this sum, David wants you to sell to him your interest in the business and sign a CNC, which the judge in the divorce proceeding agreed to require. In the CNC, you must promise "not to engage either directly or indirectly, on

In this paragraph the writer restates the facts and asks Ana to respond if those facts are not correct or complete.

her own or in the employ of another, in the health and exercise club business in any form for a period of five years in the counties of Hamilton, Hancock, Boone, Marion, Johnson, and Hendricks, plus the towns of Arcadia and Bloomtown, East Carolina."

Previously you and David purchased health clubs from sellers who signed CNCs that restricted competition only in the county in which the purchased clubs were located. Further, you planned to expand your business into those counties and towns listed in the CNC where you presently have no Centers, but you and David never took any action toward that end. David, however, has told you the inclusion of those locations in the CNC is appropriate since the Hart Fitness Centers are service-oriented and you have personal relationships with many of the Centers' clients.

This paragraph continues restating the facts as understood by the attorney

Again, my recommendations are based on my understanding of the facts obtained during our meeting. Let me know if any facts are missing or stated inaccurately.

Based on my research and my understanding of the facts as we discussed in our meeting, David's proposed CNC is likely too broad because it gives more protection to David's interests than is reasonable. The CNC restricts competition in three counties and two towns where you do not operate any Hart Fitness Centers. As a result, the business has not developed any relationships with customers in those areas. In addition, the CNC is unreasonable because it extends beyond the one-county restriction of the CNCs signed by those who previously sold their health clubs to you and David.

In this and the next 2 paragraphs the writer explains how the conclusion was reached, including both references to the law and to facts the facts Ana provided.

The agreement with the previous sellers included CNCs that restricted competition only to the county in which the purchased clubs were located. Your and David's purchase of those clubs under the limited terms in the CNCs reflects an understanding that a one-county restriction in those sales was reasonable. These past CNCs, more limited in scope than the CNC you have been ordered to sign, supports the position that a CNC restricting competition in locations beyond where the Centers are currently located is broader than necessary and unenforceable.

A single-county restriction also reflects the practice that members usually attend clubs that are closest to their homes and work. Members probably will not travel great distances to go to another club, so it's not necessary to restrict competition over a geographic area that exceeds the present Hart Fitness Center locations.

I realize that David claims this extensive coverage in the CNC is reasonable because the two of you had planned to extend the business into these new areas. David also feels it's reasonable because of your personal relationship with many of the present clients, which he believes creates a greater threat to the service-oriented business. However, courts do not favor CNCs. In your situation the two of you never took any definitive action to expand the business into the areas where you do not currently operate any Centers. Allowing the CNC to extend beyond the present locations of the Centers might limit the availability of health and exercise clubs to the public and limit competition, which encourages better service and value to the public.

In this and the next paragraph the writer recognizes the position of the opposing party – here the husband – and explains why that position will not change the outcome.

Further, the geographic area in the CNC exceeds the value of the goodwill David has in the current membership, which is what a CNC is meant to protect. Therefore, the CNC is likely overbroad for the protection of David's business interest and is unenforceable.

I recommend we first send a letter to David's attorney requesting a change in the CNC language. At a minimum, a fair amendment would be to restrict the CNC to those counties and towns only where Hart Fitness Centers are located. In the letter, I will require a response from David's attorney by the end of the day three weeks after the date on the letter. If David does not agree to the CNC terms, we may need to raise this issue in court. This would involve additional time and expense, but if you plan to continue in the health club business, you may consider this a valid issue to pursue.

This paragraph provides the recommendation and sets a time limit for a response.

I know you are anxious to get your divorce finalized, and I will make every effort to proceed as quickly as possible. Please let me know by May 19 how you would like to proceed. Again, let me know whether my version of the facts provided at the beginning of this letter are complete and accurate. My analysis and recommendation are based on the facts as I understand them.

If you would like to talk further, you may call me at (222) 547-9975, or you may email me at dsmith@smithjones.com. I would also be happy to speak with you over the internet or personally, if you prefer. If you would like to set up an internet call or a personal meeting, if you prefer. If you would like to set up an Internet call or personal meeting, please contact my assistant, Jerry Jameson, at the above phone number to schedule an appointment. I look forward to hearing from you.

This paragraph again asks Ana to respond by a certain date and reminds her that everything is based on the facts she provided. The last paragraph offers to talk and provides contact information.

With best regards,
Daniel A. Smith
Attorney at Law

The above sample client letter focuses on only a single legal issue, the enforceability of the CNC. If writing about multiple issues, the letter would be more clear by providing a roadmap in the introduction that sets out the multiple issues to be discussed in the letter and then moves through each issue separately, each with its own heading.

4. General Guidelines

a. Considerations about the structure of the document

How you communicate information and where you place that information within the document, each paragraph, and each sentence influences the way the reader interprets the message. This is equally true when writing a client letter.

When the client's news is bad, for example, paying particular attention to the organization of the letter might help to convey the information in a way the client is more likely to accept. One organizational approach is to begin the letter with general information, setting the tone, and then relaying the negative outcome message, letting the client know that more details are provided later in the letter. Once the specific negative message is conveyed, re-establish the tone and, if possible, mention that alternative positive outcomes may be possible. Then, after explaining below the reasons for your conclusion, discuss those alternative approaches that may also have a positive result. Again, end by offering to speak further with the client about the conclusions and the reasons for those conclusions.

b. Recommendations of style

(1) Be direct

To be direct may seem to contradict the recommendation made above when conveying a negative message, but that is not the case. The above recommendation refers to the placement of negative information; being direct refers to making the message clear at that point when it is conveyed to the client. No matter whether the conclusion is good news or bad news, the goal must be to answer directly the question or request posed by the client. If there is no direct answer, be direct by saying so, and then explain why no direct answer exists.

(2) Be clear

Use language that the client can understand and avoid so-called legalese, which is exaggerated legal language, including words such as *aforementioned*, *hereinafter*, and *heretofore*. No reason justifies using legalese. In fact, since the goal of all writing is to clearly communicate a message, pay particular attention to using language that is easily understood by the reader.

In addition, avoid references to technical terms. After drafting a letter, review it and edit any words that may be unfamiliar to the client. If technical terms, such as legal terms, are necessary in order to be thorough, define those legal terms within the letter, unless there's no question the reader will know what the terms mean. For example, instead of referring only to the "statute of frauds," refer to "a statute that requires some contracts to be written and signed as a way to avoid fraud." If referring to the "beneficiary of a will," refer to "a beneficiary, or one who receives benefits under a Last Will and Testament." If the definition alone does not clarify the meaning of a legal term, consider providing an example as a way to make sense of the term. This would require more words and make the letter longer. Sometimes brevity, however, must give way to clarity.

(3) Be brief whenever possible

While clarity is the overriding goal of any legal writer, be brief and concise wherever possible. Eliminate any unnecessary statements or redundancies. Strive to reduce the language without eliminating the substantive message.

(4) Finish by considering tone, purpose, and audience

Finally, be considerate of your client. Remember that every potential client has a legal problem or suspects that they have one. Ideally, respond to each in a way that recognizes the client's concerns and needs but still provides the legal information the client needs to know.

• Exercise 14-A

1. Consider Edina Broward, whose facts were introduced in Chapter 1 and raised again in exercises in Chapters 6 and 7. Edina wants to recover her famous painting that was lost decades ago and only found and identified as hers in the last year. Draft a client letter to Edina that states your opinion that a court may toll the statute of limitations until its discovery last year, allowing her to recover the painting based on the relevant case law found online in the Student Supplemental Materials for this book located on the publisher's website at http://www.aspenpublishing.com.
2. Consider the *Olson v. Redwood Mobile Homes* attractive nuisance problem first raised in an exercise in Chapter 6 and further explored in a Chapter 7 exercise. The Olsons' son Ricky drowned after trespassing onto Redwood Mobile Homes property and falling into a settlement tank. Draft a letter to Ricky Olson's parents explaining what you have learned about the case and make a recommendation to proceed toward recovery for Redwood's wrongdoing.

C. Writing Demand Letters

1. Purpose, audience, and tone

This section addresses guidelines attorneys in the United States follow when writing demand letters. A demand letter communicates with a potential adversary (audience) and makes specific requests to either take certain action or refrain from taking certain action (purpose). To accomplish this purpose, tone is highly important. When writing a demand letter, strive to be firm but not belligerent. If the tone is too aggressive, the writer may elicit a negative response that is due, at least in part, to the tone of the request rather than because the potential adversary disagrees with the substance of the demand.

A demand letter is directed to opposing counsel, if the opposing party has hired an attorney. Any attorney who wants to send a letter directly to the opposing party must first get permission from the opposing party's attorney, if the party is represented by counsel.[1] If the opposing party is not represented by counsel, any lawyer's written communication should include a clear statement telling the opposing party that the lawyer writing the communication is representing the lawyer's client, the other party in the legal matter.

2. Ethical considerations

The American Bar Association, in its Guidelines for Conduct, urges all lawyers to "treat all other counsel, parties, and witnesses in a civil and courteous manner," both in person and through any written communications.[2] The Guidelines specifically cite as inappropriate any "offensive conduct" and "disparaging personal remarks" toward all other parties involved in a dispute.[3]

As with all actions by attorneys, strive to present the specific demand in a firm yet respectful manner, to be professional, and to be honest. The reader is more likely to carefully consider the demand if the tone is one that is credible, conveying a message of professionalism and competency. The Model Rules of Professional Conduct make clear that lawyers cannot lie about the facts, the law, or what could happen should the reader not comply with the request.[4]

---

1. Model Rules of Prof'l. Conduct R. 4.2.
2. ABA Section on Litigation Guidelines for Conduct (ABA 2020), https://www.americanbar.org/groups/litigation/policy/conduct_guidelines/lawyers_duties.
3. *Id.*
4. Model Rules of Prof'l. Conduct R. 4.1.

3. What to include in a demand letter

Most demand letters contain the following sections:

a. Heading, salutation, and introduction
b. Statement of the facts and law that support your request
c. Statement of the deadline to respond
d. What will happen should the reader not comply with your request
e. Closing

a. Heading, salutation, and introduction

A demand letter contains a heading and salutation, just as in a client letter. The introduction, however, usually includes not only the purpose of the letter but also the specific request that the recipient take certain actions or refrain from certain actions.

In the sample letter about the CNC Ana has been ordered to sign, these sections might read as follows.

> Smith, Jones, & Brown, P.C.
> Attorneys at Law
> 532 Main Street
> Flora, East Carolina 57235
>
> May 12, 20xx
>
> James Fielder
> Attorney at Law
> 12 N. Main Street
> Flora, East Carolina. 57204
>
> Dear Jim,
>
> I am writing on behalf of my client, Ana Hart, who is divorcing your client, David Hart. Ana has some legitimate concerns about the CNC she is expected to sign with the settlement agreement. We are asking that the geographic scope of the CNC be revised.

b. Support for the request based on the facts and the law and the consequences of non-compliance

As in a letter to a client, follow the request with an explanation of any key facts and the law supporting the client's position. The level of detail will depend on the case and each lawyer's preference regarding how much information to reveal about the client's case. The following is an example of the support:

As presently drafted, the CNC restricts Ana's ability to work in her field of expertise in geographic areas extending beyond the counties in which Hart Fitness Centers are located. This expansive scope of the CNC makes it broader than necessary and is unenforceable. When David and Ana Hart previously purchased additional health clubs, the CNC included only the county in which each purchased club was located. The same reasonable restriction is appropriate with the CNC between Ana and David.

Key is that the party receiving the demand letter understands what the consequences will be should the demand be ignored. The consequence might be, for example, to proceed to court; to request a temporary restraining order requiring the party not to take certain actions; or to turn over a debt to a collection agency. Making any consequences clear in the demand letter demonstrates what will happen after the deadline has passed, with no need to communicate further with the opposing party. A statement of the consequences in Ana's case follows.

This compromise is essential to the divorce settlement. Disagreeing on this term may result in protracted litigation in court, which would not serve the best interests of either David or Ana Hart.

c. A statement of the deadline

Do not make an open-ended demand. After stating explicitly the request and justification for the request based on the law and facts, provide a specific timeline for what is expected from the recipient. Consider carefully by what specific date and time the reader must respond. An unreasonable time limit will more likely result in a negative response. Give opposing counsel sufficient time to talk with the client and ideally to comply with the request. If there's no reply, or the reply states that the recipient will not comply with the demand, the time limit set should be one that, once it's passed, the lawyer writing the letter is prepared for and can immediately move forward in the case.

Here is an example of this section of the demand letter.

I will need to hear from you on this matter no later than the end of the day three weeks from the date on this letter. In the meantime, if you would like to talk, please contact me or my assistant, Jerry Jameson, at (222) 547-9975, or email me directly at dsmith@smithjones.com.

d. Closing

Include a respectful closing, such as "Regards" or "Respectfully."

Respectfully,

David A. Smith
Attorney at Law

A complete demand letter based on Ana Hart's case follows.

Smith, Jones, & Brown, P.C.
Attorneys at Law
532 Main Street
Flora, East Carolina 57235

May 10, 20xx

James Fielder
Attorney at Law
12 N. Main Street
Flora, East Carolina. 57204

Dear Mr. Fielder,

I am writing on behalf of my client, Ana Hart, who is divorcing your client, David Hart. Ana has some legitimate concerns about the CNC she is expected to sign with the settlement agreement. We are asking that the geographic scope of the CNC be revised.

> This first paragraph explains why the lawyer is writing and what Ana wants.

As presently drafted, the CNC restricts Ana's ability to work in her field of expertise in geographic areas extending beyond the counties in which the Hart Fitness Centers are located. This expansive scope of the CNC makes it broader than necessary and unreasonable. When David and Ana Hart previously purchased additional health clubs, the CNC included only the county in which each purchased club was located. The same reasonable restriction is appropriate with the CNC between Ana and David.

> This paragraph explains the support for the request.

This compromise is essential to the divorce settlement. Disagreeing on this term may result in protracted litigation in court, which does not serve the best interests of either David or Ana Hart. I will need to hear from you on this matter no later than the end of the day three weeks from the date on

> This paragraph discloses what will happen if the demand/request is not met, gives a deadline for the response, and provides the lawyer's contact information.

this letter. In the meantime, if you would like to talk, please contact me or my assistant, Jerry Jameson, at (222) 547-9975, or email me directly at dsmith@smithjones.com.

Respectfully,
David A. Smith
Attorney-at-law

• Exercise 14-B

(1) Presume for purposes of this exercise that Edina Broward would like you to proceed in getting the painting returned to her. Draft a demand letter to Thomas Warren, who is not represented by an attorney. Dr. Warren lives at 232 W. Findlay Avenue, Flora, East Carolina 57468. In the demand letter include the specific demand and the facts and law to support (1) why the painting was originally Ms. Broward's, (2) why she was unable to locate the painting until after the statute of limitations passed, and (3) why, based on an exception to the statute of limitations, the painting must be returned to Ms. Broward. Close by stating when and how the painting should be returned and what will happen should the deadline not be met. Close by providing your contact information. Use the Student Supplemental Materials for this book located on the publisher's website at http://www.aspenpublishing.com.

(2) Presume for purposes of this exercise that the Olsons would like you to proceed against Redwood Mobile Homes in a wrongful death action for the drowning of their son, Ricky, in Redwood's settlement tank. Draft a letter to Monica Dhonau, President of Redwood, 1814 Colony Drive, Flora, East Carolina 57468. In the demand letter include the specific demand and the facts and law to support why, despite the fact that Ricky was a trespasser, Redwood is liable for Ricky's death because they placed concrete blocks in a stair-like fashion that drew Ricky to climb up to see what was over the fence surrounding the settlement tank, which is when he fell over and drowned. Provide a specific demand regarding compensation to the Olsons and state what will happen if Ms. Dhonau doesn't respond by a specific date and time. Close by providing your contact information. Use the Student Supplemental Materials for this book located on the publisher's website at http://www.aspenpublishing.com.

D. *Writing Emails*

Historically, professionals would draft or dictate a letter, an assistant would type up that letter, and the professional would take at least one more look and make any necessary changes to the letter before finalizing the document and placing it in the mail.

Even with the advent of the computer, writers are still more likely to initially draft a letter and read it over at least once, allowing time to let it sit, later looking at it more objectively. Sometimes letter writers are surprised to discover upon the second reading that the message reads differently than originally intended.

Of course, letters are still part of the legal world, but more and more often attorneys communicate with clients and other parties through what some might consider to be more informal modes of communication, including emails. Referring to emails as an "informal" means of communication reveals one of the potential concerns with incorporating emails into legal practice. The process of drafting, then rethinking and rewriting, may not always seem possible with email communications. Instead, business is oftentimes conducted at lightning speed. Many junior attorneys feel they are expected to be available through their smartphones twenty-four hours a day, seven days a week—while sitting in a meeting, walking down the sidewalk, or riding in a car. And the general feeling is that responses must occur immediately. The thinking part of the writing—certainly the part where the writer lets a draft sit for a period of time and then reviews it more objectively—might easily be omitted. But what seems like expediency and efficiency in responding quickly can produce negative results. What follows are a few suggestions for writing professional emails.

1. To email or not to email? Consider the message

Always make sure an email is the right choice for each communication. Generally, emails are appropriate when confirming a meeting or sharing general, non-sensitive information. However, an email may not be appropriate when giving the client bad news, conveying highly confidential information, or addressing something technical or difficult to understand, such that the client or other party would likely have follow-up questions. Perhaps in those instances it would be better to convey the information in person, to assess the individual's body language and overall reaction, or to contact the person by phone, which may be especially helpful if your goal is to soften your message. A video meeting over a computer might also be preferred over an email. A video appointment allows both parties to view one another's visual reactions to the conversation and to hear the tone in each other's voice.

Consider also which mode of communication the recipient might prefer. While most professionals these days are proficient in emails, some still prefer to avoid all things electronic, including email.

Most expect to hear quickly from the recipient after sending an email, certainly within twenty-four hours, if not sooner. If, due to the substance of the response or to other pressing matters additional time is needed to fully address the contents of an email, consider replying quickly to acknowledge receipt of the email. Then let the recipient know a response is forthcoming and when to expect that response. This allows time to consider how to respond to the email and to do so carefully. A sample quick response might be:

> Thank you for your email. I am working on responding to your questions and will get back in touch no later than October 15.

Further, the substance of the email may have unintended consequences if not phrased carefully with explicit limitations on the use of the content of the email. For example, if the substance of the email relates to contract terms, those terms may unintentionally become part of a binding contract. Emails may also be used to support a legal action, such as one in defamation, employment discrimination, or sexual harassment, or even to prove criminal liability. Email communications may also be used to help establish personal jurisdiction over a party.

In making a choice about what to include, remember that any written email may be discoverable and ultimately read in open court. First, only emails that include legal advice related to litigation or work product are privileged. But even those emails will not retain their privilege if shared willingly with a third party. The privilege exists for the benefit of the client, but if the client forwards an email to someone else, such as a client's relative or friend, the privilege is waived. For these reasons, it is wise to advise clients to not forward confidential emails and to learn whether the client's email account is accessible by others, such as a corporate account shared with the client's employer. Even an email that is inadvertently disclosed may result in a waiver of privilege.[5]

In short, while an email can be considered a casual form of communication, treat each one like a more formal document when used for business purposes. Also make careful choices, knowing that others might read the document and it may be presented as evidence in court. Having business-wide policies in place for Internet and email use may help prevent later problems.

2. Guidelines when using email communications as a professional tool

Informal emails may comprise long, rambling paragraphs or no paragraphs at all. However, readers will benefit if writers are deliberate in their approach to the presentation of any emails. Consider the following general guidelines:

5. For more on inadvertent disclosure, see John T. Hundley, Annotation *Waiver of Evidentiary Privilege by Inadvertent Disclosure — State Law*, 51 A.L.R.5th 603 (1997).

a. From and to lines

More than likely, any email address will include the name of the firm or business, which works well. Some writers, however, may write professional emails using their personal emails. If you are one of those, make sure your personal email address is appropriate. Email names such as "superbored@" and "yourspecialsomeone@" are examples of inappropriate names when sending a professional email.

Further, consider composing an email by first typing the content of the email without putting the email address in the "To" line, doing that last. This approach serves a few purposes.

- The email can't be sent accidentally before it is completed.
- Waiting to type in the recipient's email might encourage the writer to review the message at least one more time, to be sure it's as intended.
- Waiting also gives the writer time to make sure the recipient is the actual party intended to receive the email and that it's directed *only* to that party.
    - Aim not to be that attorney who sends a confidential settlement agreement to a national reporter rather than to another attorney with the same last name as the reporter who was also working on the agreement, and both names were included on the sender's online address book (and the reporter publishes that communication).[6]
    - Do not be the law clerk who replies to a listserv message about a job posting by accidentally replying to "All" (and the employer also happens to be a member of that same listserv).

The stories about these types of mistakes are endless, but all have the same result. At a minimum there's a degree of embarrassment involved; at most a client's case can be adversely affected, or the writer could lose a job.

b. The subject (Re:) line and attachments

Consider writing a subject line that is specific enough so that the reader can immediately identify the purpose of the email but is also as succinct as possible. And if there are a series of emails going back and forth between the same two parties, retain the same subject line throughout all the communications, for quicker filing purposes and easier access later on. If, however, the subject of the correspondence changes, consider altering the subject line to reflect the new topic.

Consider also adding any attachments to include with the email when filling in the subject line. If not then, consider adding the attachment when explaining the nature of the attachment in the body of the email. Oftentimes,

6. Thomas Adcock, *Elite Firm Summer Associate Sends E-Mail Boasting of Laziness to Partners* (June 20, 2003), http://www.nylawyer.com/display.php/file=/news/03/06/062003b.

email writers finish an email and send it before clicking on the paperclip to add the attachments. By adding them earlier, it may be more likely they aren't overlooked until after the email is sent. And before attaching any documents, make sure all unintentional marginal comments on the attachment have been deleted.

c. The salutation and introductory paragraph

The level of formality with a salutation in a business-related email depends on the relationship with the recipient. Begin with a salutation that reflects the relationship between the writer and the recipient. If the recipient is a stranger, consider using a more formal salutation such as "Dear Ms. Lopez." If the writer and the recipient know each other well, such as colleagues in an office, the salutation might be, e.g., "Dear Maria," or "Maria," or "Hi, Maria."

The introductory paragraph provides an opportunity to set out the purpose of the email and also to relay any conclusions reached regarding the purpose of the email. In other words, tell the reader at the beginning the reason for writing. And if replying to an email, refer to the original email received, for example, by referencing the date and key information from that original email.

If addressing multiple issues, set those out and number them in the same order in which they are addressed in the email. Then use those numbered points to create the structure of the rest of the email. Ideally, organize the information so the most important topic is addressed first. If the email response is lengthy, consider using headings when moving from one topic to the next. Finally, if making any specific requests to the recipient, state those not only at the beginning of the letter but also add a gentle reminder at the end.

d. The closing and signature

End the email by summarizing any key conclusions or points made as well as any further information needed from the recipient. If the email is to a client and further information is needed, delineate that information explicitly, ideally using numbers or bullet points, and provide any necessary and specific due dates (e.g., "receipt in my office by 5:00 p.m. on November 1," rather than "within the next two weeks"). When communicating with someone in a different time zone or country, make sure to specify to which time you are referring (e.g., "receipt in my office by 5:00 p.m. [EST] or [Beijing time]"). Finally, when finished with the email, close and include any contact information in the signature block.

e. Stylistic considerations

- *Use the format of your email to promote readability.* A message is more readable if you break up a longer message into readable blocks of text, beginning with a topic sentence or heading set apart from the text. Consider also spacing between each paragraph for readability.

- *Strive to be courteous.* The best way to avoid writing an angry email is to delay writing anything until you are no longer angry, annoyed, or inclined to vent. Also, never use offensive language (again, thinking of someone passing along the email or its being introduced in court), and avoid using **CAPITAL LETTERS OR BOLDFACE TEXT TO CONVEY YOUR MESSAGE.** It always comes across as screaming.
- *Consider the tone and professionalism.* You may be inclined to be less formal with a client you know well or an attorney representing the other party with whom you are close friends and socialize. Avoid that inclination and omit, for example, sarcastic private notes or jokes. Again, consider that any email may later be submitted as evidence in court. And generally avoid use of emoticons or e-acronyms like "btw" for "by the way."
- *Strive for clarity.* Short, concise but complete sentences are ideal. As always, be aware of the recipient and write so the recipient will be able to understand the message on one read through, without needing to reread it or to refer to a dictionary or other resource.
- *Write a clean document.* Keep the reader focused on the substance of the message rather than focusing on the quality of the writing. This shift from the words to the writer often occurs when the email is riddled with grammatical and typographical errors. Unfortunately, it's those errors that will likely be remembered long after the message matters.

Finally, make sure you say what you mean and mean what you say. Consider this actual email:

> Your food stamps will be stopped effective March 1992 because we received notice that you passed away. May God Bless You. You may reapply if there is a change in your circumstances.
>
> Department of Social Services
> Greenville, South Carolina[7]

While this is an extreme example of a message gone wrong, mistakes are made all the time and especially when a document is written hastily. While business—and life—may be moving at breakneck speed, the time taken to correct email errors later will likely far exceed the time taken to get it right the first time the email is sent. It pays to pause and count to three (or more) before clicking on the send button.

7. https://buffalonews.com/news/article_8ed216c3-e5ac-5cd2-af77-6d5648932bd9.html (March 6, 1992).

E. Writing E-Memos

Lawyers nowadays communicate legal analyses primarily by email. Emails containing legal analyses are often referred to as "e-memos." This section will address common considerations when writing e-memos and provide a sample e-memo.

1. Threshold considerations when writing e-memos

When emailing any legal analysis to another lawyer or a client, legal writers face a few threshold decisions:

- Should writers include their legal analysis in the body of the email or attach a traditional office memo to the email containing their legal analysis, or do some combination of both?
- What tone should the writer adopt? For example, should personal communications, like, "I hope you have a good day," be included in the email?
- How should legal authorities be handled? Should citations to legal authorities be included in the email? Should the writer attach legal authorities to the email?

a. Should the writer include the legal analysis in the body of the email or attach a traditional office memo to the email containing the legal analysis, or do some combination of both?

In considering whether to include the legal analysis in the body of an email or via an attached traditional memo, the lawyer should take into account the reader's preferences and needs, and the complexity of the issue being analyzed. For example, where the analysis of a complex issue requires a ten-page memo, the writer might (1) set out in the body of the email the issue and a brief conclusion that includes a summary of the reasoning supporting the conclusion, and (2) attach a traditional legal memo to the email.

When attaching a traditional legal memo to an email, be sure to let the reader know it is attached. When possible, the writer should also include a hyperlink to the memo on a cloud drive, such as a law firm's Microsoft OneDrive. When including a hyperlink, to preserve confidentiality, make sure the settings for that document allow the link to be used only by the addressee.

b. What tone should the writer adopt? For example, should personal communications, like, "I hope you have a good day," be included in the email?

The tone of an e-memo should always be professional and polite. Assume the legal reader of the e-memo is extremely busy and in need of a quick answer on the issue the lawyer-writer has been asked to research and analyze. However, legal readers are also human and work in a professional environment. In most law practice environments, legal readers can be addressed by their first name. Depending on the culture of the place where the lawyer works, the legal writer might include an opening or closing that wishes the reader a good day or acknowledges a particularly challenging or happy circumstance faced by both the reader and writer. For example, in the beginning days of the COVID-19 pandemic, many lawyers might have ended or begun emails with a remark acknowledging the very difficult and scary times they were all living in and wishing their colleague well.

c. How should legal authorities be handled? Should citations to legal authorities be included in the email? Should the writer attach legal authorities to the email?

Just like a traditional legal memo, the e-memo provides legal analysis that the client or supervising attorney needs and should be able to rely on. So, references to legal authorities should not be omitted from e-memos. E-memos should include citations. When possible, make every citation a hyperlink[8] so the e-memo reader can easily click on the citation and view the legal authority being cited. If authorities are attached, be selective about which ones to attach. Some legal readers' email systems may not accommodate attachments that exceed a specific size. If the reader prefers to or should have copies of all of the authorities, the writer, if possible, should place all of the authorities in a secure cloud drive folder, and share a secure link to that folder in the e-memo.

2. Guidance on writing the e-memo

While preferences and styles may differ among organizations and employers, the legal writer should keep in mind the following considerations when writing e-memos.

---

8. The MERRIAM-WEBSTER DICTIONARY defines hyperlink as "an electronic link providing direct access from one distinctively marked place in a hypertext or hypermedia document to another in the same or a different document." *Hyperlink,* Merriam-https://www.merriam-webster.com/dictionary/hyperlink (last visited Sept. 19, 2021).

- Is the e-memo tailored for a legal reader who needs an answer on an issue quickly? That is, is it written concisely and crisply?[9] Does it contain headings that guide the reader through the e-memo?
- Will the reader be able to easily scroll through the e-memo on their phone or tablet and grasp the legal analysis being communicated, through helpful visual breaks and headings and accessible hyperlinks that can be clicked on?
- Are the legal issue and answer on any issue, along with reasoning for the answer, included at the beginning of the e-memo?
- Has the writer cited supporting authorities in the e-memo and used appropriate citation form?
- Has the writer attached or provided a hyperlink to supporting materials and authorities that the reader may need to understand the e-memo or simply prefers to have?
- If appropriate, has the writer provided in the e-memo practical advice or a recommendation that follows from the writer's conclusion?
- Has the writer addressed the reader by name at the beginning of the email? (Examples: "Dear Phoebe," "Hi Phoebe")
- Has the writer included a concise and crisp legal analysis that uses the CREAC structure or an abbreviated form of the CREAC structure?
- Has the writer let the reader know how they can contact the writer by including a signature block with the writer's email and work phone number?
- Has the writer included any needed confidentiality alerts in the e-memo? Some employers require lawyers to include a confidentiality or privilege statement at the end of the email letting any recipient know that the e-memo is intended to be confidential.

3. *An e-memo example*

Here is an example of an e-memo communicating the objective analysis included in Chapter 6 and relying solely on *Mats Transport v. ABC Corporation*,

---

9. Professor Brad Desnoyer, based on his empirical study of e-memo preferences, advocates for conciseness and crispness in e-memos, applying the "iceberg theory" of Ernest Hemingway to the legal e-memo:

> "The Iceberg Theory is acutely applicable for those writing e-memos; Hemingway fostered his discipline 'to prune language and avoid waste motion' by writing short stories. With the 'Iceberg Theory of e-memo writing,' the writer may omit known facts, clearly understood logical steps, and overly-duplicative conclusions—while still providing sharp substantive analysis. Elegance replaces redundancies. Thus, a proper e-memo is not less rigorous than a memorandum; it is perhaps even more so. Writers must consider not only what to include but also what to exclude."

Brad Desnoyer, *E-Memos 2.0: An Empirical Study of How Attorneys Write*, 25 LEGAL WRITING 213 (2021), https://www.legalwritingjournal.org/article/24785-e-memos-2-0-an-empirical-study-of-how-attorneys-write.

824 S.E.2d 1467 (E.C. App. 1992). Keep in mind that e-memo styles and preferences can vary among employers and clients. This e-memo example addresses the issue of whether the CNC Ana has been ordered to sign is overbroad and unreasonable as to David's interest. The footnotes that appear in the example are directed to the reader of this textbook; an e-memo should not contain any footnotes.

E-memo example

To: Quinn Markham (markham.1@lawfirmx.com)
From: Kyle Pang (pang.10@lawfirmx.com)
Re: Hart matter/CNC reasonableness issue

Hi Quinn,

I hope you are well. Here's the analysis you requested:

Issue and Answer

As you may recall, the court has ordered Ana Hart to sign a CNC that would restrict competition in three counties and two towns where no Hart Fitness Centers are located. You asked me to analyze whether the CNC that Ana has been ordered by the court to sign is overbroad and unreasonable in its protection of David Hart's business interests.[10]

Yes, the CNC is probably overbroad and would be found unreasonable. In the main East Carolina case on CNC reasonableness, *Mats Transp. v. ABC Corp.*, 824 S.E.2d 1467 (E.C. App. 1992), the court emphasized its concern with geographic restrictions extending beyond the scope of the seller's business.[11]

The *Mats Transport* case. *Mats Transport* involved the sale of a trucking business. The CNC prohibited the seller from competing in the trucking business with the buyer for a period of *5 years anywhere in the U.S.* The buyer sued the seller, alleging violation of the CNC. The seller successfully moved for summary judgment, arguing the CNC was overbroad in its protection of the buyer's business interest. The court of appeals affirmed, reasoning the CNC was written as if the seller's business was a national enterprise when it had only one terminal in East Carolina, and hauled freight primarily for a few major clients in East Carolina and adjoining states. *Id.* at 1468.

The CNC Ana has been required to sign is probably unreasonable because it extends to three counties and two towns where no Hart Fitness Center. is located. Ana's case is strikingly similar to the *Mats Transport* case, where

10. For purposes of this example, assume that the reader and writer are both familiar with the detailed background facts.

11. The case citation should also be a hyperlink to the case itself.

the CNC restricted competition nationwide when the seller's business only operated out of East Carolina. Here, also, previous CNCs signed by sellers in prior sales of clubs to the Hart Fitness Center were subject only to a one-county restriction. In the context of fitness clubs, the one-county restriction is even more likely to be reasonable given that club members usually use clubs closest to their homes or workplaces.

It is unlikely but possible that the court focuses on plans for expansion and Ana's relationships with customers and finds the CNC to be unreasonable. Ana and David had planned to expand the business over the next three years into the three counties and two towns covered by the CNC. Also, Ana has developed relationships with club members, and David might be viewed by the court as having a legitimate business interest in preventing Ana from stealing away members.

However, given the court's emphasis on unreasonable geographic restrictions, the CNC is probably overbroad and unreasonable.

We should discuss with the client the possibility of preparing a motion challenging the court's order on the basis that the CNC is unreasonable.

I'm happy to help with the motion. Let me know if you have any questions. I'm available to chat by phone or Zoom tomorrow.

Thanks,
Kyle

Kyle Pang
Law Firm X
pang.10@lawfirmx.com
988-788-8888

CONFIDENTIALITY NOTICE: This email message may contain privileged or confidential material. If you are not the intended recipient, please contact the sender by reply email and immediately delete all copies of the original message and any attachments without copying or disclosing the contents. Thank you.

A lawyer or law student writing an e-memo should be sure to check with the person they are writing to regarding the date and time by which they need the e-memo, and if they have any preferences. But legal writers should not wait to hear the answers; they should work quickly and efficiently, with the goal of producing a well-researched, concise, and useful e-memo product.[12]

12. Fortunately, many legal scholars have written about and studied the topic of lawyer emails and e-memos. Law students and lawyers wishing to learn more will have many articles to choose from, including the following: Brad Desnoyer, *E-Memos 2.0: An Empirical Study of How Attorneys Write*, 25 Legal Writing 213 (2021), https://www.legalwritingjournal.org/article/24785-e-memos-2-0-an-empirical-study-of-how-attorneys-write Joe Fore, *The Comparative Benefits of Standalone*

CHAPTER SUMMARY

- Client letters are written for one or more of the following reasons: (1) to answer specific questions from the client, (2) to update the client about the case, (3) to predict a possible outcome in the case, or (4) to make recommendations as to how to proceed in the case.
- Demand letters make specific requests to either take certain actions or refrain from certain actions.
- Demand letters must include (1) the specific request, (2) the justifications for the request, (3) a clear deadline for compliance with the request, and (4) a clear statement of the consequences should the reader not comply with the request.
- When writing electronic communications, including emails and e-memos, lawyers should (1) consider readability on an electronic device, (2) pay attention to security considerations for attachments and hyperlinks, and (3) maintain a professional and respectful tone.

E-Mail Assignments in the First-Year Legal Writing Curriculum, 22 LEGAL WRITING 151, 152 (2018); Katrina June Lee, *Process Over Product: A Pedagogical Focus on Email as a Means of Refining Legal Analysis*, 44 CAP. U. L. REV. 655, 664 (2016); Ellie Margolis, *Is the Medium the Message?*, 12 LEGAL COMM. & RHETORIC: J. ALWD 1, 7-8 (2015); Kristen K. Robbins-Tiscione, *From Snail Mail to Email: The Traditional Legal Memorandum in the Twenty-First Century*, 58 J. LEGAL EDUC. 32, 48-49 (2008).

GLOSSARY

Absurd result: A ridiculous or illogical outcome.

Acronym: A word created by taking the first letter of each word in a phrase and combining those single letters into a new word.

Active voice: In grammar, the subject of a sentence is the person or entity performing the action of the verb and the verb describes the action taken.

Adjudication: A judicial decision-making process; the act of entering a judgment or a decree in a lawsuit.

Administrative agency: A department or commission in state or federal government that regulates and monitors a particular industry or public interest (e.g., the Federal Communications Commission) as provided under the law.

Admissible evidence: Evidence permitted by the court to be introduced at trial and considered by the trier of fact when making its decision.

Adversary: An opponent.

Adversary legal system: Adversary legal systems involve parties who oppose each other and state their views and arguments regarding how their dispute should be decided before an independent decision maker, usually a court. The lawyers representing the parties provide evidence, witness testimony, etc., before the court in order to prove their case. The lawyer for the opposing party may ask questions to challenge the strength of the other side's case.

Adverse possession: A system where landowners lose their legal rights to real property by allowing another to use the property in a way and for a period of time that the other acquired title to the property.

Affirm: To uphold the decision of a lower court.

Affirmative defense: A defense raised by a party in a lawsuit; the party admits that the cause of action is established, but because of the defense, the party cannot be held legally liable. Examples of affirmative defenses include self-defense in a criminal case or necessity in a trespass to property case.

Aggravated: To make worse, as in "aggravated assault" in criminal law.

Aggrieved: One who is injured or has sustained a loss.

Allegation: A claim stated in a pleading that the party making the claim intends to prove at trial.

Alternative dispute resolution (ADR): An alternative method for settling disagreements without requiring the parties to engage in formal litigation. Examples of alternative dispute resolution methods include mediation and arbitration.

Ambiguity: Lacking clarity; a term or provision is capable of two or more mutually conflicting meanings.

Analogy: A comparison that states similarities between two or more things.

Answer: A pleading that is a defendant's written response to a plaintiff's complaint; it specifically responds to each allegation raised in the complaint by either admitting, denying, or pleading that the defendant lacks sufficient knowledge to respond to the truth of the allegation.

Appeal: A legal process by which a party in a lawsuit requests a higher court to review the final judgment of a lower court within that higher court's jurisdiction.

Appearance: In a legal context, an act of coming into court or filing documents with a court by which a party to a lawsuit, in person or through its attorney, indicates an intent to participate in the lawsuit.

Appellant: The party who initiates an appeal.

Appellate court: A court in the state or federal court system that has the power to review the decisions of lower courts in its jurisdiction and decide whether these lower court decisions should be upheld, modified, or reversed.

Appellate review: The process by which an appellate court reviews a decision made by a lower court in its jurisdiction.

Appellee: The party who opposes an appeal.

Arbitration: An alternative to a court adjudication of a dispute. The opposing parties agree on a neutral person or group of persons to hear the parties' arguments and settle the dispute by issuing an award.

Arbitrator: A person or one of a group of persons chosen by opposing parties in a dispute to hear the parties' arguments and settle the dispute by issuing an award.

Assault: When one person intentionally puts another person in fear or apprehension of imminent contact.

Attribution: The process of giving credit for a thought, idea, or statement to the creator of that thought, idea, or statement. Proper attribution requires that (1) the writer must accurately report the borrowed words or ideas in the writer's paper; (2) the writer must notify the reader about any quoted words, phrases, or passages by either placing quotation marks around the quoted text, or, if the quotation is 50 or more words, by placing the quoted text in block format; and (3) the writer must accurately cite to the original source at all necessary points in the writer's paper where the writer has borrowed text or ideas.

Balancing of equities: The process by which a fact-finder in a dispute considers notions of fairness as they relate to the particular circumstances of the parties in the dispute.

Bench trial: A trial in which there is no jury and the judge decides issues of fact and makes rulings of law.

Beneficiary: A person who receives a benefit from someone or something, such as a person who receives property under the terms of a Last Will and Testament.

Bill: When the term is used in connection with legislation, it means a writing that is introduced to a legislative body as a proposed law; the legislative body considers whether it should be enacted into law.

Bill of Rights: The first ten amendments to the United States Constitution, mandating fundamental rights and protections for the people.

Binding: In the law the term "binding" is often used when discussing statutes and cases that must be reconciled in reaching a decision in a present case, e.g., binding authority.

Block format: A form for presenting a quotation of 50 or more words; the right and left margins are indented, and the quoted text is single-spaced and quotation marks are omitted.

Brief: In a legal context, a case brief is a summary of a case that states the relevant facts of the dispute, the procedural history, the procedural and substantive issues raised in the case, the court's holdings on the procedural and substantive issues, the rules favorably applied by the court, and the court's reasoning. The term "brief" also refers to a document submitted by attorneys to the court to provide support for their client's case.

Brief Answer(s): The section of a formal office memorandum where the writer answers briefly the questions posed in the Questions Presented section of the office memorandum.

Burden of proof: The responsibility of one party to prove a legal assertion in court.

Canons of construction: Persuasive rules or principles used by courts to help give meaning to ambiguous statutory language.

Case of first impression: A legal issue raised where there is no controlling law in the jurisdiction.

Cause of action: A claim or claims of wrongdoing (e.g., breach of contract, negligence, or fraud) that entitle the victim to a remedy as provided under the law.

Chattels: Personal property; things.

Chronological: In order, starting from the oldest date to the most recent date. For example, the steps in a lawsuit, in chronological order, begin with filing a complaint with a court through the trial and appellate process.

Circuit court of appeals: An appeals court in the federal court system.

Claimant: A person who makes a claim, e.g., a plaintiff in a lawsuit.

Closing argument: An attorney's final presentation to the court that summarizes the client's favorable evidence and that attempts to persuade the fact-finder to decide in favor of the attorney's client.

Common law: A body of rules and principles created by the judiciary to respond to legal issues not addressed by statute.

Complaint: In the context of a legal action, a pleading filed in a court by a plaintiff that begins the formal litigation process. The complaint establishes the jurisdiction of the court, outlines the plaintiff's claims, names the defendants, and designates the remedy sought by the plaintiff.

Concurrence: In reviewing lower court decisions, when one or more judges agree with the outcome by the majority of the judges but do not agree with how the court reasoned to the decision. The concurring judge(s) may or may not write a concurring opinion.

Congressional hearings: Proceedings held by various committees of the United States Congress to collect evidence in order to evaluate proposed legislation or other governmental action.

Conservator: An individual who guards or preserves, such as one who preserves art.

Consideration: An agreement to exchange performances or promises between two or more parties that requires the parties to act, forbear from acting, or give up a present or future right, required as part of a contract.

Constituent: One component of a larger whole, as in constituent requirements.

Constituents: The population that a legislative representative is charged to represent. For example, a U.S. senator from New York represents the interests of New York citizens (constituents) in the U.S. Congress.

Constitutional provision: A clause in a state or federal constitution. For example, the First Amendment to the United States Constitution includes a clause providing for the separation of church and state.

Counterclaim: A claim made by a defendant against a plaintiff in a lawsuit that may or may not relate to the subject matter raised in the plaintiff's complaint.

Countervailing: Opposite, as in arguments that are in opposition to others presented.

Court of last resort: The highest court of appeals within a state court system or a federal court system.

Covenant not to compete: An obligation by which the obligor promises not to engage in specific conduct that competes with the interests of the obligee for a specified period of time and within a specified geographic area.

Credibility: The degree to which one is believed; reliability; truthfulness.

Crossclaim: A claim made by a party against any co-party arising out of the subject matter of the lawsuit.

Cross-examination: At trial, the process by which the attorney for the opposing party questions a witness called by the other party to testify. This questioning takes place after the direct examination of the witness by the attorney for the party who called the witness to testify. The cross-examination can address only matters raised during the direct examination.

Decedent/deceased: A person who has died. The term is often used when discussing the Last Will and Testament of a party who has died.

Declaratory judgment: A decision made by a court during the course of a trial that can be appealed immediately.

Default judgment: A judgment entered in favor of the prevailing party when the opposing party fails to respond to the claims made by the prevailing party.

Dependent clause: In grammar, a statement that does not form a complete sentence and thus is incapable of standing alone; to be grammatically correct, it must be accompanied by an independent clause.

Deposition: A means of acquiring information during the pre-litigation, discovery process during which a party or witness is questioned either orally or in writing about matters related to the controversy.

Descent and distribution: The process of passing property after a party dies without a Last Will and Testament.

Dicta: Statements by a court in its opinion that are not part of the direct holding of the case.

Direct examination: The process at trial where an attorney questions a witness that attorney has called to testify.

Direct object: In writing, a noun or pronoun that receives the action of the verb in a sentence and answers the question *what*? or *who*? (e.g., Jack threw a knife; knife is the direct object).

Directed verdict: *See* judgment as a matter of law (JMOL).

Discovery: The evidence-gathering stage of formal litigation during which each party investigates and collects information related to any claims or defenses raised in the pleadings.

Discretionary: Optional, not required.

Dissent: To disagree with, as a judge who disagrees with, or dissents to, the majority opinion in a case.

District court: A trial court in the federal court system.

Due diligence: The degree of care a party must exercise to meet a legal requirement or obligation.

Duty of care: A level of care and caution that is owed by one party to another in certain situations. If the party fails to provide this standard of care, then the other party may be liable for the resulting harm.

Dynamic statutory interpretation: A theory of statutory interpretation that promotes the use of traditional tools of statutory construction but permits considering what the statute ought to mean if the original legislative outlook does not reflect current political, legal, or societal customs.

East Carolina: A fictitious state in the United States created for the purpose of the exercises in this book.

***Ejusdem generis*:** A canon of construction used when interpreting a statute, providing that general words following specifically listed words apply only to those items "similar in nature" to the listed words.

Elements: In the law, requirements, usually part of a test that must be met to establish liability in a cause of action.

Ellipsis: A set of three periods used within a quotation to indicate the omission of quoted material.

Enact: To pass into law, as in a statute or amendment.

Enumeration: Organizing information in a series, such as (1) . . . , (2) . . . , and (3). . . .

Equity: An ideal of justice relating to the fair treatment of individuals.

Estate: The quality and quantity of a person's ownership interest in personal property or real estate; the property owned by a decedent upon his death as well as the property acquired or received by the estate from the time of the decedent's death until the final distribution of the property to the beneficiaries.

Executive branch: One of the three branches of state government or federal government; its primary role is to enforce the statutes created by the legislative branch.

Extrinsic source canons: A canon of construction used when interpreting a statute by looking to agency interpretations of a statute, legislative history, or common law rules of other courts that have interpreted the same (or similar) statute.

Fact-based analysis: A discussion to determine whether the facts of a case satisfy an applicable statute, rule, or principle.

Fact-finder: In the U.S. judicial system, the party deciding the facts in a case presented to the court. The fact-finder may be a jury or, if no jury, a judge serving as the fact-finder.

Factors: Considerations; in a legal test, factors are multiple items that are not required but are considered and weighed in determining whether a legal test has been met.

Felony: A crime that can result in punishment for more than one year.

Final judgment: A judgment by a court that settles a disputed issue and may be appealed.

Floor debate: A debate between legislators that takes place in the hall of the legislative body, when the legislators argue in favor of or against proposed legislation, or other governmental action.

Foreign courts: Courts outside the jurisdiction of the court presiding over a dispute.

Forum: The court or jurisdiction where the legal dispute will be litigated.

Fraud: Intentional misrepresentation.

Fundamental right: A right expressed in the provisions of the United States Constitution.

General jurisdiction court: A court that can hear cases raising many different types of disputes.

Generic names: In the context of an explanation of a case, the names identifying the relationship of the parties to the dispute at issue, e.g., "buyer" and "seller" in the case of a dispute involving a sale.

Goodwill: An intangible asset of a business arising from the approval or patronage of customers because of the business's good business practice.

Gross negligence: When an actor either does something in a conscious, voluntary manner, or omits to do something in reckless disregard of a legal duty with the consequences to another party.

Hearsay: A statement made by someone other than the person testifying at trial.

Heir: A person who stands to inherit property from an estate.

Hierarchy: A classification system that ranks people or objects based on their characteristics or powers.

Holding: The answer to the issues raised in a case, based on the legal principle drawn from the opinion. *See ratio decedendi.*

Homicide: The killing of a person by another.

Hypothetical: In law, a fictitious story created to explore the law's policies and principles; theoretical.

***In pari materia*:** A canon of construction used when interpreting statutes, providing that statutes relating to the same subject matter should be interpreted similarly to avoid inconsistencies.

Independent clause: In grammar, a clause that includes both a subject and a verb and can, therefore, stand on its own.

Inference: A conclusion of fact reasonably deduced from facts already shown to be true.

Inheritance: In the context of an estate, the personal property, real estate, or money one receives upon the death of the owner.

Injunction: A court order requiring a party to a dispute to take a specific action or to refrain from a specific action.

Intangible: Something that is not physical, that cannot be touched (e.g., intellectual property).

Intentionalism: A theory of statutory interpretation that focuses on determining a legislature's intent. The intentionalist looks at the words of a statute as an expression of the legislature's meaning that can be clarified through the use of outside sources.

Interrogatories: A method of acquiring information in the litigation process through a series of written questions relating to the dispute submitted to the opposing party, who must respond in writing.

Intestacy: A situation in which a person has died without a valid Last Will and Testament.

Involuntary manslaughter: When one kills another without intending to do so; the death is a result of criminal negligence or occurs while another unlawful act is taking place. Deaths occurring as a result of an automobile accident are oftentimes ruled to be involuntary manslaughter.

Issue of fact: A question regarding the truth of an item, occurrence, or situation claimed by a party in its pleading and disputed by another party in its response pleading.

Issue of first impression: A question of law that has never been decided in a jurisdiction. *See* case of first impression.

Issue of law: A question regarding what law should be used to resolve a legal dispute or how a law should be interpreted to resolve a legal dispute.

JMOL: Judgment as a matter of law (JMOL). *See* motion for a judgment as a matter of law.

Judgment: The final decision of a court regarding a legal dispute.

Judgment as a matter of law (JMOL): *See* motion for a judgment as a matter of law.

Judgment notwithstanding the verdict (JNOV): Outdated terminology for "judgment as a matter of law."

Judicial branch: One of the three branches of state government or federal government; the courts' primary role is to interpret and apply statutes and to create laws in situations not addressed by statutes.

Judicial efficiency: A public policy concern that the judicial system function economically by avoiding duplicative actions and wasting judicial resources.

Judiciously: Using sound judgment or discretion.

Jurisdiction: The power of the court to assert authority over parties in a case (*see* personal jurisdiction) and the authority of the court to hear and decide the issues arising from the pleadings in a case (*see* subject matter jurisdiction); the geographic area in which a court may assert this authority.

Jurisprudence: The study of legal theory.

Jurist: A legal scholar.

Jury trial: A trial where the jury serves as the fact-finder in a case (as opposed to the judge) and decides issues of fact.

Justice: The term used for a judge who sits on the United States Supreme Court, or on the court of last resort in the state judicial system; a principle of fairness and equity.

Landmark decision: Major, as in a "landmark case"; a case that establishes a new rule that is then followed and subsequently cited.

Law-based analysis: A discussion to determine whether a statute, rule, or principle applies to a dispute or, if competing rules exist that may apply to a dispute, determines which rule should apply to a dispute.

Law review article: A scholarly paper published in a law school–sponsored periodical, edited by law students at that institution.

Legalese: Pretentious or meaningless legal language.

Legislative act: In the context of legislation, a law enacted by the legislature.

Legislative branch: One of the three branches of state government or federal government, such as the U.S. Congress; possesses law-making powers and enacts statutes that are subject only to constitutional restraints.

Legislative history: The official records of the legislative process that pertain to a particular piece of legislation.

Legislative intent: The reason legislators enact a bill into law.

Limited jurisdiction court: A court that can hear only disputes raising certain issues (e.g., a small claims court may hear only cases involving claims for small debts).

Living law: The legal principle that the common law is constantly evolving to integrate advances in science and technology, as well as to integrate changes in social customs and economic considerations.

Long-arm statute: A state statute that mandates that a court may exercise personal jurisdiction over a party who is outside the territorial boundaries of the court's jurisdiction, provided the party has certain contacts with the state, as stated in the statute.

Malice aforethought: Planning in advance to do something wrong.

Mandate: When used as a verb, it means to command, dictate, or require.

Mandatory precedent: Prior case decisions that must be followed by a court (e.g., a state trial court is bound by the previous decisions of the higher courts within its jurisdictional borders, as well as federal statutory and constitutional decisions of the United States Supreme Court).

Manslaughter: The killing of another. Voluntary manslaughter is an intentional killing; involuntary manslaughter is an unintentional killing.

Maxims: Rules of law.

Mediation: A non-binding method of alternative dispute resolution where the parties seek to resolve their issues through mutual collaboration and problem solving with an unbiased third party.

Mediator: An unbiased third party who assists disputing parties in resolving their issues.

Merits: A case decided "on the merits" is one that is fully tried at the trial level and is not dismissed on a procedural motion.

Model Rules of Professional Conduct: A set of ethical guidelines for U.S. lawyers published by the American Bar Association. The guidelines include some rules that are mandatory and others that are only advisory. Many states have adopted the Model Rules of Professional Conduct.

Motion: In the context of a legal dispute, an oral or written formal request made by a party to the dispute to the court, to make a ruling or to enter a judgment in the dispute.

Motion for a judgment as a matter of law (JMOL): At the end of an opposing party's presentation of its case at trial, another party may make a motion to the court to enter a verdict in the moving party's favor on the basis that "there is no legally sufficient evidentiary basis for a reasonable jury to find for [the opposing party]." Fed. R. Civ. P. 50(a)(1). If the court grants the motion, then a judgment is entered in favor of the moving party.

Motion for a judgment on the pleadings: A motion by a party made anytime between the close of pleadings and prior to the trial, asking the court to enter judgment in the moving party's favor because, based on the pleadings filed by the parties, the moving party is entitled to judgment as a matter of law.

Motion to dismiss: Responding to a pleading, a party moves the court to dismiss a claim raised in the pleading on the basis that even if the facts alleged in the pleading are true the claim raised by the pleading must be dismissed because there is no legal basis for the claim.

Moving party: A party to a legal dispute who makes a motion to the court.

No contest plea: A plea entered by a criminal defendant that allows the defendant to accept responsibility for the charge without admitting guilt. Also known as a "nolo contendere plea."

***Noscitur a sociis*:** A canon of construction used for interpreting statutes; the meaning of a word or phrase can be deduced from the words surrounding the word in question.

Nuisance: In a legal context, something that interferes with another's use and enjoyment of his property; an annoyance.

***Obiter dicta*:** That part of a court opinion that is not necessary to the holding in the case.

Objective legal analysis: A type of analysis that requires a writer to consider and present the support that exists for both sides of a disputable issue. The goal of an objective legal analysis is to inform the reader of the law on a particular issue and to predict the issue's probable outcome in a client's case.

Office memorandum: A formal objective document that analyzes and answers questions posed by a supervising attorney. Oftentimes the office memorandum will assess the strengths and weaknesses of a client's case.

Opening statement: An attorney's presentation at the beginning of the trial; provides an outline of the case to the fact-finder and states what the attorney intends to prove in the case.

Opposing counsel: The attorney representing the other party in a case. For example, an attorney representing the wife in a divorce proceeding is opposing counsel to the attorney representing the husband in the same divorce proceeding.

Oral argument: An oral presentation by an attorney to the court regarding a disputed issue in an attempt to establish the validity and superiority of the client's position and persuade the court to rule in favor of the client.

Ordinary course of business: Conducting business in a way that is in accordance with the customary way to operate that type of business.

Overrule: An act by a court to set aside or reject a prior court decision in a different case; to reject an objection made by a party during the trial.

Parenthetical: A term used to refer to the factual holding of a case when it is provided in parentheses after the case citation.

Passive voice: In grammar, the subject of the sentence is not the one performing the action of the verb and the verb is a form of "to be."

Personal jurisdiction: The power of the court to assert authority over parties in a case, which is necessary for any judgment rendered by the court to be enforceable over the parties.

Personal representative: One party who acts on behalf of another, oftentimes a party acting on behalf of the estate of one who is deceased.

Persuasive authority: Legal sources that are not binding on courts deciding future cases but that may help persuade the court to reason to a decision in a certain way. Persuasive authority may be primary authority that originates in a non-binding jurisdiction, or it can be any non-primary source.

Persuasive precedent: Decision-making rules a court may follow from lower courts in its jurisdiction or from courts outside the jurisdiction.

Plagiarism: The intentional or unintentional use of someone else's written or spoken words or ideas without proper attribution to the source.

Plain Error Doctrine: A doctrine providing an exception to the general rule that if a party fails to object, the alleged error is considered waived. If a party can establish the existence of exceptional circumstances that affect substantial rights resulting in a miscarriage of justice, then the alleged error may not be waived.

Plain Meaning Rule: Rule of statutory interpretation that states a court will first look to the language of the statute itself to determine its meaning, and, if the statute is clear in its plain meaning, the court will not look outside the language of the statute to determine the statute's meaning. Under the Plain Meaning Rule a court will consider commonly accepted English principles of grammar, syntax, and punctuation to determine the meaning of a statute's words, as understood by a reasonable person.

Pleading: Documents filed with a court at the beginning of a formal litigation process that establish the claims and defenses of the parties. A pleading includes documents such as a complaint, answer, crossclaim, counterclaim, and any replies to crossclaims or counterclaims.

Precedent: Holdings in prior cases used by a court to reach a decision in a current case.

Predeceased: A person who has died, or is treated as though he or she died before the decedent.

Preempt: To override; to take the place of.

Preponderance of the evidence: A majority; more than 50 percent. For example, the burden by some plaintiffs to prove their case is by a preponderance, or majority, of the evidence.

Pretext: Pretext occurs when persons say they are doing something for one reason, but they are really doing it for a different reason that they are unwilling to admit. For example, in an employment situation an employer may claim to have fired an employee because the employee did not arrive to the office on time, when the firing really occurred because the employee reported to the government that the employer was doing something illegal (known as a whistleblower).

Pretrial conference: A conference between the attorneys involved in a case and the judge that is held before the trial of the case to assist in the management and speediness of the trial.

Primary authority: The main source of the law: constitutions, statutes, case law, and administrative regulations based on statutes.

Procedural law: Laws governing the process for determining the parties' rights and obligations in a legal dispute.

Procedural posture: The identification of the motion that is the basis for the appeal for review of a case. For example, if a case was fully tried at the trial level, the appeal will be based on the final outcome in the case (also known as a "decision on the merits"). If the case was dismissed based on one of the procedural motions available to a party, such as a summary judgment motion (*see also* motion for judgment as a matter of law), the procedural posture on appeal will be whether the summary judgment motion was properly granted.

Proceeds: In the law, usually refers to money or assets.

Promulgate: To proclaim, announce, or make public.

Prong: One part of something larger, as in one requirement of a three-pronged (requirement) test.

Property settlement: In a dissolution of marriage proceeding, an agreement that divides the property of the divorcing couple between them.

Prototypes: Original models designed and created prior to the mass production of goods.

Proximate cause: One of the requirements to prove negligence, specifically, that an actor's breach of a duty resulted in an injury that was reasonably foreseeable.

Public policy: Principles that concern the society as a whole; a principle of law that promotes the protection of the public's well-being as opposed to the interests of a private person, entity, or group.

Purposivism: A theory of statutory interpretation that focuses on determining the purpose or goal of a statute. After determining the purpose of the statute, the purposivist interprets the statute consistent with that purpose.

Question(s) Presented: The section of an office memorandum that frames the disputable legal issues being addressed in the office memorandum.

RJMOL: *See* renewed motion for a judgment as a matter of law.

***Ratio decidendi*:** The court's decision on a contested legal issue in a case. *See* holding.

Rebuttal: Evidence that disproves or contradicts any evidence.

Reconciled: How one thing is consistent with another; for example, showing how the decision in a new case is consistent with the holdings in prior cases binding on the court in the new case.

Remand: In the context of a legal dispute, a decision by a higher court to send the case back to a lower court for the lower court to take additional action in the case.

Remedy: In the context of a legal dispute, a means by which a wrong is made right or compensation is given to the victim of the wrongdoing, e.g., an injunction or payment of money.

Removal: In the context of a legal dispute, the process of having a case that was filed in one court moved to another court. For example, a defendant may request the removal of an action originally filed in a state court moved to federal court if the case involves a question of federal law. Only the defendant can request a removal.

Renewed motion for a judgment as a matter of law (RJMOL): A renewed motion made by the losing party after the jury returns its decision; the losing party requests that the judge enter a judgment in the moving party's favor, despite the jury's verdict against that party.

Res judicata: A judicial doctrine that prevents the parties from litigating the same issues again when a final judgment has been issued by a court with appropriate jurisdiction over the parties and over the subject matter of the action. Res judicata is an affirmative defense to any second action on the same issue involving the same parties.

Restatement of Law: A collection of common law rules covering various areas of law, such as contracts and torts, published by the American Law Institute and written by scholars in the field, with commentary.

Restitution: When the party must return any benefit received under the contract.

Reverse: In the context of an appeal of a case, to set aside the ruling of the lower court in that case.

Rule explanation: A concise description of a relevant court decision, used to help the reader better understand the rule by showing how a prior court applied the rule in an issue identical or similar to the issue being analyzed.

Secondary sources: Anything that is not primary authority. The most common legal secondary sources include legal encyclopedias, law review articles, books, and restatements of law.

Service of process: The formal process whereby all defendants to an action are served with a copy of the complaint (or some other legal notice), along with a summons to appear in court and respond to the plaintiff's claims.

Slayer: Someone who has killed another.

Slayer statute: Statute that prevents a person who kills another from benefiting from the victim's death. The specific requirements vary from state to state.

Socratic method: A teaching method through which a professor instructs by asking questions of students, rather than just lecturing.

Sovereign authority: The power of each nation to decide its own course of action and govern its own people and territory.

Standard of Review: The extent of an appellate court's reviewal power when determining whether a lower court's decision was or was not correct.

Stare decisis: A legal doctrine that requires a court to reconcile a new decision with that court's prior decisions and higher court decisions in the same jurisdiction involving similar issues and substantially similar facts.

Statement of Facts: The section of the formal office memorandum that sets out the legally significant facts of a client's case, along with necessary background facts.

Statute of Frauds: A U.S. statute designed to avoid fraudulent acts by setting out certain requirements that must be met to enforce contracts for the sale of goods over $500.

Statute of limitations: A statutorily imposed time limit for filing a complaint.

Statutory provision: A clause in a statute.

Statutory scheme: The statutory scheme of a statute may include (1) any statutory definitions of terms used in the statute in question, (2) other statutory provisions related to the statute in question, (3) any codified preamble that pertains to the statute in question, and (4) the title of a legislative act that includes the statute in question.

Strictly construe: To interpret a term or clause narrowly.

Subject matter jurisdiction: The authority of the court to hear and decide the issues arising from the pleadings in a case.

Substantive law: Law found in statutes, regulations, constitutions, and common law; helps determine the parties' rights and obligations at issue in a legal dispute.

Substantive policy canons: Canons of construction used in interpreting statutes that focus on matters such as constitutional concerns, the common law prior to the statute's enactment, and specific statutory policies; these canons do not focus on the meaning of statutory text or what the legislature intended when it drafted the text.

Summary judgment: A judgment entered by a court, upon a party's summary judgment motion, dismissing a lawsuit because no genuine issue of material fact existed as to any or all claims or defenses, so the moving party is "entitled to judgment as a matter of law." Fed. R. Civ. P. 56(c).

Syllogism: A logical argument where two premises support a conclusion. The typical example cited is: "All men are mortal (major premise); Socrates is a man (minor premise); therefore, Socrates is mortal."

Tabulation: A formatting technique that sets off each enumerated item from the surrounding text by placing it in a separate, indented block.

Target audience: The people or segment of the population that writers are attempting to reach with their writing.

Textual canons: A canon of construction used in statutory interpretation focusing on the legislature's choice of certain words, the syntax used in the statutory language, or the relationship of the words or phrases in the question to words or phrases found in other provisions of the same statute or similar statutes.

Textualism: A theory of statutory interpretation that focuses on the plain meaning of a statute and textual canons.

Thesis statement: A statement that introduces a legal issue and also provides the conclusion on that legal issue.

Thirteenth Circuit: A fictitious federal circuit that includes the fictitious state of East Carolina; used for purposes of examples and exercises in this book.

Threshold issue: An issue that should be decided by the court first.

Transcript: In the context of a legal dispute, the official record of a proceeding.

Transitional words: Words used to notify the reader that a change in focus (transition) is taking place.

Trespass: To invade.

Uniform Resource Locator (URL): An Internet address; the string of letters, words, and numbers that usually begins with "http."

Vacuum: In the law, writers may refer to something being considered "in a vacuum." This means that the reference is being considered in isolation of everything else—it will be considered on its own.

Venue: The location of the suit; out of all the courts with personal and subject matter jurisdiction over a dispute, where the lawsuit may be brought.

Verdict: A jury's decision on issues of fact in a trial.

Voir dire: An examination of potential jurors by the attorneys or the judge to determine whether the potential jurors will be fair and impartial when weighing the evidence in a trial.

Voluntary manslaughter: When one kills another intentionally, but there are reasons to lessen the crime that would otherwise be considered murder. Deaths occurring during a heated fight, for example, may fall within voluntary manslaughter.

Warrant: In the law, a formal document that authorizes someone to take a certain action, such as a warrant for a person's arrest.

Writ of certiorari: An order issued by an appellate court after exercising its discretion to review a lower court's decision in a case. The writ orders the lower court to certify the record of the case's legal proceedings in that lower court and present the certified record to the appellate court.

INDEX